PUBLICATIONS OF THE BUREAU OF BUSINESS
AND ECONOMIC RESEARCH
UNIVERSITY OF CALIFORNIA, LOS ANGELES

Previously published in this series:

THE NATURE OF COMPETITION IN GASOLINE DISTRIBUTION AT
THE RETAIL LEVEL
by Ralph Cassady, Jr., and Wylie L. Jones (1951)

THE PACIFIC COAST MARITIME SHIPPING INDUSTRY, 1930–1948
VOLUME I: AN ECONOMIC PROFILE
by Wytze Gorter and George H. Hildebrand (1952)

THE ROLE OF MERGERS IN THE GROWTH OF LARGE FIRMS
by J. Fred Weston (1953)

THE PACIFIC COAST MARITIME SHIPPING INDUSTRY, 1930–1948
VOLUME II: AN ANALYSIS OF PERFORMANCE
by Wytze Gorter and George H. Hildebrand (1954)

THE MEXICAN PETROLEUM INDUSTRY, 1930–1958
by J. Richard Powell (1956)

THE PERSECUTION OF HUGUENOTS AND FRENCH ECONOMIC DEVELOPMENT,
1680–1720
by Warren C. Scoville (1960)

"DISGUISED UNEMPLOYMENT" IN UNDERDEVELOPED AREAS
by Yong Sam Cho (1963)

THE DEVELOPMENT OF THE SPANISH TEXTILE INDUSTRY, 1750–1800
by James Clayburn La Force, Jr. (1965)

Economic Development and Export Growth

PUBLICATIONS OF THE
BUREAU OF BUSINESS AND ECONOMIC RESEARCH
UNIVERSITY OF CALIFORNIA, LOS ANGELES

Economic Development and Export Growth

A STUDY OF NORTHERN RHODESIA, 1920–1960

BY

ROBERT E. BALDWIN

UNIVERSITY OF CALIFORNIA PRESS

Berkeley and Los Angeles 1966

UNIVERSITY OF CALIFORNIA PRESS
BERKELEY AND LOS ANGELES

CAMBRIDGE UNIVERSITY PRESS
LONDON, ENGLAND

© 1966 BY THE REGENTS OF THE UNIVERSITY OF CALIFORNIA
LIBRARY OF CONGRESS CATALOG CARD NUMBER: 66-13091

Acc
HC
517
Z26
B3

LIBRARY
FLORIDA STATE
TALLAHASSEE, FLORIDA

PRINTED IN THE UNITED STATES OF AMERICA

To Janice and the children

BUREAU OF BUSINESS AND ECONOMIC RESEARCH
UNIVERSITY OF CALIFORNIA
LOS ANGELES

James M. Gillies, *Chairman*
Werner Z. Hirsch
H. Laurence Miller, Jr.
George W. Robbins
Warren C. Scoville
Harold M. Somers
Ralph Cassady, Jr., *Director*

*The opinions expressed in this study are those of the author.
The functions of the Bureau of Business and Economic
Research are confined to facilitating the prosecution of in-
dependent scholarly research by members of the faculty.*

Preface

Most of the basic research for this study was undertaken between September, 1960, and August, 1961, while I was a Foreign Area Training Fellow under the auspices of the Ford Foundation. Except for two months in the United Kingdom, the year was spent in the Federation of Rhodesia and Nyasaland. A brief visit to the Federation was also made in July of 1962.

Since 1961 the political structure of the area has radically changed. The Federation has been dissolved, and Northern Rhodesia has achieved political independence under the name of Zambia. No attempt is made to integrate the economic changes associated with these recent events into the main historical analysis of the book, as such a project would not be feasible without spending a fair amount of additional time in Zambia. Furthermore, it is still too soon to expect the policies of the new government to have had very much effect on the country's economic development. The period covered in the study, consequently, starts in the 1920's and ends about 1960.

I am indebted to many people for their cooperation and the kindnesses shown me in the undertaking of this study. First to be thanked, of course, is the Ford Foundation, which was willing to finance not only me but my wife and four children for a year in Africa. The Bureau of Business and Economic Research and the African Studies Center, both at the University of California, Los Angeles, also have been very generous in giving financial assistance for research assistants. I shall always be grateful to James S. Coleman, Director of the African Studies Center, for encouraging me to study economic development in Africa. In addition, the research committee of the Graduate School at the University of Wisconsin provided summer support to me while completing the manuscript. A year spent in the federal government working on the Kennedy Round of tariff negotiations delayed completion of the manuscript by at least a year, and the grant from Wisconsin was very valuable.

In the Federation the cooperation and assistance of government officials and private individuals was excellent. William L. Taylor, Professor of Economics at the University College of Rhodesia and Nyasaland, very generously arranged for office and library facilities at the university and even for a university flat for the family. The many stimulating discussions at the university with him as well as with Robin Johnson, Selby Ngcobo, J. van Velsen, and John Scott were invaluable in giving a better perspective on African development. Discussions with George Hay of Reed College and Ronald Jones of the University of Rochester, two other American economists who were in the Rhodesias at the time, also proved highly valuable.

A good part of the material in the study could not have been obtained without the help of the copper companies. Both Anglo-American Corporation of South Africa and Roan Selection Trust were willing to make significant efforts to provide the information I requested. F. Taylor Ostrander of American Metal Climax in New York kindly arranged for my contacts at Roan Selection Trust, at whose head offices in Salisbury H. R. Finn was particularly helpful. He furnished me with an office for a short time, permitted me to go over early company records, and made excellent arrangements for my trips to individual copper mines, and William Sampson gave me the benefit of his many keen insights into the economics of the Rhodesian copper industry. Among the many people who provided very useful information at the various mines on the Copperbelt, I especially wish to thank E. C. Bromwich, Chief of the Study Department at Roan Antelope Copper Mines; K. J. M. MacDonald, Accountant at the Rhokana Corporation; T. W. Jones, Assistant African Personnel Manager at Rhokana; D. D. Guest, Mine Secretary at Mufulira Copper Mines; and A. C. Annfield, Secretary of the Northern Rhodesia Chamber of Mines.

Much of my time was spent going over government reports at the National Archives of the Federation of Rhodesia and Nyasaland. The library staff was always most patient and helpful. In addition, I had the good fortune of becoming acquainted with L. H. Gann, who was working at the archives on a history of the Federation's three territories. His two books on the history of Northern Rhodesia are the definitive works in the field, and it was most helpful to be able to check historical points with him.

I have been most fortunate in having the assistance of four exceptionally able graduate students over the last five years. They are Antony Sutton, Walter Miklius, Robert Bray, and Malcolm

Dole. It is impossible to express fully my appreciation and affection for all of them. I am especially indebted to Malcolm Dole who undertook most of the statistical analysis, checked the footnotes and prepared the bibliography, and, most important, made many valuable comments on the manuscript.

Finally, I wish to thank Ralph Cassady, Jr., Director of the Bureau of Business and Economic Research, for encouraging me to submit the study for publication. His staff, especially Pat Hay, has directed the details of preparing the manuscript from map making to checking footnotes with admirable efficiency. Joan Harbaugh of the Bureau has spent many hours typing the manuscript and has done an excellent job.

I am grateful to the editors of the *Economic Journal* for permission to reproduce in substantially the same form my article, "Export Technology and Development from a Subsistence Level," Vol. LXXIII (March, 1963).

R. E. B.

University of Wisconsin
Madison, Wisconsin

Contents

Tables

Figures

1

Development through
Export Expansion

A Survey of Theories

Economists have long recognized that export expansion often plays a key role in initiating development.[1] Of the changes in the state of Europe that trade with the Americas touched off, Adam Smith, for example, stresses as the "most essential" the "opening [of] a new and inexhaustible market to all the commodities of Europe" that lead to "new divisions of labour and improvements of art."[2] Classical economists actually use two different theories in analyzing foreign trade. The first—and the one that tends to dominate economic thinking even today— deals with trade among developed countries. This theory assumes a given state of technology and a fixed supply of productive factors that are internationally immobile. David Ricardo's brilliant exposition of the doctrine of comparative costs epitomizes this static approach.[3] Classical writers analyze trade between devel-

---

[1] A. J. Youngson (*Possibilities of Economic Progress* [Cambridge: Cambridge University Press, 1959], pp. 269–280) has an excellent discussion of the importance of export trade in stimulating the development of certain advanced countries.

[2] Adam Smith, *An Inquiry into the Nature and Causes of the Wealth of Nations* (New York: Modern Library, 1937), p. 416.

[3] David Ricardo, *Principles of Political Economy and Taxation*, Everyman's Library (London: J. M. Dent and Sons, 1911), pp. 77–93.

oped nations and those less developed economies that are present or former colonies quite differently, however. As John Stuart Mill points out with regard to colonial areas, "These are hardly to be looked upon as countries carrying on an exchange of commodities with other countries, but more properly as outlying agricultural or manufacturing establishments belonging to a larger community. Our West India colonies, for example, cannot be regarded as countries, with a productive capital of their own. . . . All the capital employed is English capital; almost all the industry is carried on for English uses. . . . The trade with the West Indies is therefore hardly to be considered as external trade, but more resembles the traffic between town and country, and is amenable to the principles of the home trade." [4] In other words, the early economists recognize the necessity of abandoning the assumption of factor immobility when analyzing trade between developed and developing areas. Instead, they stress the importance of the international transfer of capital, technology, and labor for creating significant export industries in the latter areas.

In this classical model the mechanism by which international factor movements stimulate growth in a free market system is simple and direct.[5] The new technology and labor skills, together with the larger world markets, raise profit rates in the less developed countries and broaden their opportunities for specialization and division of labor. Additional capital flows into the areas from abroad to take advantage of these new opportunities, and the profits from previous investments in the underdeveloped countries are also reinvested. This greater stock of capital leads to still further division of labor and use of improved productive techniques. The rise in income levels, as well as the spread of the monetary sector, also creates market opportunities for the establishment of domestic industries that direct their output toward local markets. Consequently, by utilizing natural resources more fully, by organizing the existing labor force more efficiently, by increasing the supplies of skilled labor and the quantity of capital equipment, and by introducing improved productive techniques, a gradual and cumulative process of

---

[4] John Stuart Mill, *Principles of Political Economy*, ed. W. J. Ashley (London: Longmans Green, 1940), pp. 685–686.

[5] The development theories of the classical economists, as well as those of the neoclass:cal economists and Marxians are analyzed in much greater detail in Gerald M. Meier and Robert E. Baldwin, *Economic Development: Theory, History, Policy* (New York: John Wiley & Sons, 1957), chaps. 1–3.

growth—opened up from abroad—becomes institutionalized within these countries.

There are, however, two important restraints on this semi-automatic development process. The first is the existence of diminishing returns in the agricultural sector. With unchanged techniques, successively more intensive use of labor and capital with a fixed amount of land results in smaller and smaller increments of output. The only way to prevent this factor from causing eventual stagnation is to introduce technological improvements. But even Adam Smith, who is among the most optimistic of the classical economists concerning the prospects for technological improvements, does not regard technological progress as an indefinite offset to stationary conditions. He thought these conditions eventually would come about, when a nation attained "that full complement of riches which the nature of its soil and climate, and its situation with respect to other countries, allowed it to acquire." [6] But they would not emerge until the developing countries had passed through the manufacturing and commercial stages of growth outlined by Smith.

The second restraint relates to the level of wages and population growth. Most classical writers adopted a Malthusian view of the connection between wages and population growth. Specifically, there is a certain real wage, fixed by custom and habit, at which the population will neither increase nor decrease. When wages exceed this level, the death rate drops because of better living conditions, and the population expands. On the other hand, when wages fall below this "natural" level, the population declines as deaths exceed births. The offset to wages hovering at or below the natural level is the same as that which prevents historical diminishing returns, namely, sufficient improvements in productive techniques. By maintaining both the incentive for capital accumulation and the source of investment funds, that is, profits, these improvements act to raise the rate of accumulation and thus the demand for labor. If capital is accumulated rapidly, it is possible that the depressing tendency exerted on wages by an expansion in the labor force is more than counteracted by the strong demand for labor. Per capita income of the working class can then remain above its natural level.

Neoclassical economists devised a much more elegant analysis of the growth process, but they still retain the emphasis of the classical writers upon capital accumulation. They drop, however,

---

[6] Smith, *op. cit.*, p. 94.

the simple, mechanistic view of the saving and investment process used by the earlier economists. Instead, both saving and investment intentions are made functions of the interest rate. Within a given state of technology, the accumulation process is viewed as a process by which the rate of interest gradually declines as successively less profitable investment opportunities are exploited, until the interest level is too low to induce continued net saving. At this stage the stationary state of the classical writers is reached.

There are important differences between classical and neoclassical analysis concerning the prospects of reaching this stage. Neoclassical writers visualize the demand for investment funds to be highly responsive to small decreases in the interest rate. If the habit of thrift is well established among the people, capital accumulation can proceed at a rapid rate for long periods, even without technological progress. When one adds to this view of the development process the neoclassical notion that the pace of technological progress tends to be high, their optimistic view of development prospects becomes very evident. Not only is the rate of increase in the total product likely to be high, but per capita income also grows rapidly in the neoclassical model. The reason for this is that neoclassical economists no longer link population growth in a dependent manner with the accumulation process itself. Instead, they believe that population changes depend upon a host of complex sociological variables, and therefore that it is best to take population changes as "givens," determined outside the scope of economics.

The essential conclusion emerging from neoclassical growth analyses is that development is a cumulative and harmonious process. The creation of a modern export sector in less developed countries is an important means of fostering this cumulative growth process. The growth impetus derived from this sector is viewed as spreading throughout the rest of the economy and initiating modernization and more rapid development in the other sectors.

The major dissenter from the generally optimistic views of both classical and neoclassical writers concerning growth prospects in the less developed countries was, of course, Marx. The Marxian analysis of export expansion and development is as follows. Instead of fostering development, the establishment of a modern export industry that is based upon capital and skilled labor from an advanced country tends to destroy the prospects for diversified growth in a less developed country. For example, mass-produced, cheap manufactured goods flood the markets of the underdeveloped country and destroy its traditional handicraft industries. This not only eliminates the only economic sector potentially qualified to establish domestically owned and operated manufacturing industries, but swells the pool of cheap labor available for work in the foreign-directed, primary-product, export industry. It is in the latter industry that the advanced country uses its political and economic power most ruthlessly. Prices paid peasant producers for their export products, and the level of wages paid workers employed by foreign-owned enterprises, are kept low by means of monopolistic powers possessed by large foreign-owned trading and producing companies. Furthermore, by manipulating local laws and economic policies, a colonial power is able to thwart any attempts on the part of the indigenous population to break out of their position of weakness. The result is that the masses of people in the less developed country benefit little or not at all by the creation of a modern export sector. Many actually suffer severely in the development process. Foreign capitalists and their governments, on the other hand, reap enormous profits. But, instead of being reinvested, most of the profits are removed in order to build additional industrial enterprises in the already advanced nations. Capitalistic development in advanced countries eventually destroys itself, of course, despite the attempts of such countries to save themselves by means of overseas exploitation. But, the less developed nations never even get a chance to go through the process of creating a diversified industrial economy.

Modern Analyses

It is unfortunate that at the end of World War II, when interest in accelerating growth in the less developed countries began to emerge as a major economic and political topic, the two mainstreams of economic thought on the subject were represented by such extremes as the neoclassical and Marxian positions. Development theory is only a small part of neoclassical economics; unfortunately it had not received much attention by most economists in this school of thought. The growth process in less developed nations is pictured by these economists as being essentially the same as in advanced nations. In particular, although the process of capital accumulation is described as occurring gradually, the prevailing view seems to be that within a reasonable period of time, and without any special difficulties, underdeveloped countries will reach the income levels enjoyed by the advanced countries. The Marxists go to the other extreme, contending that development through export expansion in the less developed areas only benefits the advanced countries.

It became evident to postwar economists attempting to understand the growth process that neither analysis was particularly relevant to the current underdeveloped world. Many underdeveloped countries had received substantial inflows of capital from abroad and established significant export industries, and yet they had failed to develop broadly.[7] Export growth had not initiated in them the general growth predicted by the neoclassical model. Yet some countries had achieved this goal through export development,[8] and the rest were clearly better off than in the absence of the transfer of capital, labor, and techniques from abroad.

The attempts of modern economists to explain better the actual experience of the less developed economies by supplementing these theories or substituting new ones can be divided into three categories.[9]

The first focuses upon sociological and cultural obstacles to growth. One of the most direct exponents of this view is J. H. Boeke, who bases much of his analysis upon Dutch experience in Indonesia.[10] According to Boeke, capitalistic methods of production and distribution fail to spread from export industries established and directed by Western entrepreneurs because of the absence of the cultural prerequisites for Western capitalism. Western economies are based upon unlimited wants, a money economy, and large-scale organization. Boeke claims that the people in Southeast Asia possess limited wants, and that therefore the supply curve of effort for the typical individual is backward-bending. The small-scale producers who dominate production likewise are not profit-oriented and are unwilling to assume

---

[7] Most of the countries in Southeast Asia, Latin America, and Africa fit this description.

[8] Canada, Australia, Argentina, and the Union of South Africa are examples from this group.

[9] See Gerald M. Meier, *International Trade and Development* (New York: Harper and Row, 1963), chap. 7, for a more detailed analysis of modern development theories than is presented here.

[10] J. H. Boeke, *Economics and Economic Policy of Dual Societies* (New York: Institute of Pacific Relations, 1953).

the risks of utilizing the better production and organization techniques introduced from advanced Western economies.[11] Money is the medium of exchange in comparatively few open markets. In short, the Boeke explanation for the failure of modern economic techniques to spread from the export sector to the other parts of an underdeveloped economy is simply that the basic values and attitudes of the indigenous population are incompatible with the type of behavior required to introduce and successfully maintain production based on the advanced techniques of developed economies. Classical and neoclassical writers, and even Marx, assume that the cultural prerequisites for capitalist development are already present in the economies about which they theorize.[12] Those who stress the significance of the absence of such factors in the less developed nations can say that the development models of these writers, who overlook the absence of cultural prerequisites, are not applicable to the underdeveloped countries.[13]

No one will deny the importance of changes in social norms and values in fostering economic development. At the same time, however, most students of the subject would say that authors such as Boeke greatly overemphasize the rigidity of traditional attitudes and social institutions.[14] The evidence collected by other scholars who have studied Southeast Asia suggests, for example, that the people of this region do respond to price incentives in the manner postulated by neoclassical economists. The people are not as oriented to economic incentives as those in the advanced nations, but the point is that their attitudes and values act to slow the development process rather than block it com-

---

[11] A well-known addition to this list of attitudes on the part of the people in less developed countries which allegedly inhibit growth would be the notion of the "demonstration effect." Supposedly, the relatively low saving-income ratio in poor countries is explained by the desire of the people to enjoy the new foreign-produced consumption goods that they learn about in their contact with advanced countries (R. Nurkse, *Problems of Capital Formation in Underdeveloped Countries* [Oxford: Basil Blackwell, 1953], chap. 3).

[12] It was J. A. Schumpeter, however, who best appreciated the significance of these prerequisites for capitalist development (*Capitalism, Socialism and Democracy* [New York: Harper, 1947]).

[13] An outstanding, comparatively recent analysis of the growth process that emphasizes such factors is Everett E. Hagen, *On the Theory of Social Change* (Homewood: Dorsey Press, 1962).

[14] See Benjamin Higgins, *Economic Development: Problems, Principles, and Policies* (New York: W. W. Norton, 1959), chap. 12, for a critical evaluation of Boeke's thesis.

pletely. These attitudes seem to retard rather than prevent more rapid growth, and they are changed by the development process itself.[15]

A second category of explanations points to the existence of certain unfavorable market conditions and forces as the causes of the lack of significant growth in many less developed nations. The explanation suggested by Raul Prebisch[16] and H. W. Singer[17] is probably the most widely known analysis in this category. They maintain that developed countries, by exercising their monopoly powers, have brought about a significant long-run decline in the terms of trade, that is, the ratio of export to import prices, of the less developed nations. Their argument goes as follows. In recession periods the large-scale, monopolistic manufacturers typical of developed countries reduced output rather than prices. In prosperous periods, on the other hand, the industrial producers not only increased production but also, under the bargaining pressures from well-organized labor unions, raised money wages, and thus prices. Unfortunately, neither producers nor workers in the less developed countries usually possessed sufficient monopoly power to influence the world prices of the items they produced. In direct response to world demand conditions, primary-product prices fell sharply in recession periods and rose again in the prosperity phase of the international business cycle. The net long-run result has been that the prices of manufactures have risen relative to the price of primary products and, therefore, under-developed countries have been able to purchase comparatively less and less imported manufactured commodities with a given quantity of their exports of primary goods. Had this relative decline in purchasing power not occurred, development would—according to Prebisch and Singer—have spread from the export sector throughout the rest of the underdeveloped economies.

The terms-of-trade argument is on shaky grounds both theoreti-

---

[15] For a balanced, scholarly appraisal of the significance of social factors in the growth process, see Bert F. Hoselitz, "Social Implications of Economic Growth," *Economic Weekly* (Feb. 14, 21, 1959), reprinted in T. Morgan, G. W. Betz, and W. K. Choudhry, eds., *Readings in Economic Development*, no. 9 (Belmont, Calif.: Wadsworth, 1963), pp. 78–94.

[16] Raul Prebisch, *The Economic Development of Latin America and Its Principal Problems* (New York: United Nations, Department of Economic Affairs, 1950).

[17] H. W. Singer, "The Distribution of Gains between Investing and Borrowing Countries," *American Economic Review*, XL (May, 1950), 473–485.

cally and empirically.[18] Only two comments are made here, however. Even if the statistical evidence put forth by the proponents of the argument is accepted, it does not mean that the less developed countries have suffered an absolute loss in real income through international trade. On the contrary, the introduction of better techniques in the export sector, and the tremendous improvements in the quality of the manufactured goods imported from advanced countries, have resulted in substantial real-income gains from trade for these nations. Had developments in the advanced countries not resulted in the alleged deterioration in trading terms, these gains, of course, would have been greater. But substantial gains versus even more substantial trading gains should not be confused with no gains versus some gains.

The apparent decline in international trading terms is better regarded as a result of the inability of development to spread throughout these economies than as a cause of the lack of general growth. Because the best available techniques and market opportunities tend to be utilized in most sectors of developed economies, productive resources in these economies are flexible and mobile. Resources are shifted comparatively quickly out of industries with declining profit opportunities and into those with expanding profit prospects. But, because in the less developed countries the export sector and a few closely related industries are the only ones to use modern efficient productive techniques, resources are not very mobile in these economies. For example, when substitutes are discovered for some primary commodity that advanced countries have been importing from less developed countries, the latter are unable to shift easily to another promising product. There is nowhere to go, as their ability to utilize modern methods and compete in international markets does not extend beyond one or two export items. Because they are not developed, such countries tend to be at a disadvantage in terms of maintaining their export prices relative to those of the advanced countries.[19]

[18] See, for example, Gottfried Haberler, "Terms of Trade and Economic Development," in *Economic Development for Latin America*, ed. Howard Ellis (New York: St. Martin's Press, 1961), pp. 275–297; R. E. Baldwin, "Secular Movements in the Terms of Trade," *American Economic Review*, XLV (May, 1955), 259–269; Meier, *op. cit.*, pp. 55–66, 175–176; M. June Flanders, "Prebisch on Protection: An Evaluation," *Economic Journal*, LXXIV (June, 1964), 305–327; T. Morgan, "The Long-Run Terms of Trade between Agriculture and Manufacturing," *Economic Development and Cultural Change*, VIII (Oct., 1959), pp. 1–23.

[19] Charles P. Kindleberger, *The Terms of Trade* (New York: John Wiley & Sons, 1956), pp. 253–257.

In addition to the terms-of-trade effects of monopolistic activities by developed countries, it is frequently alleged that foreign-owned enterprises dominate the export sector in less developed nations, and use their monopoly positions in a manner adverse to the development of these countries.[20] For example, foreign-owned trading firms charge higher-than-competitive prices for the imported consumer goods they sell to the indigenous people. At the same time they purchase the export goods produced by peasant producers at monopsonistic prices. In cases where the export industry is directly owned by foreigners, such as mining concerns and plantations, market power is exerted by paying local workers lower wages than the competitive level. These activities reduce the spending power of the indigenous population and curtail the stimulating effect local purchases might have in inducing additional growth. The enlarged profits accruing to foreign firms by these monopolistic policies are not plowed back into the underdeveloped economy but are, instead, sent abroad. In short, the potential for additional growth existed as the underdeveloped countries expanded their export sectors, but this growth potential was not fulfilled because of the monopolistic actions of foreigners.

As with the terms-of-trade argument, one should not conclude that the monopolistic actions by the developed countries resulted in an absolute worsening in the economic conditions of the less developed nations. These actions may have limited the gains of the indigenous people—it will be claimed that this was in fact the case in Northern Rhodesia—but less developed countries still were far better off economically after the expansion of their exports than before. Furthermore, although it is easy and convenient to think in such terms, one should not consider all foreigners from advanced countries as members of a giant and single-purposed monopoly. In most economic areas there was active competition among foreign investors and entrepreneurs. The obvious exceptions should not be magnified into being the general rule.

A final group of theories concerning the failure of development to spread from the export sector concentrates on special factors affecting the basic productive elements of an economy—natural resource conditions, the rate of population growth, and the nature of technology. One of the best known of this class of

---

[20] See, for example, H. M. Myint, "An Interpretation of Economic Backwardness," *Oxford Economic Papers*, VI (June, 1954), pp. 132–163; Paul A. Baran, *The Political Economy of Growth* (New York: Monthly Review Press, 1957), pp. 83–91.

theories—and the one of most interest for the approach followed here in analyzing Northern Rhodesia's development—contrasts the factor proportions technologically required in the export sector with the supply of productive factors actually available in the less developed nations.[21] According to this factor-proportions theory, the technological nature of the production function in the industrial export sector is such that relatively fixed proportions of capital and labor are required for production. Furthermore, the necessary proportion of capital to labor tends to be high. In the rural sector, on the other hand, factor coefficients are not technologically fixed. Capital and labor can be substituted for each other over a wide range of factor proportions in order to produce a specified output level.

The factor-proportions approach begins the explanation of the growth experience of the less developed nations by noting that the export industries in these countries were created by means of investment from the advanced colonial powers. The activities of the colonial countries extended beyond investment in the export industry. They became involved in the political and social structure. One very important effect of this general involvement was a sharp reduction in the death rate of the indigenous population. Such activities as establishing law and order, undertaking public-health measures, and eliminating periodic famines within parts of the countries resulted in a population explosion in these areas. The increase in the labor force was faster than the rate of capital formation (and thus the rate at which new jobs were created) in the industrial sector. Relatively more and more workers were therefore forced into the rural sector. As capital accumulation was very slow in this sector, the additional labor was absorbed only by increasing the ratio of labor to land and capital. Finally, as the land became used more and more intensively, the marginal productivity of labor fell to zero. Disguised unemployment in the rural economy was the eventual result of the opening up of an industrial export sector.

The factor-proportions approach is highly suggestive, but it leaves a number of loose ends. Why, for example, are not other industries created in response to the nonlabor input requirements of the initial export industry, and to the consumption spending of the workers employed in this industry? Or why do not rural

---

[21] See Higgins, *op. cit.*, chap. 14; R. S. Eckaus, "Factor Proportions in Underdeveloped Areas," *American Economic Review*, XLV (Sept., 1955), 539–565.

producers introduce advanced productive techniques and also undertake rapid capital accumulation? Such developments would tend to prevent the disguised unemployment that eventually occurs in the model. The answer usually given is that, although some of these reactions occur, the population explosion more than offsets these effects. This answer is insufficient in view of the fact that very rapid population increases occurred with the successful development of most of the developed countries.

The analysis of Northern Rhodesian growth that follows draws upon elements in all three groups of explanations of the development process. Particular sociological and cultural factors that influenced the nature of the country's growth are stressed as well as certain market conditions that developed within the economy. Most of the emphasis, however, is upon the basic productive characteristics of the economy. In particular, a theory of growth is formulated in which the technological nature of the production function is the key relationship. This theory is presented in chapter 3 and then tested against Rhodesian growth experience throughout the rest of the study. Other possible explanations of this growth are also examined. These include both those that emphasize the impeding effects of monopolistic actions by special groups and those that point to the obstacles caused by the limited wants of the indigenous population.

The analysis is in the neoclassical tradition in that the tools of neoclassical economics are used, but the crude capital accumulation model of the main writers in this tradition is considerably refined in applying it to the underdeveloped countries. A disaggregative dynamic approach is used in which the demand and supply effects caused by the establishment of a particular export industry are analyzed in terms of the specific commodities and factors affected. The development process is like a complex, automatic machine with feedback mechanisms. For advanced countries a few simple aggregative relationships may suffice to depict this growth machine. But, for less developed countries simple relations are inadequate for covering large numbers of development cases. It is necessary to analyze the component parts of the growth mechanism. And in so doing, general principles must be established. If this is not done, one is merely describing and not theorizing about development. In the model presented here, certain characteristics of the production functions of the export sector provide the basis for generalization and yet enable the development process to be considered on a disaggregative industry level. Before presenting the theory and testing it against Rhodesian development experience, the next chapter outlines the main features of this country's growth between 1920 and 1960.

2

Forty Years of Rhodesian Growth

An Introductory Survey

A BRIEF ACCOUNT OF POLITICAL CHANGES

Northern Rhodesia ended its status as a British protectorate on October 24, 1964, and—under the name of the Republic of Zambia—began its history as an independent nation. It had been more than seventy years since the British government first extended its power over the region in 1891.[1] The Crown did not, however, directly take over the administration of the country at that time. The British South Africa Company, which was organized by Cecil Rhodes, was given this function under a Royal Charter granted in 1889. Before 1911 the area was divided into two parts, North-Western Rhodesia and North-Eastern Rhodesia, each of which was separately administered by the company. The two territories were combined in 1911 under the name of Northern Rhodesia. The British South Africa Company relinquished its

---

[1] For a history of Northern Rhodesia up to 1914, see L. H. Gann, *The Birth of a Plural Society* (Manchester: Manchester University Press, 1958). The same author presents a history of the country up to 1953 in *A History of Northern Rhodesia* (London: Chatto and Windus, 1964). A few of the many other detailed accounts of political developments in Northern Rhodesia during the period covered by this study are: Edward Clegg, *Race and Politics* (London: Oxford University Press, 1960); Richard Gray, *The Two Nations* (London: Oxford University Press, 1960); Colin Leys and Crawford Pratt, *A New Deal in Central Africa* (London: Heinemann, 1960); P. Keatley, *The Politics of Partnership* (Baltimore: Penguin Books, 1963); Philip Mason, *Year of Decision: Rhodesia and Nyasaland in 1960* (London: Oxford University Press, 1960); C. H. Thompson and H. W. Woodruff, *Economic Development in Rhodesia and Nyasaland* (London: E. Dobson, 1954).

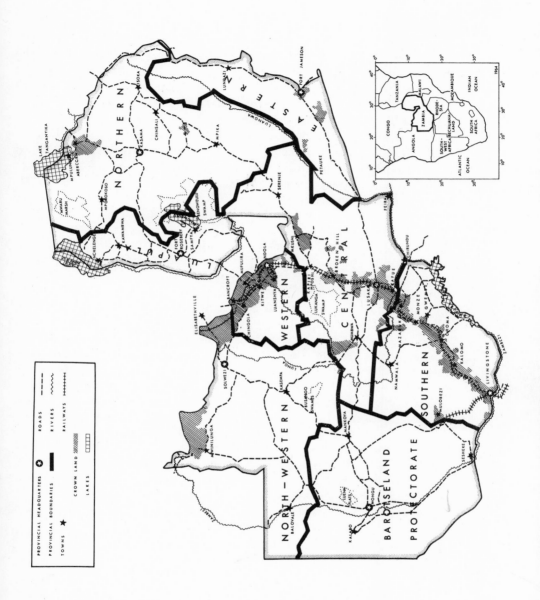

NORTHERN RHODESIA (Zambia), 1960.

SOURCE: Based on map drawn by Survey Department, Lusaka, 1960.

administrative control in 1924, at which time a governor was appointed and a legislative council established.

In 1953, Northern Rhodesia, Southern Rhodesia (now Rhodesia), and Nyasaland (now Malawi) formed the Federation of Rhodesia and Nyasaland. The federal government's responsibilities included such matters as external affairs, defense, immigration, public health, non-African education, and (in Northern Rhodesia and Southern Rhodesia) non-African agriculture. The individual territorial governments exercised residual powers in such fields as law and order; taxation other than the income tax, sales taxes, customs, excise and export duties; labor; mining; African education; African agriculture; and provisional, district, and native administration. The federation was dissolved at the end of 1963.

Within Northern Rhodesia successive constitutional changes after 1924 gradually increased the relative importance of elected (in contrast to appointed) members of the Legislative Council. But until 1958 the electoral law had remained virtually unchanged since 1925. In practice it left almost all Africans without a vote. Thereafter, however, events moved fairly rapidly toward independence under an African government. An African coalition government emerged from the general elections of 1962, and a new constitution, giving internal self government and based on the principle of one man–one vote, was put into effect in 1963. The elections of early 1964 resulted in a clear victory for the United National Independence Party and its leader, Kenneth Kaunda. The new government immediately made a formal request to the British government for independence, and Zambia with Dr. Kaunda as its president came into existence in October of the same year. It was made clear from the outset of the conferences resulting in independence that the new state would seek membership in the British Commonwealth.

THE NORTHERN RHODESIAN ECONOMY IN THE 1920's

A worldwide ranking of countries for the early 1920's, starting with the most economically backward, would certainly find Northern Rhodesia near the beginning of the list.[2] Economic

---

[2] The term "backwardness" is used as a description of the economic characteristics that affect the productive efficiency of a country's people. It denotes that levels of technological knowledge, general education, health, basic diet, and so on, among most of the people are low in comparison with the so-called advanced countries, such as the United States and Great Britain.

life for most of the nearly 1 million Africans was not too different from the primitive state that David Livingstone observed during his famous journeys through the territory seventy years earlier.[3] Europeans (only 3,000 lived there in 1921) had achieved remarkable results in eliminating the slave trade, preventing tribal wars, and spreading Christianity, but the economy was still such that more than 96 percent of the population lived in the rural subsistence sector.

Economic Activity in the European Sector

The European population was very small in number and concentrated in area. For example, in 1921, 82 percent of the Europeans lived in the country's southern and central districts where the three main towns—Livingstone (the capital at that time), Lusaka (the capital since 1935), and Broken Hill—were located.[4] Furthermore, most of those who did not actually live in these three towns resided within only a few miles of the railway line connecting them.[5] The railroad, which ran from Livingstone in the south, through Lusaka and Broken Hill, to the Congo border in the north, was the artery of European economic life. It was constructed shortly after the British South Africa Company was given the power to administer the area in 1899 and 1900.[6] The railroad reached Livingstone in 1905 and Broken Hill in 1906.

---

[3] Livingstone was by no means the first non-African to explore the region, but his travels provided the rest of the world with the first authentic information on Northern Rhodesia. From the 1790's onward, Portuguese explorers and traders traveled through parts of the country and Arab slave traders also operated in the northeastern part of the country. See Gann, *The Birth of a Plural Society.*

[4] The 2 administrative districts (out of a total of 10 in the territory at that time) were Batoka and Luangwa (*Blue Book for the Year Ended 31 December 1924,* no. 1, Northern Rhodesia [Livingstone: Government Printer, 1925], p. 2). Forty-one percent of all the European population in the country resided in Livingstone, Lusaka, Broken Hill, and Fort Jameson—a community of 66 Europeans located near the Nyasaland border ("Census of Northern Rhodesia Taken 3 May 1921," Northern Rhodesia [National Archives of Rhodesia and Nyasaland, Salisbury, Item No. A 3/19/2/5], p. iii).

[5] One other group in the economy that should be mentioned is the Indian population. Although very small in numbers (56 in 1921), this group played an important role as storekeepers, traders, and hawkers who dealt primarily with the African population.

[6] The charter of the company issued in 1889 dealt mainly with Southern Rhodesia and did not specify a northern boundary. The Barotseland North-Western Order in Council of 1899 and the North-Eastern Rhodesia Order in Council of 1900, however, explicitly extended the company's sphere of administration north of the Zambezi River. In 1911 North-Western and North-Eastern Rhodesia were combined into Northern Rhodesia.

The 506-mile-long line was finally completed to the Congo border in 1909.[7] Except for an insignificant distance of macadam all-weather roads (42 miles in 1925)[8] it was the only reliable means of transportation in the territory for many years.

The main nontertiary economic activity undertaken by Europeans was agriculture.[9] One-third of the European males listing an occupation in the 1921 census were farmers. Most of these 504 farmers lived along the line of rail south and north of Lusaka, and cultivated maize (corn) as their main crop. In 1921, the 29,000 acres under maize cultivation yielded a crop of 145,000 bags of 200 pounds each. Of these, 68,000 bags were exported (mainly to the copper mines in the Congo), 18,000 bags were consumed on the farms, and 59,000 bags were sold locally.[10] Other minor amounts of European farm income were derived from cattle, garden crops, and groundnuts. The only other significant European farming area was around Fort Jameson[11] where in 1921 there were 30 tobacco farmers. The 1924 flue-cured tobacco crop of 1.1 million pounds was exported for £91,000 and amounted to 60 percent of the total export value of agricultural products that year.[12] Transportation difficulties in this area were considerable, and only a product of high value in terms of its weight, such as tobacco, was profitable. Tobacco had to be sent about 300 miles by motor truck to Nyasaland, railed to Muraco in Mozambique, off-loaded, and transported by barge across the

---

[7] *Mining Developments in Northern Rhodesia*, Rhodesian Anglo-American (London, 1929).

[8] *Northern Rhodesia Report for 1926*, Colonial, no. 1380, Great Britain, Colonial Office (London: H.M.S.O., 1928), p. 18. There were only 1,875 miles of road suitable for motor traffic in 1924, and there were no bus or trucking companies (*Blue Book . . . 1924*, Section F$_a$3).

[9] "Census . . . 1921," table 16.

[10] S. Milligan, *Report on the Present Position of the Agricultural Industry and the Necessity, or Otherwise, of Encouraging Further European Settlement in Agricultural Areas*, Northern Rhodesia (Livingstone: Government Printer, 1931), p. 6, hereafter referred to as the *Milligan Report*. The price of maize averaged 11s. 5d. per bag between 1919 and 1929.

[11] The size of the European population in the Tanganyika District (20,311 square miles) in 1927 illustrates the extent of settlement in the rest of the country. There were 43 Europeans of whom 11 were women. The occupations of the males were: 12 missionaries, 9 farmers and ranchers, 8 administrative officers, and 3 commercial men or traders. The native population was estimated to be 106,500 ("Report of the Native Reserves Commission, 1927," Northern Rhodesia, Native Reserves Commission, Tanganyika District [National Archieves of Rhodesia and Nyasaland], pp. 13–14).

[12] *Blue Book . . . 1924*, Sections V2 and T.

Zambezi, and then finally shipped by rail to the port of Beira, also in Mozambique.[13]

Mining activities engaged only 133 Europeans in 1921 and involved mainly the production of lead and zinc at Broken Hill. The 1924 export value of metals (mostly lead) was £161,000. This sum, plus the £153,000 of agricultural exports, constituted about 70 percent of the total export value of £456,000 in that year. Copper production was very small, contributing only £7,000 to total exports. The Bwana Makubwa mine near the Congo border produced a modest amount of copper during World War I, but extraction difficulties forced its shutdown from 1920 to 1926.

Manufacturing and construction were even less important than mining as industries of European employment. The former industry employed 58 Europeans and the latter 52 at the 1921 census date. The Zambezi Sawmills near Livingstone was the only significant manufacturing establishment.[14]

Tertiary activities, consisting of administration and defense, transportation, trade, and other services, actually represented the main category of economic activity for Europeans. Fifty-four percent of those gainfully occupied were involved in these pursuits.[15]

Even though the European population was small and mostly confined to a small geographical area, a not insignificant number of Africans participated in the European directed and financed economic activities just described. By this time, the migration system, under which Africans sought employment for short periods, for example, a year, on European farms or in urban areas, was well established.[16] In 1921 36,000 African men worked for wages.[17] Their main forms of employment were: farm laborers

---

[13] "Agricultural Report, 1926," Northern Rhodesia, Department of Agriculture (National Archives of Rhodesia and Nyasaland).

[14] This firm mainly produced railway sleepers.

[15] Trade (mostly in transit) with the Congo was especially important. In 1924 the Beira and Mashonaland Railway and the Rhodesia Railways, whose 2,462 miles of line ran from Vryburg in the Union of South Africa and Beira in Mozambique through Southern Rhodesia up to the Congo, earned half of its revenue from this traffic (*Report of the General Manager for the Railway: Financial Year Ended 30th September 1925*, Beira and Mashonaland and Rhodesia Railways [Bulawayo, 1926], p. 6).

[16] This migration system will be discussed extensively in chapter 5.

[17] "Census . . . 1921," pp. 74–75. The number of women accompanying the men was only 1,200.

(38.5 percent), domestic servants (10 percent), mine laborers (7 percent), railway workers (3.9 percent), and carriers and porters (3.4 percent). Monthly wage rates for these workers mostly ranged between 5 and 10 shillings ($1.21–$2.42) in cash, plus rations (mainly food) equivalent to perhaps another 7 shillings ($1.70).[18]

Besides obtaining employment within Northern Rhodesia, large numbers of Africans accepted jobs outside the territory. For example, in 1921 the Rhodesian Native Labour Bureau recruited 13,000 individuals for employment in Southern Rhodesian mining and farming, and Robert Williams and Company recruited 7,260 for employment in the Katanga copper mines in the Congo.[19] A small number were also hired by recruiters for work on the sisal plantations in Tanganyika. On their own initiative, many more workers migrated to these same countries without a labor contract.[20] A total of 36,000 adult males—about the same number as those working in urban areas within the country—were known to be at work outside the country in 1921, and the census-takers believed this number to be an underestimate of the actual figure.

Data covering earnings of Europeans in the early twenties are difficult to obtain except for information provided by the administrator and by Rhodesia Railways. The lowest-paying government occupation was a Grade I teacher (£210–240 annually), and the highest was the administrator's position (£1,500 an-

---

[18] Wage sources: *Estimates of Revenue and Expenditure for the Year Ended 31 March 1923*, British South Africa Company (Livingstone: Government Printer, 1922); *Blue Book . . . 1924*, Section W.

[19] "Annual Report for the Year Ended 31st March 1922," Northern Rhodesia, Secretary for Native Affairs (National Archives of Rhodesia and Nyasaland), pp. 5–6.

[20] The term of the labor contract under the recruiter arrangement was 1 year in Southern Rhodesia and 6 months in Katanga. Deferred wage payments and repatriation were parts of both contracts. It was estimated in 1926 that about £54,000 was brought back in cash to Northern Rhodesia by recruited workers and another £25,000 by those returning independently ("Report upon Native Affairs for the Year 1926," Northern Rhodesia, Native Affairs Department [Livingstone], p. 10). The Secretary for Native Affairs described the employment-seeking trip of these Africans as follows: "The Native inhabitant of the Tanganyika Plateau today walks three hundred miles or more to find employment at sixpence a day rather than be content with twopence nearer home whether it be Northwards to the sisal plantations of Tanganyika Territory, Westwards to the Katanga, or Southwards to the Mines at Bwana M'Kubwa or Broken Hill. It takes him three weeks or more to complete his journey and with a scant and uncertain supply of food on the way he not seldom arrives and engages upon labor to which he is utterly unaccustomed in a half starved and emaciated condition" ("Report upon Native Affairs for the Year 1927," p. 23).

nually).[21] Typical annual wages between these extremes were: junior clerks (£300–460); warrant officers, noncommissioned officers, and constables (£250–450); native commissioners (£325–550); Grade IV (highest) teachers (£340–380); assistant printers (£440); and medical officers (£600–850). In the railroad industry annual wages were, for instance, £270 for a mainline fireman and £363 for a Class I carriage and wagon examiner.[22] On the basis of this scanty evidence, probably no adult European male received full-time earnings less than £200 a year, and most probably earned between £275 and £400. This compares with an average earnings figure of £150 for artisans in the British building trades in 1924.[23]

This large intercountry disparity was partly a result of the difficult living conditions in Rhodesia. For example, the death rate among the comparatively young European population was 13.4 per thousand, with blackwater fever and malaria being the greatest killers.[24] The incidence of illness from such diseases as malaria, bilharziasis, and tropical ulcers was high. As late as 1930, more than half of Ndola's white population contracted malaria during the malaria season. Educational facilities in the country were also very poor, and in the early twenties only 40 percent of the European children between 5 and 15 years of age attended school.

African Health and Educational Conditions

If living conditions for Europeans at this time can be described as rugged, for Africans they must be characterized as appalling. The most striking contrast between the two groups relates to health conditions. Whereas the infant mortality rate among Europeans was around 11 percent,[25] it was apparently well over 50 percent for the African population.[26] In 1925, for example, the infant mortality rate on certain government stations was listed as 42 percent for Africans, but the medical officer remarked that the actual rate "is considerably higher than these figures

---

[21] *Estimates of Revenue and Expenditure . . . 1923.*

[22] *Interim Report of Commission To Report on Railway Dispute,* Southern Rhodesia (Salisbury: Government Printer, 1927).

[23] Calculated from data obtained in *Ministry of Labour Gazette,* Great Britain, Ministry of Labour and National Service (Jan., 1927), p. 11.

[24] *Medical Report on Health and Sanitary Conditions for the Years 1925 and 1926,* Northern Rhodesia (London: Crown Agents for the Colonies, 1928), p. 22. The median age in 1921 was 27 years.

[25] *Ibid.,* p. 19.

[26] "Report upon Native Affairs . . . 1926," p. 23.

would indicate" and noted that it had been estimated to be as high as 70 percent.[27] Even if an African was fortunate enough to survive his first year, his future was still likely to be one of debilitating disease and early death. Malaria was a standard disease for almost all. At the Katanga mines 60 percent of African children ages 1–5 in 1923 were found with malaria parasites in their blood,[28] and even in the early 1940's 50 to 60 percent of the children on the Northern Rhodesian Copperbelt suffered from the disease.[29] A study in one district revealed that "a minimum of 25 percent of the total native population is affected with yaws in one of its forms."[30] This disease, which resembles syphilis, causes grotesque deformations through the appearance of ulcers on the face, limbs, and other parts of the body.[31] Syphilis itself was also common. Among the Lungu tribe near Lake Tanganyika, 50 percent of the population suffered from this malady.[32] Two other prevalent debilitating diseases were bilharziasis and hookworm. In 1914 a doctor discovered "no less than 30 per cent" of the prisoners in the Salisbury (Southern Rhodesia) jail were infected with bilharziasis,[33] and a routine examination of African patients in the Livingstone hospital in 1926 indicated that 90 percent had hookworm disease.[34] There were also 3,100 known cases of leprosy among the African population in 1925, and the medical officer believed that an effective survey would at least double this figure. Sleeping sickness was yet another terrible disease afflicting Africans, although by this time its incidence apparently was quite low and confined mainly to the area along the Luangwa River in the east.[35] In addition to these more unusual maladies, pneumonia and influenza were widespread.

The high incidence of sickness and death is not hard to under-

---

[27] *Medical Report . . . 1925 and 1926,* p. 17.
[28] Sir Malcolm Watson, *African Highway* (London: John Murray, 1953), p. 194.
[29] *Ibid.,* p. 183.
[30] *Medical Report . . . 1925 and 1926,* pp. 125–142, appendix by Dr. J. A. Acheson on 2,279 consecutive cases of yaws treated in Kasempu District of Northern Rhodesia, 1925–1926.
[31] See M. Gelfand, *The Sick African* (3d ed.; Cape Town: Juta, 1957) for a medical analysis of yaws as well as the other tropical diseases mentioned in the text. As an example of a case "which may be met with every day of the week" even in the late forties, Gelfand describes a native patient who simultaneously is "suffering from sleeping sickness, hookworm disease, bilharziasis, pellagra, and possibly chronic malaria as well" (*ibid.,* p. 31).
[32] "Report of the Native Reserves Commission, 1927," p. 17.
[33] M. Gelfand, *Tropical Victory* (Cape Town: Juta, 1953), p. 203.
[34] *Medical Report . . . 1925 and 1926,* p. 14.
[35] *Ibid.,* p. 15.

stand, when one considers the lack of medical assistance available to the African population. As late as 1928 there were only fifteen medical officers in the territory, and these spent most of their time working with the European population.[36] In 1925 the 9 native hospitals treated only 5,610 Africans as inpatients. Seven of these hospitals were near the main centers of European settlement.[37] The only other qualified doctors available to the general public were those at the 10 or so small missionary hospitals.[38] Africans did have their own medical specialists,[39] but contrary to a frequently expressed popular belief, their methods were not very effective. Treatment consisted more of attempts to heal by suggestion than by the use of drugs.[40]

Harsh working conditions in the mines contributed to the high disease and death rate. Not only were the recruits young men who probably were as healthy as any group in the African population, but any individual in obvious ill health was rejected through medical examinations before beginning employment. Those who became ill were given medical treatment at the mine hospitals. All this notwithstanding, at the Broken Hill lead and zinc mine, the death rate among Africans was 29.2 per thousand in 1922, and among those recruited to work in the copper mines in Katanga Province in the Congo, the rate was 24 per thousand. Pneumonia was listed as the most important cause of death.

Education is another field that demonstrates the extent of backwardness in the early 1920's. With the exception of the Barotse National School, all African educational facilities until 1924 were operated and financed by various missionary societies. The government did not spend funds on African education until 1925, at which time it made a contribution of £348 to the missionary schools. By 1929 the figure had reached £8,493. Barotseland was the only district in the country where a certain proportion (10

---

[36] *Medical Report on Health and Sanitary Conditions for the Year 1928,* Northern Rhodesia (London: Crown Agents for the Colonies, 1929), p. 15.

[37] In 1929 the medical director described the facilities at all but two native hospitals as unsatisfactory (*Medical Report on Health and Sanitary Conditions for the Year 1929,* Northern Rhodesia [London: Crown Agents for the Colonies, 1930], p. 31).

[38] *Ibid.*

[39] See Edwin W. Smith and A. M. Dale, *The Ila-Speaking Peoples of Northern Rhodesia* (London: Macmillan, 1920), Vol. I, chap. x, for a description of medical activities among the natives.

[40] C. M. Doke, *The Lambas of Northern Rhodesia* (London: George G. Harrap, 1931), pp. 274–275.

percent) of the native tax was returned to the Paramount Chief.
It was from these funds that the Barotse school was established
and maintained. In 1926 the average number of students in attendance in the Barotse National School and its outschools was
about 360 boys with only 9 of these in Standard IV (the equivalent of the fifth and sixth grades).[41] Throughout the rest of the
territory, the 6 missionary societies, with 207 European teachers,
performed a remarkable job, but naturally they were primarily
concerned with religious education. Average attendance in 1924
was listed as 40,000, but this figure is misleading. Most of these
students attended village schools that frequently ran only for a
few weeks during the year. Furthermore, as the Director of
Native Education notes in his 1929 report: "The work of a
village teacher was principally of a religious nature, and as a rule
only the elements of the three R's were taught. Even on the
stations,[42] with a few outstanding exceptions, the primary aim of
education was to produce evangelistic teachers, competent to
teach the scripture and elementary reading and writing in the
vernacular and of sufficiently reliable character to be sent out
in charge of village schools." [43] The number of natives acquiring
vocational skills was also small.[44] In short, the level of African
education in the early twenties was extremely rudimentary, and
literacy in English was generally not an educational objective.
Probably much less than 1 percent of the African population
could read and write English.

African Agriculture

A survey of economic conditions for the African population in
the twenties is not complete without a description of agricultural
techniques. Although progress toward the use of better farming
techniques has been made since then, especially in the line-of-rail
and Eastern Province areas, the practices discussed are still used
extensively in the subsistence sector. The most famous type of
subsistence agriculture practiced in the twenties was undoubtedly

---

[41] "Annual Report on Native Education, 1926," Northern Rhodesia (National
Archives of Rhodesia and Nyasaland), Appendix III.

[42] The reference is to the missionary stations of which there were 75 in 1926.
The village schools were free, but the station schools with educational facilities
up to Standard IV charged an average of £2 per year (*Annual Report of the
Director of Native Education for the Year 1929*, Northern Rhodesia [London:
Crown Agents for the Colonies, 1931], p. 11).

[43] *Ibid.*, p. 2.

[44] "Report upon Native Affairs . . . 1926," p. 6.

the so-called chitemene system. This ash-cultivation method has been aptly termed "slash and burn" or "Guy Fawkes" farming. It was prevalent in much of North-Eastern Rhodesia and also the northern sections of North-Western Rhodesia.[45] Agriculture as practiced today by the Mambwe tribe,[46] located in the woodland areas near the Tanganyika border, illustrates the essentials of the chitemene system.[47] Between July and September the men of the tribe lop off the trees of the surrounding forest preparatory to the establishment of a new garden. If the forest is abundant, only the branches are cut off; if not, the trees are cut to within about 4 feet of the ground. Any trees or branches in excess of 4 inches in diameter are cleared and set aside for fencing the garden. The women then collect the cut branches and carry (not drag, since some of the leaves would fall off) them to the site of the new garden. They are stacked in a circular pile to a height of about 2 feet over the garden site, which covers an area of about 1.75 acres. The branches are left to dry until the end of October, when the windy season has passed and the rains are about to commence. At this time the pile is fired by the men, after which the garden is ready for sowing. Pumpkins and squashes are planted around the edges of the garden and castor-oil seeds around any anthills or charred tree stumps. Near the

---

[45] A complete classification of native agricultural systems was undertaken in two ecological surveys: C. G. Trapnell and J. N. Clothier, *The Soils, Vegetation and Agricultural Systems of North-Western Rhodesia* (2d ed.; Lusaka: Government Printer, 1957), and C. G. Trapnell, *The Soils, Vegetation and Agriculture of North-Eastern Rhodesia* (Lusaka: Government Printer, 1953). The first report was based on fieldwork from 1932–1934 and the second on investigations carried out during 1937, 1938, and 1940.

[46] For an analysis of the tribal structure of Northern Rhodesia, see J. Moffat Thomson, *Memorandum on the Native Tribes and Tribal Areas of Northern Rhodesia*, Northern Rhodesia, Native Affairs Department (Livingstone: Government Printer, 1934).

[47] The agriculture of these peoples was described in 1932 by U. J. Moffat, "Native Agriculture in the Abercorn District," in *Second Annual Bulletin of the Department of Agriculture*, Northern Rhodesia (Livingstone: Government Printer, 1933), pp. 55–62, and more recently by W. Watson, *Tribal Cohesion in a Money Economy* (Manchester: Manchester University Press, 1958). Although Watson's fieldwork was done in 1952–1953 and Moffat's from 1928 on, the descriptions of the system are identical. The description in the text is based mainly on Moffat's investigations. Other descriptions of the chitemene system in this general area made before and during the twenties are contained in T. C. Moore, *Report on the Possibilities of Developing a Cotton Growing Industry on the North-Eastern Plateau and Neighboring Valleys of Northern Rhodesia*, Northern Rhodesia, Agriculture Department (Livingstone: Government Printer, 1926); "Report of the Native Reserves Commission, 1927," pp. 17–23; C. Gouldsbury and H. Sheane, *The Great Plateau of Northern Rhodesia* (London: Edward Arnold, 1911), pp. 291–308.

end of December, finger millet seed is scattered in the ashes.
Except for construction by the men of a 4- or 5-foot fence around
the garden to protect it from all wild animals but elephants, no
other work is necessary before harvesting. The burning eliminates
the necessity of weeding and no other cultivation is done. In
May or June the women harvest the millet crop, while the men
build platforms for drying it. New millet gardens are made
every year, with an average of 10 acres of woodlands required
for 1 acre of garden. A garden is not abandoned, however, for
the initial millet crop is followed in successive years by groundnuts and then by beans on mounds.[48] The life of a garden is
three or four years.

Although thought to be incredibly wasteful [49] by most Europeans, who believe its usage is attributable mainly to the laziness
of the natives, agricultural officers discovered the chitemene system to be surprisingly productive. In a series of experiments,
the ash-cultivation method was found to yield three times the
amount of millet produced by preparing the seed beds in the
normal manner for cereal crops, that is, by hoeing.[50] Burning
the branches appreciably enhanced the phosphate and potash
status of the soils, increased the degree of calcium saturation, and
corrected the acid condition of the soil.[51]

The chitemene system was well adapted to the resource conditions of the twenties, because woodlands were still relatively
abundant in most of these areas. The technique made extensive
use of the comparatively cheap woodlands, and was therefore
economically efficient. But it apparently was insufficient for large-
scale village production, for too large an area of woodlands was
required. So much time and effort would be involved just traveling from the village to the gardens that it seems doubtful if
farmers could produce enough output to match, for example,
the income they could earn in urban employment. The chitemene

---

[48] Trapnell, *op. cit.*, p. 49. Sometimes the mounds are spread and millet sown
again.

[49] For a typical European view, which describes the system as "disastrous" in
terms of the deforestation and depletion it causes, see *North Charterland Concession Inquiry: Report to the Governor of Northern Rhodesia by the Commissioner, Mr. Justice Maugham*, Colonial, no. 73, Great Britain, Colonial Office (London: H.M.S.O., 1932), p. 3.

[50] Moffat, *op. cit.*, p. 61.

[51] H. B. Stent, "Observations on the Fertilizer Effect of Wood Burning in the
'Chitemene' System," in *Second Annual Bulletin of Department of Agriculture,
Northern Rhodesia* (Livingstone: Government Printer, 1933), p. 49. Unfortunately
the amount of labor time used in the different experiments is not reported.

method also was uneconomic in areas of heavy population expansion. Subsistence farmers in these regions turned to hoe cultivation.

Hoe cultivation also has been employed for many years in the southern plateau area to the west of the railroad line where trees were more sparsely scattered. The burning of trees in this area is undertaken more with a view to clearing the land rather than to fertilizing it.[52] Hoe cultivation, unlike the chitemene system, produced considerably lower yields than were obtainable by using the more advanced European techniques. One set of experiments showed, for example, the yield with hoeing to be about two bags (200 pounds each) of maize per acre, whereas if manure was added and contour ridges established, the per acre output jumped to around six bags.[53]

The grassland cultivation of the central Barotseland plain is another distinct technique of farming and represents the most complex type of subsistence agriculture in the country. A variety of different types of gardens is made, each of which is dependent upon the nature of the soil and the amount of moisture available.[54] Along the floodplains of the Zambezi River, for example, there are small gardens of maize and kaffir corn which are enriched by the alluvium of each annual flood and by the manure of staked cattle. In the watershed plains, on the other hand, trenches about one and a half feet wide are dug between long strips of hoed grass, and the soil from the trenches is then piled upon the strips of hoed grassland. The tribes in this area remain in one place instead of moving their villages every four or five years because of the loss of soil fertility, as do most of the tribes in the country.

The cattle-raising area within the territory is limited by the widespread prevalence of the tsetse fly (the carrier of cattle trypanosomiasis as well as human trypanosomiasis or sleeping sickness). There were four main fly-free areas in the mid-1920's:[55] most of Barotseland; the region flanking the railway line from

[52] Trapnell and Clothier, *op. cit.*, p. 22; Trapnell, *op. cit.*, pp. 38–39.

[53] *Annual Report for the Year 1940*, Northern Rhodesia, Department of Agriculture (Lusaka: Government Printer, 1940), p. 4.

[54] Besides the work of Trapnell and Clothier (*op. cit.*), agriculture in this region has been described by Max Gluckman, *The Economy of the Central Barotse Plain*, Rhodes-Livingstone Papers, no. 7 (Livingstone: Rhodes-Livingstone Institute, 1941), and D. U. Peters, *Land Usage in Barotseland*, Rhodes-Livingstone Communication, no. 19 (Lusaka: Rhodes-Livingstone Institute, 1960).

[55] *Medical Report . . . 1925 and 1926* notes that two-thirds of the territory is fly infested and that no district or even subdistrict is entirely free.

Livingstone to Broken Hill; the area around Fort Jameson; and a region running along the Tanganyika border near Abercorn.[56] Three of these four areas were the major regions of European agriculture.

African agriculture, in the early twenties, was nonmarket oriented in all but a few areas. Africans rarely dealt with the money economy, but there were some market-oriented activities.

The largest and most remunerative cash activity in the country was the fishing industry.[57] It was centered in the northeast along the Luapula River and around Lakes Mweru and Bangweulu and found its market outlet in the Katanga mines of the Congo. The district commissioner at Fort Rosebery estimated that 800 tons of dried fish were exported to the Congo in 1926.[58]

A smaller fishing industry flourished on the Kafue River in the vicinity of the railway line and in the Zambezi Valley. Trade in grains was confined to those Africans who lived in the vicinity of mines, plantations, or government stations.[59] The almost complete lack of suitable transportation facilities to the line of rail prevented any other markets from developing.[60] As one report on the northeastern plateau states:

Natives carry meal up to sixty miles to sell a basket full, which realizes about one shilling. It is not surprising that the native is not inclined to grow grain, have it ground and carry roughly four loads of fifty pounds per annum, to some distant market to obtain sufficient money to pay his tax alone. The result is that they usually plant sufficient for their own use. If the crop is a good one, they will sell the surplus, if not, they seek work from white people, usually as carriers, or suffer hunger to some degree.[61]

The African cattle industry was of some importance, although the existence of the tsetse fly confined it mainly to Barotseland. In 1926 the number of African-owned cattle was estimated as

---

[56] *Report of the Commission Appointed To Enquire into the Financial and Economic Position of Northern Rhodesia,* Colonial, no. 145, Great Britain, Colonial Office (London: H.M.S.O., 1938), pp. 8–10, hereafter referred to as the *Pim Report;* Trapnell and Clothier, *op. cit.,* pp. 25–26; Trapnell, *op. cit.,* p. 39.

[57] "Report upon Native Affairs for the Year 1928," p. 13.

[58] "Report upon Native Affairs for the Year 1927," p. 15.

[59] "Report upon Native Affairs for the Year 1926," p. 13.

[60] *Annual Report for the Year 1929,* Northern Rhodesia, Department of Agriculture (Livingstone: Government Printer, 1930), p. 5.

[61] Moore, *op. cit.,* p. 24. The tax for each male was 7s. 6d., and the price the native received for millet meal at that time was one-half pence per pound (*ibid.,* p. 45).

289,000.[62] Cattle were the only important liquid asset that an African could accumulate in the subsistence economy and were regarded as the main measure of wealth. Bride payments and other contractual obligations were made in cattle, and in earlier years apparently were slaughtered for food only at the time of special occasions or famines. By the twenties they were raised more and more frequently for sale in the monetary sector,[63] and by 1930 half the cattle sold were African owned.[64]

Except for the activities above, trade was confined to relatively small quantities of otter skins (the only African product exported overseas)[65] taken from the swamps south of Lake Bangweulu, salt, and tobacco. In some areas, village trade in locally produced iron hoes, spears, axes, and pottery continued, but most of the traditional native industries were displaced by European trade goods.[66]

THE RISE OF THE COPPER INDUSTRY

From the backward, rural territory just described, Northern Rhodesia was transformed, within two decades, into one of the most rapidly growing economies in the world. Since 1945, for example, real gross domestic product (in the monetary sector) has grown at an average annual rate of 8.5 percent (table 2-1), and for the period 1938 (the first year for which national income estimates exist) to 1961 the growth rate averaged 5.8 percent.

Copper as a Natural Resource

The impetus for this outstanding growth performance came almost entirely from the creation of a large-scale copper industry.[67]

---

[62] "Report upon Native Affairs for the Year 1926," Appendix I.

[63] Audrey I. Richards, *Land, Labour and Diet in Northern Rhodesia* (London: Oxford University Press, 1939), p. 195.

[64] *Milligan Report,* p. 19.

[65] "Report upon Native Affairs for the Year 1926," p. 14.

[66] *Ibid.,* pp. 13–14; G. Cooper, "Village Crafts in Barotseland," *Rhodes-Livingstone Journal,* XI (1951), 47–60; M. P. Miracle, "Plateau Tonga Entrepreneurs in Historical Inter-Regional Trade," *Rhodes-Livingstone Journal,* XXVI (Dec., 1959), pp. 34–50.

[67] To supplement the brief account in the text of the history of the copper industry, consult these selected sources: Kenneth Bradley, *Copper Venture* (London: Mufulira Copper Mines, 1952); L. H. Gann, "The Northern Rhodesian Copper Industry and the World of Copper: 1923–1952," *Rhodes-Livingstone Journal,* XVIII (1955), 1–18; Sir Ronald L. Prain, *The Copperbelt of Northern Rhodesia* (London: Royal Society of Arts, 1955). The *Rhodesian Mining Journal* also contains a number of articles in its 1929 volume which deal with the early history of the mines.

TABLE 2-1

NORTHERN RHODESIA'S GROSS DOMESTIC PRODUCT AND GROSS CAPITAL
FORMATION IN THE MONEY ECONOMY, 1938–1961
(in millions of pounds)

Year	(1) Gross domestic product (current prices)	(2) Gross domestic capital formation (current prices)	(3) Percentage $\frac{(2)}{(1)}$	Gross domestic[a] product (1949 prices)
1938	12.7	6.0	47.2	30.3
1945	15.0	1.6	10.7	28.6
1946	17.6	2.2	12.5	29.2
1947	27.2	4.4	16.2	32.1
1948	34.1	8.7	25.5	39.8
1949	43.9	12.0	27.3	43.9
1950	58.7	15.1	25.7	48.1
1951	85.7	19.3	22.5	55.1
1952	96.7	26.8	27.7	59.8
1953	112.4	28.9	25.7	72.9
1954	126.5	42.1	33.3	80.1
1955	154.9	47.5	30.7	76.5
1956	174.3	59.6	34.2	90.5
1957	137.3	60.1	43.8	95.1
1958	117.0	51.9	44.4	87.2
1959	164.2	43.7	26.6	106.2
1960	184.3	40.7	22.1	116.2
1961	175.3	41.2	23.5	116.1

[a] There is no satisfactory deflator of gross domestic product available for Northern Rhodesia, and the figures can only be regarded as rough estimates. The method used here was to deflate that portion of gross domestic product attributable to the mining industry by an appropriate index of mineral prices. The rest of the domestic product was deflated by an index of prices for domestic expenditure in the federation for 1954–1961, and by an index of consumer prices in Northern Rhodesia for the other years. The difficulty with this procedure is that prices of imported commodities enter into the deflator. For example, in view of a worsening in the terms of trade of about 25 percent between 1939 and 1945, it is difficult to judge whether the apparent decline shown in the table in real gross domestic product between these years is in fact significant. Copper production was 9 percent less in 1945 than in 1938 (the latter year was not surpassed in the postwar period until 1949), but a careful analysis is needed to determine whether the decline was enough to decrease the overall product figure.

SOURCES: Figures for 1938 taken from or estimated on the basis of Phyllis Deane, *The Measurement of Colonial National Incomes*, National Institute of Economic and Social Research, Occasional Paper, no. 12 (Cambridge: Cambridge University Press, 1948), chap. 3, and *Colonial Social Accounting* (Cambridge: Cambridge University Press, 1953), chap. 5. An estimate of depreciation allowances was added to the figure covering the monetary sector in these sources; data for 1945–1953 from *The National Income and Social Accounts of Northern Rhodesia, 1945–1953*, Federation of Rhodesia and Nyasaland, Central Statistical Office (Salisbury: Government Printer, 1954), table 2; the 1954–1959 figures are from *National Accounts of the Federation of Rhodesia and Nyasaland, 1954–*

TABLE 2-1—*Continued*

1959, Federation of Rhodesia and Nyasaland, Central Statistical Office (Salisbury: Government Printer, 1960). Gross domestic product data (1960 and 1961) and gross domestic capital formation (1954–1961) estimated from *National Accounts of the Federation of Rhodesia and Nyasaland, 1954–1960*, Federation of Rhodesia and Nyasaland, Central Statistical Office (Salisbury: Government Printer, 1961). Except for minor differences, the figures from all sources are based on similar methods of calculation. African subsistence output is excluded from total gross domestic product to obtain gross domestic product in the monetary sector.

The existence of copper was known, of course, long before the present industry developed. For centuries Africans worked the copper deposits of Northern Rhodesia and those just across the border in the Katanga Province of the Congo Republic. One of the main uses of copper was to fashion crosses and bars for use as mediums of exchange. It was not until around the turn of the century that European prospectors entered the area and discovered several of the ore bodies that are now mined. But even the extension of a railroad from Broken Hill to the Congo border in 1909 did not stimulate production on a large scale. Only one mine, Bwana Makubwa, was at all significant before the 1930's, and it never sustained a profitable level after World War I. The high costs of extracting copper from the comparatively low grade of oxide ore finally forced its closure in 1930.

The apparent existence in Northern Rhodesia only of oxide ores, averaging but 3 to 5 percent copper, meant that prospects were poor for the development of a copper industry. In Katanga, a copper industry developed rapidly because of the presence of large supplies of oxide ores that averaged around 15 percent copper. Ores of 6 to 7 percent copper actually were discarded in the Congo at this time as too poor to treat.[68] What was not realized was that, unlike the Katanga ore bodies, the deposits in Northern Rhodesia changed to copper sulphides of about 3 to 5 percent at moderate depths. Sulphide ores can be fed directly into smelting furnaces after the crushing and concentrating process, whereas with oxide ores a leaching process is necessary to extract the copper. In the twenties the cost of processing sulphide ores was much lower than handling oxide ores of equal copper content. Thus, the discovery of extensive sulphide ores opened up a highly lucrative investment opportunity in Northern Rhodesia.

Exploration and Growth

Several factors were responsible for the intensive copper exploration that began in 1925. In 1923 the British South Africa Com-

---

[68] *Mining Developments in Northern Rhodesia*, p. 11.

pany, in contrast to its policy in Southern Rhodesia, decided to grant exclusive prospecting rights over large areas. This policy, in conjunction with a rise in copper prices during the twenties, as the electrical and automotive industries expanded throughout the world, attracted powerful financial companies who were prepared to undertake exploratory drilling on a large and systematic scale. The perfection of the flotation process during the second decade also gave a boost to the entire industry. This method of concentrating copper ore was much more economical than the use of vibrating tables. Another factor especially important for Northern Rhodesian development was the great improvement in methods of malarial control. Malaria and blackwater fever were rife on the Copperbelt, and without the control knowledge obtained by Sir Ronald Ross and Sir Malcolm Watson in the Malay Peninsula of Southeast Asia, it would have been difficult to attract a sizable European labor force.

Development work on four mines—Roan Antelope, Mufulira, Rhokana, and Nchanga—began in the late twenties. The first two are controlled by Rhodesian Selection Trust (now Roan Selection Trust), a holding company in which the American Metal Climax Company of New York has a 50.6 percent ownership interest. Rhokana and Nchanga, on the other hand, are controlled by the Anglo-American Corporation of South Africa. Despite its name, this is a British and South African firm that also controls large mineral interests in the Republic of South Africa. Roan Antelope and Rhokana began operations in 1931, but the depression postponed the opening of Mufulira until 1933, and Nchanga until 1939. Additional mines were put into operation in the 1950's. Chibuluma, a Rhodesian Selection Trust mine, started production in 1956, and Bancroft, an Anglo-American firm, opened in 1957. The latter mine soon closed because of the depressed copper market and technical difficulties, but reopened in 1959. In 1963, Rhodesian Selection Trust announced the start of development work on still another new mine in the area, Chambishi.

The rapid growth of Northern Rhodesian copper production is shown in table 2-2. Output rose from a negligible quantity in 1930 to 138,000 long tons in 1934, and then remained approximately at this level through 1937. Production rose sharply thereafter, reaching a peak of 251,000 long tons in 1943. Technical difficulties in the mines and a decline in wartime demand for copper gradually reduced production to 182,000 tons in 1946. A

TABLE 2-2

NORTHERN RHODESIAN COPPER PRODUCTION
FOR SELECTED YEARS

Year	Thousands of long tons	Percentage share of free-world market[a]
1926	1	—
1930	6	.56
1934	138	13.38
1938	213	13.42
1942	247	9.92
1946	182	11.05
1950	276	13.21
1954	379	16.16
1958	374	13.23
1960	579	15.68

[a] Free-world production defined as total world less U.S.S.R. and Yugoslavia.

SOURCES: Copper production for Northern Rhodesia from Annual Reports, 1926, 1930, 1934, 1938, 1942, 1946, 1950, 1954, Northern Rhodesia, Mines Department (Lusaka: Government Printer); *Year Book*, 1958, 1960, Northern Rhodesia Chamber of Mines (Kitwe, Rhodesian Printers); free-world production from *Mineral Resources of the United States*, 1926, 1930, U.S. Department of Commerce, Bureau of Mines (Washington: Government Printing Office); *Minerals Yearbook*, 1934, 1938, 1942, 1946, 1950, 1954, 1958, 1960, U.S. Department of the Interior, Bureau of Mines (Washington: Government Printing Office).

slow recovery took place after the war, but not until the devaluation of the pound in 1949, when the pound price of copper increased 44 percent overnight, did another rapid expansion occur. From a level of 213,000 tons in 1948, output rose to 379,000 tons in 1954. Between 1954 and 1958 the general level of production changed very little, and it was not until 1959 that further significant growth began to take place.

As the percentage figures on the Northern Rhodesian share of the world copper market indicate, the territory has continued to grow in relative importance as a world supplier since the early thirties. Only the United States, with a production of about 1,100,000 long tons, exceeded Northern Rhodesia's output of 566,000 long tons in 1960. Following Northern Rhodesia in order of importance were Chile (497,000 long tons), Canada (364,000 long tons), the Congo Republic (296,000 long tons), and Japan (184,000 long tons). Total free-world production in that year was

3,594,000 long tons.[69] In recent years the Rhodesian share of the free-world market has averaged about 16 percent. The completion of all expansion progress now under way will raise the capacity of the Northern Rhodesian mines to 690,000 long tons by 1970.[70] As world consumption of copper has been increasing at an average rate of about 4 percent annually,[71] the Rhodesian market share will decline to roughly 12 percent by 1970 if no further expansion occurs. It is unlikely that the Northern Rhodesian copper companies will allow their market share to fall, and also improbable that their share will increase significantly. The outlook is that the market share will not change significantly over the next ten years.

The world's major copper companies have long attempted to cooperate in controlling the total supply of copper on the international market. A formal international copper cartel actually existed when the modern Rhodesian mines began production in the early thirties, and they were assigned a specific production quota. But, being small producers with a considerable expansion potential—at low costs—the Rhodesian mines refused to accept their quota, and the international cartel broke down.[72] A few years later Roan Antelope played a leading part in the formation of a new international cartel that operated from 1935 to 1939.[73] Since then, there has been no formal international agreement, but rather the type of informal control over supply that is so familiar in American oligopolies. Given the low price elasticity of world copper demand (estimated to be about −0.3 by the Rhodesian companies), the slow growth in world consumption, and the large increase in world capacity which can be made without increasing costs substantially, major world producers apparently have found it mutually profitable to limit the world supply of copper. The Northern Rhodesian firms, especially Rhodesian Selection Trust, have become the output leaders, and have initiated several cutbacks in world production. They are earning a comfortable return (between 1958 and 1960 net profits averaged

---

[69] *Year Book,* 1961, Northern Rhodesia Chamber of Mines (Kitwe: Rhodesian Printers), p. 18.

[70] *First Report on a Regional Survey of the Copperbelt, 1959,* Northern Rhodesia (Lusaka: Government Printer, 1960), p. 4.

[71] Sir Ronald L. Prain, "The Copper Industry: Some Factors Affecting Its Future," in his *Selected Papers* (London: B. T. Batsford, 1961), II, 57–67.

[72] Alex Skelton, "Copper," in *International Control in the Non-Ferrous Metals,* eds. W. Y. Elliott *et al.* (New York: Macmillan, 1937), p. 472.

[73] *Report on the Copper Industry,* U.S. Federal Trade Commission (Washington: U.S. Government Printing Office, 1947), p. 238.

16 percent of the estimated market value of the industry's mining investment) [74] under present market-sharing arrangements, and apparently will not attempt to enlarge their market share significantly in the future. If this is so, the Northern Rhodesian economy cannot count on an increase of copper production of more than about 4 percent annually in the foreseeable future.

The Dominance of Mining

The domination of the Northern Rhodesian economy by the mining industry manifests itself in almost every aspect of the economic structure. For example, an average of 46.5 percent of the territory's gross domestic product originated in this one industry between 1954 and 1961 (table 2-3). Although her figures

TABLE 2-3

INDUSTRIAL ORIGIN OF THE GROSS DOMESTIC PRODUCT
OF NORTHERN RHODESIA, 1954–1961
(percentage distribution)

Industry	1954	1955	1956	1957	1958	1959	1960	1961
Agriculture								
Non-African	2.0	1.6	1.8	2.7	2.1	2.4	2.1	2.8
African	11.0	8.8	8.4	10.6	11.2	9.5	9.3	9.8
Mining and quarrying	52.4	56.8	54.0	39.0	32.6	45.4	47.5	44.1
Manufacturing	4.0	3.9	4.4	6.4	7.1	5.6	5.5	5.9
Building and								
construction	6.1	6.2	6.7	8.6	9.7	5.8	4.5	4.1
Electricity and water	.4	.4	1.6	1.9	2.5	2.0	2.3	2.2
Transport and								
communications	3.4	3.4	3.7	5.2	5.3	5.0	5.1	5.1
Distribution	5.7	5.1	5.1	6.5	6.4	5.2	5.4	5.6
African rural household								
services	6.6	5.4	4.9	6.4	7.9	7.0	6.2	6.9
All other	8.4	8.4	9.4	12.7	15.2	12.1	12.1	13.5
Total	100.0	100.0	100.0	100.0	100.0	100.0	100.0	100.0

SOURCE: *National Accounts of the Federation of Rhodesia and Nyasaland, 1954–1961*, Federation of Rhodesia and Nyasaland, Central Statistical Office (Salisbury: Government Printer, 1962), p. 72.

are not strictly comparable with those of the Central Statistical Office, Phyllis Deane found that in 1938, 54.8 percent, and in 1948, 47.4 percent, of net domestic product was attributable to

[74] Investment data from *First Report on a Regional Survey of the Copperbelt, 1959*, p. 4; net profits computed from income-tax payments as listed in *Year Book*, 1960, Northern Rhodesia Chamber of Mines (Kitwe), table 4, p. 23.

the mining industry.[75] Still another sign of the great importance of the mining industry appears in the export statistics of the economy. Between 1945 and 1953 copper exports accounted for an average of 86.5 percent of the value of all exports. Other mineral exports added another 8.8 percent to total exports. The fact that exports of mineral commodities equaled 69.3 percent of Northern Rhodesia's gross domestic product during these years demonstrates the importance of the copper industry in the entire economy.[76] After federation in 1953, these figures were no longer available, but there is no reason to believe that they changed to any significant extent.

The copper industry is also mainly responsible for the favorable postwar trend in Northern Rhodesia's terms of trade. Because of the sharp rise in copper prices, the ratio of export to import prices rose 80 percent between 1945 and 1953.[77] Separate figures for Northern Rhodesia are not available for later years because of federation,[78] but price data for the entire federation (probably much the same as for Northern Rhodesia alone) show a decline of about 20 percent between 1953 and 1961.[79]

The manner in which mining dominates the industrial struc-

---

[75] Phyllis Deane, *Colonial Social Accounting* (Cambridge: Cambridge University Press, 1953), p. 67.

[76] Export statistics from A. G. Irvine, *The Balance of Payments of Rhodesia and Nyasaland, 1945–1954* (London: Oxford University Press, 1959), pp. 223–224; gross domestic product data, including an estimate for the African subsistence sector, from *National Income and Social Accounts of Northern Rhodesia, 1945–1953*, Federation of Rhodesia and Nyasaland, Central Statistical Office (Salisbury: Government Printer, 1954), pp. 23–25.

[77] Irvine, *op. cit.*, p. 248.

[78] A terms-of-trade series covering Northern Rhodesia for the period before 1944 also is not available. But if copper prices are used to represent export prices, and if consumer prices of clothing, footwear, and household stores are used to approximate import prices, Northern Rhodesia's trading terms appear to have worsened about 25 percent between 1939 and 1945. There has also been an apparent decline in the commodity terms of trade between just before the recession of the early thirties (say 1928) and 1939. Copper prices fell very sharply in the early thirties, and in 1939 were still almost 25 percent below the 1928 level. An index of import prices does not exist, but if retail prices in South Africa are used to give a rough indication of the change in these prices, the terms of trade decreased about 20 percent between 1928 and 1939. A careful study of the terms of trade over the entire period is needed before any firm statements on the matter can be made, but there does not appear to have been any major change in commodity trading terms between the late twenties and the early sixties.

[79] *National Accounts of the Federation of Rhodesia and Nyasaland, 1954–1961*, Federation of Rhodesia and Nyasaland, Central Statistical Office (Salisbury: Government Printer, 1962), p. 8; export and import prices as reported by Irvine (*op. cit.*, p. 453) were used to run the data back to 1953.

ture is perhaps best indicated by gross-output figures for several leading industries together with the direct purchases from these sectors by the copper companies (table 2-4). Not only is metal mining by far the most important in gross-output terms, but most of the other significant industries are highly dependent upon the mining industry in a direct manner: electric power, rail transportation, timber, ferrous and metal products, and the government itself are outstanding cases. It is no exaggeration to state that without the copper industry the Northern Rhodesian economy would still be a very backward, rural economy, with European interests confined to the lead and zinc mine at Broken Hill and to tobacco growing along the line of rail.

The mining industry is the major purchaser of the outputs of most of the significant industries in Northern Rhodesia, but the share of total nonwage expenditures by the mines within Northern Rhodesia is still small. Of the main supplies used for operational purposes in the copper mines—explosives, timber, coal, furnace and firebricks, mill balls (used to crush ore), rails and fittings, and steel—about 15 percent of the timber is cut within the territory,[80] and a large share of the mill balls are manufactured in Northern Rhodesia. The rest of the articles are imported. Among the remaining stores used by the industry, the main items produced or processed to any appreciable degree within the country are clothing and clothes; limestone, cement, crushed stone, and sand; oxygen; bolts, nuts, rivets, and washers; and foodstuffs. No more than between 15 and 20 percent of the nearly £23 million spent by the copper companies on such operational stores in 1960 went for commodities processed in the manufacturing or mining sector of the economy.[81] The raw materials for such industries as clothing and steel fabrication are imported. The mines purchase a notable amount of repair and distributive services from small firms within the Copperbelt area and, of course, substantial amounts of electricity and railway services. With regard to capital outlays, all but a negligible part of the equipment purchased is imported. The mines do make considerable payments to the building and construction

---

[80] "Sixth Annual Report, 31st March 1960," Rhodesia Congo Border Timber Company (Kitwe, 1960). This company, which is owned jointly by Rhodesian Selection Trust and Anglo-American Corporation of South Africa, purchases almost all the timber requirements for the copper industry.

[81] The figures for expenditure on supplies are taken from *Year Book*, 1960, table 15. Purchases within Northern Rhodesia are estimated from the record of such payments by Mufulira and the issues by the stores department at Roan Antelope.

TABLE 2-4

Estimated Copper Companies' Purchases from Northern Rhodesian Industries,[1] 1956–1957[a]

Industry	Gross output of Northern Rhodesian industries (thousands of pounds)	Gross output of Northern Rhodesian industries purchased directly by copper companies (thousands of pounds)	Percent of gross output purchased directly (percentages)	Purchases as percent of gross copper output (percentages)
Mining and quarrying				
Metal mining	136,470	b	b	b
Stone quarrying	154	32	21	b
Manufacturing				
Grain mill products, slaughtering, dairy, and other food manufacturing	4,426	528	12	.4
Alcohol, beer, soft drinks, etc.	1,831	b	b	c
Manufactures of textiles, wearing apparel, and footwear	317	44	14	c
Manufactures of wood and cork, except furniture	739	195	26	.1
Vulcanizing and chemical products	679	161	24	.1
Bricks and structural clay	411	23	6	c
Cement and other nonmetal products	1,724	30	2	c
Ferrous and metal products	2,040	1,146	56	.8
Repair of equipment and motor vehicles	2,639	82	3	c
Printing and other manufacturing industries	822	6	1	c
Total manufacturing	15,628	2,171	14	1.6
Electricity and water				
Electricity	9,777	6,150	63	4.5
Water	337	b	b	b
Construction				
Payments to contractors	28,247	8,128	29	b
Railway services	6,553	3,991	61	2.9
Government tax revenue originating in Northern Rhodesia	48,500	32,100	66	23.5
African wages in monetary sector	26,000	6,300	24	4.6
Total European wages and salaries	41,800	15,700	38	11.5

ª Since the census of 1956–57 covers one year of data spanning both calendar years, an average for the calendar years 1956 and 1957 is given, if possible, for sources that present data on this basis.

ᵇ Not known.

ᶜ Insignificant.

SOURCES: Gross output data for all sectors except railway services, government tax revenue, and wages from *The Censuses of Production of the Federation of Rhodesia and Nyasaland, 1958–1959*, Federation of Rhodesia and Nyasaland, Central Statistical Office (Salisbury: Government Printer, 1961), pp. 43–47, and information provided privately by Central Statistical Office. Railway services: revenue for 1957 from "Annual Report," 1957, Rhodesia Railways (Bulawayo); total revenue allocated to Northern Rhodesia based on territorial allocations given in "Annual Report," 1954, Rhodesia Railways (Bulawayo), p. 37. Government tax revenue and part paid by mining companies based on table 8-2, p. 190 (see explanation presented there). Wages: data from *National Accounts of the Federation of Rhodesia and Nyasaland, 1954–1959*, Federation of Rhodesia and Nyasaland, Central Statistical Office (Salisbury: Government Printer, 1960), p. 69.

Purchases by copper companies: timber purchases: data covering 1960 from "Sixth Annual Report, 31st March 1960," Rhodesia Congo Border Timber Company (Kitwe, 1960). The 1960 expenditure per ton of copper produced was used to obtain the 1956–57 figure. Rail services purchased: information privately supplied by Northern Rhodesia Chamber of Mines. Electric power: figures based on "Directors' Report and Accounts, Year Ended December 31, 1957," Rhodesia Congo Border Power Corporation (Kitwe). The ratio of actual 1957 calendar-year purchases to 1957 gross output was applied to 1956 gross output to obtain estimated 1956 purchases. These two figures were then averaged. Payments to contractors from *Annual Report*, 1956, 1957, Northern Rhodesia, Mines Department (Lusaka, Government Printer). Most of these payments apparently were for construction work. Grain mill products, slaughtering, dairy, and all other food products: average cost of food provided Africans for 1956 and 1957 from *Year Book*, 1956, 1957, Northern Rhodesia Chamber of Mines (Kitwe). African and European wages: *Year Book*, 1956, 1957, Northern Rhodesia Chamber of Mines. All other mine purchases: Mufulira Copper Mines kindly compiled a schedule of estimated payments to Northern Rhodesian firms for 1959 and 1960. These were averaged and allocated by industry. It was assumed that the same relationship that existed between these industry expenditures and Mufulira's average 1959–1960 copper output also applied in 1956–1957. To obtain purchases by the entire industry, account was taken of Mufulira's share of total copper output. As the mines vary in their expenditure patterns, these figures are very rough.

industry within the country, and in 1959 the copper firms paid out about £4 million to this industry.

There are few domestic manufacturing activities left to be counted, once the local industries from which the copper companies make significant purchases are enumerated. A small furniture industry, a sugar refinery, several beer and soft-drink establishments, bakeries, confectionery firms, printing establishments, grain mills, slaughtering houses, and a dairy industry constitute most of the remaining list of secondary industries. The rest of the economy consists of the retail- and wholesale-trade sector, firms supplying financial services, government activities, and a commercial agricultural sector.

ECONOMIC DUALISM

The copper industry transformed Northern Rhodesia from a comparatively stationary economy into a rapidly growing one, and it now dominates the nation's industrial structure. However, development has been confined to a very small part of the total economy.

Population

A modern, highly mechanized industry has been superimposed upon a rural, backward economy, 72 percent of whose population still is engaged in subsistence production.[82] The narrowness of the development base is vividly seen when traveling within the country. Along parts of an approximately 20-mile stretch on both sides of the railway running from Livingstone to the Copperbelt there are several modern towns and many modern farms. Most of the main road running through this area has a bituminous surface—even if only 12 feet wide in parts. But, beyond this region, there are thousands of villages following agricultural techniques much the same as those practiced for hundreds of years. Village life has been much affected by the migration of the men —and to a lesser extent their wives and children—to the monetary sectors of the economy, but the African rural sector is still subsistence oriented. The villages that can be reached by road

---

[82] Subsistence population data from *National Accounts of the Federation of Rhodesia and Nyasaland, 1954–1959*, Federation of Rhodesia and Nyasaland, Central Statistical Office (Salisbury: Government Printer, 1960), p. 64.

are connected to the line of rail only by gravel and earth roads.[83]

Thus, the Northern Rhodesian economy fits the dualistic pattern found so often in underdeveloped countries. A modern, developed economy exists in the midst of a subsistence economy, apparently without stimulating development in the latter sector. Northern Rhodesia differs from most such dual economies because not only was the capital required to establish the developed enclave imported, but also a significant part of the labor involved in operating it. In 1959 there were 73,000 Europeans among the country's 2,360,000 people. The growth of this population as well as of the African, Asian, and Coloured population (defined by Rhodesian authorities as persons of mixed race other than those living amongst and in the manner of Africans) is shown in table 2-5. The major gains in European population occurred in the

TABLE 2-5

THE POPULATION OF NORTHERN RHODESIA, 1911–1959

Year	European	Coloured[a]	Asian	African (estimated)
1911	1,497	b	39	820,000
1921	3,634	145	56	980,000
1931	13,846	425	176	1,330,000
1946	21,907	804	1,117	1,660,000
1951	37,079	1,112	2,524	1,890,000
1956	65,277	1,577	5,450	2,100,000
1959	73,000	10,000		2,280,000

[a] The "coloured population" is defined by Rhodesian authorities as persons of mixed race other than those living amongst and in the manner of Africans.

[b] Data not available.

SOURCES: *Census of Population 1956*, Federation of Rhodesia and Nyasaland, Central Statistical Office (Salisbury: Government Printer, 1960), p. 3; *Report: Appendix VI—Survey of Developments Since 1953*, Great Britain, Advisory Commission on the Review of the Constitution of the Federation of Rhodesia and Nyasaland, Cmnd. 1149 (London: H.M.S.O., 1960), p. 327. These population estimates, especially the earlier years, must be taken as very rough estimates. For an attack on the validity of the population figures for both Africans and Europeans, see R. R. Kuczynski, *Demographic Survey of the British Colonial Empire* (London: Oxford University Press, 1949), II, 402, 409, 421.

twenties, during the development of the copper mines, and after World War II, when mining activity again expanded rapidly.

---

[83] In 1960 there were in Northern Rhodesia 711 miles of bituminous surface roads, 1,977 miles of gravel roads, and 18,738 miles of earth roads (*Annual Report for the Year 1960*, Northern Rhodesia, Ministry of Transport and Works [Lusaka: Government Printer, 1961], p. 44).

Among the 65,000 Europeans present in 1956 only 16 percent had resided in the federation ten or more years.[84]

Income Differences

Only about 3 percent of the total population is European, yet these people constitute about 11 percent of the entire labor force engaged in the money economy, and 15 percent of the labor force in the mining industry.[85] Almost all the skilled labor, as well as much of the semiskilled labor employed in the economy, is European. In recent years there have been some attempts—notably by the copper companies—to advance Africans into jobs with a greater skill content, but the number of Africans in jobs that can be termed as all "skilled" is still insignificant. There is, consequently, a definite racial division of the labor force into two, largely noncompeting groups. The wage level for European workers was determined initially by the prevailing level in the countries where they were recruited, and by the additional sum needed to induce them to forego the social and economic facilities of more developed countries. The African wage rate, on the other hand, was related to the much lower alternative income that could be earned in the subsistence sector. The great wage differential that these considerations brought about in the twenties and thirties would not have continued in the forties and fifties, if free and open markets had existed (see chap. 4). By means of government policies and union actions, however, the European population managed to maintain its income level far above that for Africans (table 2-6).

A more detailed view of the income differences is shown in tables 2-7 and 2-8. These present the available data on the income distribution of the economically active European, Asian, and Coloured population, as well as of the Africans employed in the country's 8 main urban areas. Table 2-9 represents an attempt to estimate the distribution of family income for the entire population. Figure 1 depicts the results of table 2-9 graphically, and compares the relationship for Northern Rhodesia with that existing in the United States. The income inequality in Northern Rhodesia is striking. Four percent of the wealthiest families, in which there are only a handful of Africans, received 35 percent of all personal income in 1959.

---

[84] *Census of Population 1956,* Federation of Rhodesia and Nyasaland, Central Statistical Office (Salisbury: Government Printer, 1960), pp. 62, 66.

[85] Labor-force percentages computed from table 2-6.

TABLE 2-6

AFRICAN AND NON-AFRICAN EARNINGS AND EMPLOYMENT BY INDUSTRY, NORTHERN RHODESIA, 1961

Industry	Africans		Non-Africans	
	Number	Average earnings (in pounds)	Number	Average earnings (in pounds)
Agriculture	40,300	54	670	956
Mining and quarrying	37,800	293	6,840	2,326
Manufacturing	21,600	137	3,430	1,493
Building and construction	30,000	120	2,400	1,434
Electricity and water	2,900	124	510	1,875
Wholesale and retail trade	14,400	124	4,990	976
Finance and insurance	500	146	1,260	1,056
Transport and communications	10,300	168	2,900	1,349
Government administration	20,600	149	3,040	1,365
Education	9,300	176	1,310	1,121
Health	6,200	122	1,140	1,256
Private domestic services	33,400	81	100	622
Other services	10,800	113	2,270	992
Total	238,100	139	30,860	1,476
Subsistence population	1,692,000	18		

SOURCES: *National Accounts of the Federation of Rhodesia and Nyasaland, 1954–1961*, Federation of Rhodesia and Nyasaland, Central Statistical Office (Salisbury: Government Printer, 1962), pp. 84–85. Subsistence population and per capita (not per employed person as in the other industries) income refers to 1959 and is from *National Accounts of the Federation of Rhodesia and Nyasaland, 1954–1959*, Federation of Rhodesia and Nyasaland, Central Statistical Office (Salisbury: Government Printer, 1960), p. 64.

TABLE 2-7

INCOME DISTRIBUTION OF NON-AFRICAN MALE POPULATION,
NORTHERN RHODESIA, 1956

Annual income class (in pounds)	European males		Asian and coloured[a] males	
	Number	Percent	Number	Percent
Under 50	113	.59	27	1.19
50–99	219	1.14	31	1.36
100–149	159	.83	71	3.12
150–199	149	.77	123	5.41
200–249	196	1.02	173	7.60
250–299	169	.88	175	7.69
300–349	233	1.21	211	9.27
350–399	222	1.15	207	9.10
400–449	234	1.22	178	7.82
450–499	254	1.32	194	8.53
500–599	426	2.21	203	8.92
600–699	732	3.80	149	6.55
700–799	944	4.91	101	4.44
800–899	1,326	6.89	70	3.08
900–999	1,618	8.41	76	3.34
1,000–1,099	1,847	9.60	64	2.81
1,100–1,199	1,161	6.03	20	.88
1,200–1,299	1,621	8.43	36	1.58
1,300–1,399	755	3.92	10	.44
1,400–1,499	1,156	6.01	19	.84
1,500–1,999	3,201	16.64	57	2.50
2,000–2,999	1,857	9.65	36	1.58
3,000–3,999	312	1.62	16	.70
4,000–4,999	137	.71	14	.62
5,000–7,499	110	.57	10	.44
7,500–9,999	40	.21	2	.09
10,000–14,999	25	.13	1	.04
15,000 and over	22	.11	1	.04
Total	19,238	99.98	2,275	99.98
Median income	£1,521		£433	

[a] The "coloured population" is defined by Rhodesian authorities as persons of mixed race other than those living amongst and in the manner of Africans.

SOURCE: *Census of Population 1956*, Federation of Rhodesia and Nyasaland, Central Statistical Office (Salisbury: Government Printer, 1960), pp. 121, 122, 124. Those in the lower income groups represent mainly part-time workers and new immigrants who had worked less than a year.

TABLE 2-8

INCOME DISTRIBUTION OF UNRATIONED[a] AFRICAN FAMILIES AND SINGLE PERSONS
IN THE URBAN AREAS, NORTHERN RHODESIA, 1960[b]

Annual income class (in pounds)	Families		Single persons	
	Number	Percent	Number	Percent
48 or less	990	1.34	3,470	10.18
More than 48 to 72	11,980	16.18	11,770	34.52
" " 72 to 96	13,860	18.72	6,830	20.03
" " 96 to 120	12,230	16.52	3,930	11.52
" " 120 to 144	12,300	16.61	3,380	9.91
" " 144 to 168	8,720	11.78	1,850	5.42
" " 168 to 192	5,430	7.33	1,030	3.02
" " 192 to 216	3,100	4.19	560	1.64
" " 216 to 240	1,570	2.12	440	1.29
" " 240 to 264	1,120	1.51	220	.64
" " 264 to 288	730	.99	190	.56
Over 288	2,000	2.70	430	1.26
Total	74,030	99.99	34,100	99.99
Median income	£116		£77	

[a] An unrationed employee does not receive any part of his wage in kind, for example, in the form of meat or mealie meal.

[b] The copper bonus of 46 percent of basic wages for the year ending June 30, 1960, is not included in these income figures. The figures also exclude 13,620 self-employed and unemployed Africans, and 4,060 employees receiving rations, who were covered in the survey.

SOURCE: *Report on Northern Rhodesia African Demographic Surveys, May to August, 1960,* Federation of Rhodesia and Nyasaland, Central Statistical Office (Salisbury, 1961), pp. 58–59.

Another outstanding feature of income flows in the economy is the comparatively small share of employee compensation in gross domestic product. Between 1954 and 1961, wages and salaries averaged 48 percent of gross national product, whereas profits and property income averaged 52 percent.[86] In the United States labor's share in the gross domestic product is about 65 percent. The large property income generated within Northern Rhodesia, coupled with the importance of foreign investment in the country's main industries, creates a significant difference between domestic product and national product. National product refers to the income earned by residents of the territory and consequently excludes income earned by foreign-owned factors of

[86] *National Accounts of the Federation of Rhodesia and Nyasaland, 1954–1961,* pp. 71, 73. Income from unincorporated enterprise was divided between profits and property income, and wage and salary income in the same proportions as that existing for all industries, excluding mining.

TABLE 2-9

DISTRIBUTION OF FAMILY INCOME, NORTHERN RHODESIA, 1959

Annual income class (in pounds)	Percent of families in each class	Percent of income in each class	Cumulative percentages for families	Cumulative percentages for income
Under 50	14.67	3.73	14.67	3.73
50–99	40.09	19.11	54.76	22.84
100–149	24.81	19.70	79.57	42.54
150–199	9.18	10.21	88.75	52.74
200–249	4.45	6.36	93.20	59.11
250–299	1.61	2.82	94.81	61.93
300–349	.57	1.19	95.38	63.12
350–399	.28	.66	95.66	63.78
400–449	.19	.51	95.85	64.29
450–499	.17	.53	96.02	64.82
500–599	.27	.94	96.29	65.76
600–699	.32	1.30	96.61	67.06
700–799	.28	1.36	96.89	68.42
800–899	.33	1.76	97.22	70.18
900–999	.37	2.22	97.59	72.40
1,000–1,099	.41	2.72	98.00	75.12
1,100–1,199	.25	1.83	98.25	76.95
1,200–1,299	.16	1.28	98.41	78.23
1,300–1,399	.16	1.35	98.57	79.58
1,400–1,499	.24	2.22	98.81	81.80
1,500–1,999	.66	7.39	99.47	89.19
2,000–2,999	.38	6.11	99.85	95.30
3,000–3,999	.07	1.48	99.92	96.78
4,000–4,999	.03	.86	99.95	97.64
5,000–7,499	.02	.95	99.97	98.59
7,500–9,999	.01	.48	99.98	99.07
10,000–14,999	.005	.41	99.98	99.48
15,000 and over	.004	.52	99.99	100.00
Total	99.99	100.00		

SOURCES: It was assumed, as is usual for Northern Rhodesia (see *Report: Appendix VI—Survey of Developments Since 1953*, Great Britain, Advisory Commission on the Review of the Constitution of the Federation of Rhodesia and Nyasaland, Cmd. 1149 [London: H.M.S.O., 1960], p. 404), that the African subsistence family comprises 5 members. The distribution of income for the 640,000 families in this sector is based upon the per capita subsistence income figure for 1959 given in *National Accounts of the Federation of Rhodesia and Nyasaland, 1954–1959*, Federation of Rhodesia and Nyasaland, Central Statistical Office (Salisbury: Government Printer, 1960), p. 64. It is also based upon the pattern of income distribution around this mean income that A. M. Morgan Rees and R. H. Howard found for a sample of African farmers in their study, "An Economic Survey of Commercial African Farming among the Sala of the Mumbwa District of Northern Rhodesia," in *Agricultural Bulletin*, no. 10, Northern Rhodesia, Department of Agriculture (Lusaka: Government Printer, 1955), p. 49. For the 265,000

TABLE 2-9—*Continued*

Africans employed for wages, 112,000 are covered by the 1960 survey cited in table 2-8. These figures have been modified to include the copper bonus received by African workers in the industry for the year ending June, 1960. As the wages of workers outside the 8 urban areas are lower than the general average within these towns, the income distribution for single workers in the 8 towns has been used to estimate the income distribution of those not covered by the survey, except agricultural workers. The latter group of 45,000 workers has been distributed about their average 1959 income on the basis of the range of agricultural wages given in *Annual Report, 1960,* Northern Rhodesia, Department of Labour (Lusaka, Government Printer, 1961).

It is impossible to obtain income by families for both Africans and Europeans employed in the monetary sector, so the unit of measurement used for both these groups is a wage-earner rather than a family. The 33,000 Europeans, Asians and colored people (male and female) employed in 1959 have been distributed into income groups according to the same percentages that existed at the time of the 1956 census. The average income of this group in 1959 was approximately the same as in 1956, although the latter year was influenced by an exceptionally high copper bonus.

production. National product is computed by deducting net income paid abroad from the economy's domestic product. Between 1951 and 1953—the last years for which separate data on Northern Rhodesia are available—net domestic product averaged £93.1 million and net national income (or product) only £67.4 million.[87] Thus, over 17 percent of the income earned within the country was remitted abroad in the form of net interest, net dividends, and net profits.

Housing

There are specific indicators of economic and social welfare which emphasize the dualistic nature of the economy. One such indicator is the difference in housing conditions for Europeans and Africans. In the subsistence sector almost all African housing still consists of huts. The sides of these dwellings are made of poles and grass, and are frequently covered with clay. The roofs are constructed of grass.[88] Urban Africans fare better: about 90 percent dwell in brick or concrete houses with asbestos, iron, or concrete roofs; the number of rooms per housing unit averages about 2.6 and the persons per room 1.5.[89] Of the Europeans residing in private homes and flats, only about 10 percent were

---

[87] *National Income and Social Accounts of Northern Rhodesia, 1945–1953,* Federation of Rhodesia and Nyasaland, Central Statistical Office (Salisbury: Government Printer, 1954), p. 23. The figures relate to the money economy.

[88] A family usually occupies more than one hut.

[89] "Report on Northern Rhodesia African Demographic Surveys, May to August, 1960," Federation of Rhodesia and Nyasaland, Central Statistical Office (Salisbury, 1961), p. 24.

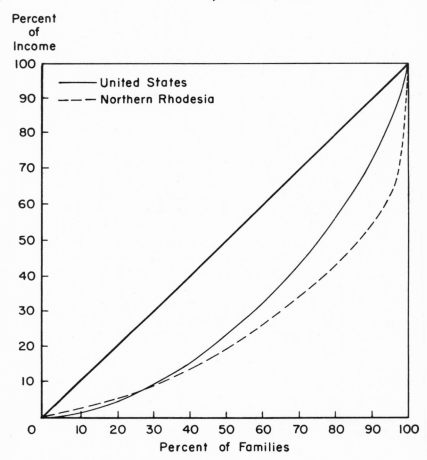

FIG. 1. Inequality of income in United States and Northern Rhodesia.

Source: *Statistical Abstract of the United States, 1962,* U.S. Department of Commerce, Bureau of the Census (Washington: Government Printing Office, 1962), no. 442, p. 329; table 2-9, p. 46, above.

living in conditions of at least 1.5 persons per room.[90] The size
of a typical room in an African house also is much smaller than
in a European home. Nearly 25 percent of the urban African
population has 40 square feet or less per person in which to
dwell.[91] Electric-light facilities are gradually being provided for
Africans living in urban areas, but in 1960, 68 percent of these
people were still without electricity.[92] In rural areas, of course,
there are no electric facilities for the African population.

Education

Education is another field where the dualistic features of the
Northern Rhodesian economy are clearly revealed. For European
children, education is compulsory between the ages of 7 and 15,
and the federal government, in whose jurisdiction non-African
education lay, pursued a vigorous policy of school expansion.
Between 1950 and 1959 the number of schools increased from
37 to 68.[93] By 1959 the teacher-student ratio in the primary
schools of the federation was 1:27.5, and in secondary schools
1:17.1. These ratios compare with 1:29.6 in England and Wales
and 1:35.4 in Australia for primary schools, and 1:20.4 in England and Wales and 1:22.8 in Australia for secondary schools.[94]

Great strides were taken after World War II in improving
African educational facilities, but in 1960 there were sufficient
places for only 15 out of 100 rural children to reach Standard VI
(approximately equivalent to the eighth grade) and 2 or 3 out of
each 100 to reach secondary school.[95] The structure of African
primary and secondary education in 1937, 1944, and 1960 (table
2–10) shows that the educational pyramid is still very heavily
weighted toward the lower levels. This is consistent with the
government's long-standing primary objective of providing four
years of education (through Standard II) for all Africans. The
pursuit of this policy raised the percentage of school-age children
enrolled in schools from 34 percent in 1944 to 60 percent in

[90] European housing data from *Census of Population 1956*, pp. 14–15.

[91] "Report on Northern Rhodesia African Demographic Surveys, May to August,
1960," p. 28.

[92] *Ibid.*, p. 29.

[93] *Annual Report on Education* for each year from 1954 to 1960, Federation of
Rhodesia and Nyasaland (Salisbury: Government Printer).

[94] *Annual Report on Education*, 1959, p. 38.

[95] *Triennial Survey, 1958–1960*, Northern Rhodesia, Ministry of African Education
(Lusaka: Government Printer, 1961), p. 19.

TABLE 2-10

ENROLLMENT OF AFRICANS IN PRIMARY AND SECONDARY SCHOOLS, NORTHERN RHODESIA, 1937, 1944, AND 1960

Class		1937		1944		1960	
		Number	Percent	Number	Percent	Number	Percent
Primary							
Substandard	A	15,113	50.92	52,776	51.64	69,234	23.86
	B	6,525	21.99	19,527	19.11	60,001	20.68
Standard	I	3,773	12.71	13,527	13.24	53,115	18.31
	II	2,168	7.30	8,099	7.92	51,317	17.69
	III	1,223	4.12	4,342	4.25	19,943	6.87
	IV	611	2.06	2,425	2.37	17,491	6.03
	V	154	.52	830	.81	8,679	2.99
	VI	110	.37	620	.61	7,756	2.67
Subtotal		29,677	99.99	102,146	99.94	287,536	99.10
Secondary							
Form	I	nil	nil	} 30	.03	1,311	.45
	II	"	"			747	.26
	Remove[a]	"	"	} 19	.02	235	.08
	III	"	"			139	.05
	IV	"	"			111	.04
	VI (1st year)	"	"			28	.01
	VI (2d year)	"	"			28	.01
Subtotal		0	0	49	.05	2,599	.90
Grand total		29,677	99.99	102,195	99.99	290,135	100.00

[a] This class is in session for 6 months and links the Northern Rhodesia school year ending in June with the "Cambridge" year ending in December.

SOURCES: A. W. Frisby, *African Education Development Plans 1945–1955*, Northern Rhodesia (Lusaka: Government Printer, 1945), p. 4, and *Triennial Survey, 1958–1960*, Northern Rhodesia, Ministry of African Education (Lusaka: Government Printer, 1961), p. 17.

1960.[96] As discussed in chapter 8, the approach of concentrating on four years of education for all does not, however, maximize the rate of return on educational investment (pp. 207–213). Moreover, in view of the growing role that Africans were playing in government, the fact that in 1960 2,599 students were enrolled in secondary schools with only 26 taking courses of higher education suggests an alarming misallocation of resources.[97] Fortunately, the Ministry of Education was giving priority to a rapid expansion of secondary education.[98] A gift of £650,000 and a low-interest loan for an additional £650,000 by the copper companies in 1960 greatly facilitated this change in policy.

Health Facilities

Health facilities are much better for the non-African population than for the African, although again there has been a tremendous improvement in medical services for the latter since the twenties and even since the mid-thirties (pp. 21–23). In 1937 the *Pim Report* described medical services for the European population as "reasonably adequate" but deplored those existing for Africans.[99] At that time there were only about 70 government and missionary posts in the entire territory—a condition that left more than half the country without European medical services of any description. Out of the 12 government medical stations at that time, 10 were located to serve primarily the interests of Europeans, and the medical officers at most of these stations were so occupied by the claims of the European population that they rarely visited the nonurban Africans within their districts.[100] Furthermore, medical conditions prevailing in 5 of the African hospitals at these government stations, which were visited by the Pim Commission, were termed "bad." By 1958 there were 13

---

[96] A. W. Frisby, *African Education Development Plans, 1945–1955,* Northern Rhodesia (Lusaka: Government Printer, 1945), p. 36; *Triennial Survey, 1958–1960,* p. 19. The proportions of African employees possessing no formal education were 56 percent at Roan Antelope, 71 percent at Rhokana, and 48 percent at Mufulira, as of December 31, 1961 (*Report of the Commission Appointed To Inquire into the Mining Industry in Northern Rhodesia,* Northern Rhodesia [Lusaka: Government Printer, 1962], p. 44).

[97] *Triennial Survey, 1958–1960,* p. 36; *Report: Appendix VI—Survey of Developments Since 1953,* Great Britain, Advisory Commission on the Review of the Constitution of the Federation of Rhodesia and Nyasaland, Cmd. 1149 (London: H.M.S.O., 1960), p. 197, hereafter referred to as the *Monckton Report.* By June, 1959, only 35 Africans had completed courses of higher education.

[98] *Triennial Survey, 1958–1960,* p. 10.

[99] *Pim Report,* p. 290.

[100] *Ibid.*

government hospitals for non-Africans, and 17 hospitals, clinics, and other institutions for Africans.[101] The number of beds per 1,000 people in the country was 10.3 for Europeans and 3.5 for Africans.[102] The mines played a considerable role in the increase of hospital facilities, and in 1960 provided almost 20 percent of all hospital beds in the territory. By greatly improved health and accident-prevention programs, they also sharply reduced the number of deaths owing to accidents and sickness among their African workers. Between 1956 and 1960 the annual average of deaths among African employees per 1,000 was 1.25 from mine accidents and 3.30 from all causes.[103]

Despite the stepped-up improvement in health services, there is still an extremely high incidence of disease among rural Africans. For example, in one district in the Luapula Province it was discovered that 40.7 percent of all schoolchildren between 6 and 10 years of age had malaria.[104] In the same district the bilharziasis infection rate was 14.3 percent among schoolchildren living in the plateau area, and 28.9 percent among those residing in the valley, and almost 100 percent of the population in the area suffered from hookworm. The same district also had an infant mortality rate of 43 percent of all births.[105] This rate is not much less than the 50 percent figure frequently cited during the twenties. Throughout the whole territory, however, the infant mortality rate for Africans was 259 per 1,000 live births in 1950.[106] This still represented one of the highest rates in the world. Leprosy and trypanosomiasis (sleeping sickness) also exist within the territory. In 1959 the number of cases of leprosy averaged 7 per 1,000 people, with Barotseland possessing a rate of 15.1 per 1,000. The number of reported cases of trypanosomiasis in the same year was 57.[107] Tuberculosis is another widespread disease,

[101] *Monckton Report*, pp. 138, 140.

[102] *Report of the Commission of Inquiry into the Health and Medical Services of the Federation 1959*, Federation of Rhodesia and Nyasaland (Salisbury: Government Printer, 1960), p. 85.

[103] Calculated from *Year Book*, 1960, pp. 36, 42.

[104] Dean A. Smith, *Report of a Nutrition and Health Survey in the Kawambwa District*, Northern Rhodesia (Lusaka: Government Printer, 1950), p. 2.

[105] *Ibid.*, pp. 3–4.

[106] "Report on the 1950 Demographic Sample Survey of the African Population of Northern Rhodesia," Southern Rhodesia, Central African Statistical Office (Salisbury, 1952), p. 22.

[107] *Annual Report on the Public Health of the Federation of Rhodesia and Nyasaland, 1959*, Federation of Rhodesia and Nyasaland (Salisbury: Government Printer, 1960), pp. 11–12.

although there are no adequate statistics on its extent among the African people.

The European population also suffers to a surprising extent from some of these diseases. The European malaria rate, for example, was 7.4 per 1,000 in 1959,[108] and a 1956 study showed 3.1 percent out of a sample of 5,303 people to be infected with bilharziasis.[109] One statistic that shows a sharp difference between Europeans and Africans is the infant mortality rate. This was 20.1 per 1,000 in 1959 for the European sector.

Malnutrition may contribute to the high susceptibility of Africans to disease. There is a dearth of information on the diet of rural Africans, but what there is does suggest that malnutrition is widely prevalent. Audrey Richards, in her study of the Bemba in Northern Rhodesia, found the average calorie intake to be only 1,706 per man per day.[110] Another study made by Betty Thomson in the Serenje District in 1947 reinforces these conclusions. Three villages were studied and a so-called required nutrient intake was compared with the actual intake. Table 2–11 presents the

TABLE 2-11

ACTUAL AND "REQUIRED" NUTRIENT INTAKE IN AN AFRICAN VILLAGE, NORTHERN RHODESIA, 1947

Nutrients	Actual	"Required"
Calories	1,392.0	2,298.0
Protein (gm)	42.1	63.0
Calcium (gm)	1,202.0	984.0
Vitamin A and carotene (I.U.)	2,337.0	3,210.0
Iron (mg)	22.7	11.4
Riboflavin (mg)	.5	1.6
Ascorbic acid (mg)	15.5	41.8

SOURCE: Betty Preston Thomson, *Two Studies in African Nutrition*, Rhodes-Livingstone Papers, no. 24 (Manchester: Manchester University Press, 1954), Appendix III.

results of this survey for a typical village. On the basis of accepted medical standards, it indicates serious deficiencies with respect to the intake of calories, protein, riboflavin, and ascorbic acid. One interesting fact that emerged from the study was that the extent

[108] *Ibid.*, p. 8.
[109] *Ibid.*
[110] Richards, *op. cit.*, p. 39.

of the malnutrition was not evenly distributed among family members. In general, the men obtained an adequate diet. Women and children were the ones who bore the brunt of the malnutrition.[111]

Among those employed in the monetary sector malnutrition was a less serious problem. The government long required employers who furnish their employees with rations to meet certain minimum dietary standards. For the year July, 1938, to June, 1939, the average daily calorie intake of workers at the copper mines was as follows: Mufulira, 4,886; Roan Antelope, 4,063; Nchanga, 4,008; and Rhokana, 3,567.[112] On the basis of the Rhokana diet, it was found that the average recruit increased his weight from 126.5 pounds to 128.9 pounds between arrival and actual engagement (a period of about 2 weeks). He lost about 1 pound during his first month of work, but gradually regained this in subsequent months until by about the sixth month he reached 129 pounds.[113]

In 1960 the first comprehensive diet study of all African urban workers was made by the Central Statistical Office. The calorie intake among families whose income was less than £9 12s. 6d. per month was only 90 percent of that required (calculated from table 2-12). The protein intake for this group was also less than

[111] Betty Preston Thomson, *Two Studies in African Nutrition*, Rhodes-Livingstone Papers, no. 24 (Manchester: Manchester University Press, 1954), p. 51.

[112] "Compound Manager's Report on Native Diet, Year Ended 30 June 1939," Rhokana Corporation, Nkana.

[113] The diet study also compared the weights of employees at the time of their arrival according to the areas from which they came. If there were no significant genetic differences affecting weight potential, these data provide a rough indicator of relative African living standards among regions. The group that weighed the most upon arrival (between 131 and 132 pounds), and therefore presumably possessed the highest living standard, came from the Mankoya and Lealui districts in Barotseland and the Kasempa district in the central part of the North-Western Province. In the 129- to 131-pound weight class were workers who migrated from the Broken Hill (Central Province) and Ndola (Western Province) districts. These figures reflect one clear-cut relationship discovered in the study: that laborers recruited from urban areas weighed more than workers coming directly from the rural villages. The latter group gained more weight over the year, however. The weight class, 126.7–128.7 pounds, comprised Balovale and Mwinilunga in the North-Western Province, Mumbwa to the west of Broken Hill in the Central Province, Fort Jameson in the Eastern Province, and the Isoka, Mpika, and Chinsali districts in the Northern Province. Below this weight level (in the 123.7–126.7 pound weight class) were two general regions. One includes the Luapula Province and the western part of the Northern Province, that is, Fort Rosebery, Kawambwa, Mporokoso, and Luwingu; and the other covers the region to the west and north of Fort Jameson, that is, Serenje and Lundazi. No districts from the Southern Province were listed in the company's classification of new arrivals.

TABLE 2-12

DAILY NUTRIENTS CONSUMED AT DIFFERENT INCOME LEVELS BY URBAN AFRICAN FAMILIES, NORTHERN RHODESIA, 1960[a]

Nutrients	Reference scale[b]	Under £6 15s. 6d. per month	£6 15s. 6d. to £9 11s. 0d. per month	£9 12s. 6d. to £11 10s. 6d. per month	£11 11s. 0d. to £14 6s. 6d. per month	Over £14 6s. 6d. per month
Calories	2,860.0	2,590.0	2,620.0	2,790.0	2,860.0	3,010.0
Proteins (gm)	85.0	75.0	78.0	84.0	82.0	88.0
Fat (gm)	—	43.0	46.0	51.0	51.0	56.0
Calcium (mg)	400.0	530.0	750.0	730.0	640.0	680.0
Iron (mg)	12.0	29.0	28.0	28.0	30.0	31.0
Vitamin A (I.U.)	3,500.0	1,400.0	1,300.0	1,300.0	1,300.0	1,600.0
Thiamin (mg)	1.5	2.7	2.7	2.8	2.8	2.8
Riboflavin (mg)	1.6	.8	.8	.8	.8	.9
Niacin (mg)	17.0	15.0	15.0	17.0	15.0	18.0
Ascorbic Acid (mg)	25.0	19.0	19.0	22.0	19.0	24.0

[a] The data refer to unrationed families and are measured in terms of man units.
[b] The reference scale calculated by the Ministry of Health refers to the requirements for a man of 25 who works 8 hours a day in a job that is not sedentary but does not involve more than occasional periods of hard physical labor.

SOURCE: "First Report on Urban African Budget Surveys Held in Northern Rhodesia, May to August, 1960," Federation of Rhodesia and Nyasaland, Central Statistical Office (Salisbury, 1960), p. 28.

required. There was a shortage of vitamin A, riboflavin, and ascorbic acid among all income groups. For single men, on the other hand, the quantity of nutrients received was adequate at all income levels.

A final set of data that brings out sharp differences between the African and European populations of Northern Rhodesia are the vital statistics of the two groups. A complete census of Africans has never been made, but on the basis of a sample survey in 1950 the annual rate of increase for the African population appears to be about 2.5 percent. In that year the overall birth rate was 56.8 per 1,000 and the death rate 32.2 per 1,000.[114] The rate of increase among Europeans also is high. Indeed, the 1959 rate of 2.7 percent is greater than that for the African population. The birth and death rates that result in this rate of natural increase differ a good deal from their African counterparts. In the European sector, the birth rate was 31.4 per 1,000, and the death rate only 4.1 per 1,000.[115] The gradual aging of the European population may reduce its birth rate and increase its death rate, whereas the extension of medical facilities for the African population is likely to cut its death rate sharply. There is some positive correlation between birth and death rates among the provinces,[116] but the country very likely will face the problem of a rapid increase in the rate of population growth as development continues.

An interesting aspect of this probable rise in the natural growth rate of the African population is the higher fertility rate in urban areas compared with the rural areas. The number of births per adult woman in 1950 was .173 in the rural villages and .246 in the main towns.[117] Much of this difference is accounted for merely by the presence in the towns of a greater proportion of women in the fertile age groups. J. Clyde Mitchell, however, who found a similar relationship in his 1951 Copperbelt study, reworked the fertility rates on the basis of the age composition for women in rural and urban areas that existed in the Union of South Africa in 1936.[118] He found that even after this adjustment, the urban fertility rate was .251 compared to a rural rate of .230. He also uncovered no relationship between the fertility rate and the length of residence by women in urban areas. Fur-

---

[114] "Report on the 1950 Demographic Sample Survey . . . ," p. 8.

[115] *Annual Report on the Public Health of the Federation . . . 1959,* p. 3.

[116] "Report on the 1950 Demographic Sample Survey . . . ," p. 22.

[117] *Ibid.*

[118] J. Clyde Mitchell, "An Estimate of Fertility among Africans on the Copperbelt of Northern Rhodesia," *Rhodes-Livingstone Journal,* XIII (1953), 18–29.

ther urbanization apparently will not reduce the rate of growth of the African population.

Having briefly traced the growth of the copper industry and shown that the development it created has been confined to a relatively small proportion of the population, the next step in the analysis is to present a theory that accounts for the dualistic nature of the growth process in Northern Rhodesia. Such a theory is outlined in the next chapter. It is designed to cover not only those export-oriented developing nations that are based upon minerals but also those that specialize in labor-intensive agricultural commodities.

3

Export Technology and Development from a Subsistence Level

A Theory of Growth

INTRODUCTION

The most striking characteristic of economic development in Northern Rhodesia has been its unevenness. In the industrial sector and in areas of European agriculture, rapid expansion based upon the use of modern technological knowledge has been achieved. The European population, which holds the skilled jobs in such regions, enjoys living standards that compare favorably with the most advanced countries of the world. The introduction of advanced knowledge into these areas nevertheless has failed to lead to any significant spread in the use of better productive techniques into the traditional African economy. Subsistence agricultural producers, employing techniques that have remained essentially unchanged for years, still dominate the country by weight of number. Most of them do participate, for short periods, as unskilled workers in the "money economy," but when they return to their villages, they revert to traditional agricultural methods. As a result, growth in the rural sector has been negligible.

Wide disparities in the level of technology employed in the various productive sectors is characteristic of most underdeveloped countries. In some industries the production functions used in selecting particular factor combinations embody the most advanced levels of technology known. In other fields the choice of productive methods is based upon a state of technology that for centuries has hardly changed. Technological diversity is not, of course, a feature unique to the present group of underdeveloped nations. Throughout the period of early Western development, many notable instances of lags in the use of improved techniques existed among, or within, countries. Even today such lags are found in most advanced economies. But it is in the economy of the underdeveloped country where differences in the level of technology employed are most pronounced and where this phenomenon, therefore, attracts the most attention.

Why does technological diversity occur and why does it persist for such long periods? A few industries utilizing modern technology grow very rapidly in the economy of many underdeveloped countries, but their expansion is not accompanied by, nor does it lead to, the adoption of better techniques throughout the rest of the economy. Since a significant rise in per capita income levels depends on more advanced productive techniques and new labor skills, a study of the factors that determine the extent and speed of the adoption of new techniques and skills is a key topic of development theory.

This chapter presents a development theory for an initially backward, subsistence economy into which a substantial foreign-financed and foreign-directed export industry is introduced.

Factors Determining the Type of Export Industry Initially Established

The rate of growth in most underdeveloped nations was negligible before the introduction of modern techniques in the few industries where they currently are employed. The typical economy was largely self-sufficient, and agriculture dominated the list of economic activities. Opportunities for specialization and internal trade were limited by narrow markets, and by relatively high costs of transportation in comparison with production costs. The resulting low level of income permitted such a small volume of savings that it was difficult to provide the growing population with sufficient capital even to maintain per capita income levels. Moreover, the general backwardness of the population acted as an effective barrier to the discovery and introduction of improved productive techniques. In short, the typical underdeveloped country at this stage was caught in a low-level equilibrium trap.

Had entrepreneurs from advanced nations not become increasingly interested in the economic opportunities of such underdeveloped countries, the prospects for any significant growth in these areas would have remained poor for many years. But economic relations between the two groups of countries did increase, especially in the period of colonialism, and with the closer relations came the possibility of raising income levels appreciably by utilizing more advanced technological knowledge. The opportunity of securing capital, as well as managerial and skilled labor, from abroad also acted to raise the economic potential of the poor countries.

Capital and Labor

The traditional assumption of international trade theory—that capital and labor are immobile among countries—is completely inappropriate at this stage in an analysis of growth patterns. To ignore the actual inflows of capital and skilled labor into the developing nations when accounting for the changes in their productive structures is to miss a crucial factor. A more useful and realistic assumption is simply that it was necessary to pay a return higher than that prevailing in developed areas to attract capital and labor to the underdeveloped countries. For example, an increase in wages was required to induce skilled workers to migrate from developed countries in order to compensate them for such factors as poorer health and educational facilities, the loss of family and social relations, the higher cost of many articles in their customary budgets, and the more restrictive list of alternative employment opportunities. The cost of moving and the lack of detailed knowledge about the new areas also acted as barriers to migration. A similar condition prevailed with respect to capital movements: a higher return on capital was necessary to compensate for the greater risks involved in most investments.

At the time that economic interest in the underdeveloped areas first gained impetus, the costs of unskilled labor and of a wide variety of natural resources—at prevailing exchange rates—were much lower than in the developed nations. It was therefore profitable to introduce improved techniques into productive lines that used these low-cost factors in quantity. The cost situation with respect to skilled labor was a different story. In terms of existing labor that could perform skill-requiring tasks, or could be trained to do so, the supply price in efficiency units was much greater in the underdeveloped countries. The advanced countries therefore tended to possess a cost advantage in the commodities, produced under modern techniques, which involved a relatively large amount of such skilled labor. The lower cost of capital funds also operated to give the advanced countries a comparative cost advantage in productive lines involving high capital-labor ratios and in those requiring highly durable capital equipment.

Because of these relationships, the types of commodities that proved most profitable as export lines in the poor nations were ones that technologically tended to be highly-using of unskilled labor or of a particular natural resource. Such products as tobacco, tea, rubber, coffee, and sugar were attractive, because their production tended not only to involve the use of a high labor coefficient over a wide range of relative factor prices, but also to fit especially well the climatic conditions prevailing in many of these countries.[1] Also, many of their specific capital and material inputs were items that could be produced cheaper locally than in the richer countries. For example, the clearing and improving of land, the building of processing and storage facilities, and the long period of cultivation needed in some cases before a crop

---

[1] Data pertaining to the magnitude of the labor coefficients in major export industries of underdeveloped countries are not extensive nor very reliable. But there is no doubt that the coefficients for such commodities as tobacco, tea, rubber, coffee and sugar are significantly greater than for the other main group of export industries developed in the poor countries, namely, mineral products such as oil, copper, bauxite and iron ore. For example, about 1940, the number of men employed per $1,000 of output per year was 6.0 in the tea industry of Ceylon, 2.1 in the Cuban sugar-growing industry, and 2.6 in the rubber industry of Malaya (R. E. Baldwin, "Patterns of Development in Newly Settled Regions," *Manchester School of Economic and Social Studies*, XXIV [May, 1956], 163). Other examples are a coefficient of 3.5 for the rubber industry in West Africa and 1.6 for tobacco farming in Southern Rhodesia (*Statistical and Economic Review*, no. 7, United Africa Company [March, 1951], p. 13; M. R. Colebrook, "Economic Factors in Farm Planning," *Rhodesia Agricultural Journal*, LVII [March-April, 1961], 110). Illustrations of the number of workers used per $1,000 of output per year in mineral industries are .033 and .026 for the oil industry in Venezuela and Saudi Arabia, respectively; .07 for bauxite production in British Guiana; .13 for the copper industry of Northern Rhodesia; and .31 for iron-ore production in India (*Anuario Petrolero y Minero de Venezuela, 1952*, Venezuela, Ministerio de Minas e Hidrocarburos [Caracas, 1957], pp. 17–18; *1956 Report of Operations to the Saudi Arab Government*, Arabian American Oil Company [Saudi Arabia, April 15, 1957]; "Report of the Lands and Mines Department for 1959," British Guiana [Georgetown, British Guiana, 1960], p. 8; *Report on the Census of Industrial Production, 1956–1957*, Federation of Rhodesia and Nyasaland, Central Statistical Office [Salisbury: Government Printer, 1958], recomputed data not as yet published; R. A. Gopalaswami, *Census of India*, 1951, Vol. I, Part II-B [Calcutta: Government of India Press, 1954], p. 212; "Statistical Outline of India, 1959," Tata Industries [Bombay: Bombay House, 1959], p. 13).

could be harvested were activities in which the elasticity of substitution of unskilled labor for capital goods and for skilled labor
was relatively high.

Natural Resources

Mineral products—such as oil, copper, bauxite, and iron ore—
also proved to be greatly profitable as export lines in many underdeveloped areas. The availability of a cheap supply of some natural resource was more important than the prevalence of inexpensive unskilled labor in attracting these industries. Such mineral products generally were relatively highly-using of skilled
labor and also of specific capital goods or material inputs, which
in turn required comparatively large quantities of skilled labor
to produce. Natural resource conditions, therefore, had to be sufficiently favorable to offset the cost disadvantage imposed by the
need to import relatively large quantities of capital goods and
skilled labor.

The extent to which export commodities were processed in the
underdeveloped areas depended mainly upon the nature of their
labor, material, and capital requirements and upon their comparative costs of transportation to international markets. When
further processing required large amounts of skilled labor or
specialized capital goods and did not significantly reduce the
weight of the product, it was usually cheaper to undertake these
activities where the main markets existed.

Marketing Facilities

The size and nature of the export market were of major importance in encouraging investment by foreigners in products
for export rather than for domestic consumption. Usually a
very large growth in the export activity could be made with
production within the country still constituting only a small
fraction of total consumption of the item in advanced areas.
The ability to expand greatly the production of one or two
commodities, without causing any significant decline in the
international price, made it possible to introduce specialized
marketing facilities on a scale sufficiently large to take advantage
of the considerable economies of scale associated with harbor and
dock facilities, railroads, financial services, storage facilities, and
so on. Since the expansion of exports required only the development of marketing arrangements to send the products out of the
country, instead of the complete marketing structure required to

reach the individual consumer, exports had an advantage over domestic production.

Internal transportation and other marketing facilities were so crude and the size of the market so small within the subsistence economies that foreign-directed production aimed at capturing internal markets could not, in many cases, even compete successfully with existing local production. This was particularly evident in any attempt to penetrate the market for foodstuffs in rural areas. The consumers themselves produced most of the agricultural products they consumed. Within a geographical area, the size of the money market for foodstuffs, therefore, was relatively small. The costs of transporting and distributing agricultural products to such areas nullified the lower production costs under modern techniques. Under such conditions the investment necessary to improve the transport system was not forthcoming. Nor was the establishment of productive units in the midst of the backward rural producers attractive. Marketing costs for servicing a given area were less than if production was located a considerable distance from the rural markets, but the cost of obtaining the capital equipment and materials involved in modern productive practices, and the cost of many of the consumption items in foreigners' budgets, were higher. And so, at first, foreigners did not find it advantageous to set up agricultural units to tap rural markets. When this type of production did prove profitable, it was because a transport system based upon an export commodity had developed and brought about this incidental benefit. There were, however, many manufactured goods, such as textiles, cooking utensils, and simple agricultural implements, produced with the use of modern techniques, which were sold successfully in the rural sector. The reasons probably were that marketing costs amounted to a smaller fraction of the price of manufactured than of agricultural goods at the then prevailing price pattern, and that the decreases in production costs and improvements in quality were greater for manufactured goods under modern techniques than for most agricultural commodities. At first, most of these commodities were not produced in the underdeveloped countries. Factor endowments relative to the factor requirements for these goods were more favorable in developed than underdeveloped countries.

The initial magnitude of the development impact on backward areas from more advanced areas depended mainly upon the opportunities that existed for the expansion of the export sector.

When resource and market conditions were highly favorable, large export industries were established and the size of the subsistence sector was reduced drastically within a relatively short time. In other cases, economic opportunities for the development of exports were slight. A host of noneconomic factors, such as the political and social institutions prevailing in the advanced and underdeveloped countries, were also important in determining the extent and rate at which foreigners introduced new techniques into the poor regions. The main concern here is not with the elements influencing the absolute size of the export industry initially established, but with those factors affecting further growth once an export industry of a certain size in terms of the annual value of its output, was introduced.

THE SPREAD OF NEW TECHNIQUES AND LABOR SKILLS

The extent to which new techniques and skills actually were diffused in the underdeveloped areas depended to a marked degree upon the technological characteristics of the production function for the export industry.

Market Opportunities

The dispersion of new techniques was far from an automatic process. Merely informing indigenous producers about the existence of new productive methods accomplished little. The money market for their commodities had to be expanded. For example, it did not stimulate the use of new practices to show rural producers that they could produce a given quantity of an output for a lower real cost, when they consumed most of their output themselves. Their income elasticity for the food items they produced was usually extremely low, as was their marginal utility for leisure. The prospect of larger amounts of food production and leisure time, consequently, did not induce the rural producers to adopt new techniques, in the face of the sacrifices necessary to learn new labor skills and acquire new capital goods, and of the greater risks involved in production. On the other hand, their preferences for the money economy's manufactured goods were such that they were willing to incur these costs, provided they could sell their additional agricultural output in the monetary sector. An increased market demand also was necessary to enable the producers to purchase the equipment associated with the employment of the new techniques. They could not obtain the required capital goods prior to market expansion owing to the lack of well-organized capital markets and their low volume of savings. It was when the market price for their output increased and their cash income rose that they obtained the means at least to begin to purchase some of these capital items. The acquisition of new labor skills by the local people was another crucial requirement for the introduction of new techniques into sectors outside the export industry. These techniques could not be introduced on a profitable scale unless the quality of the labor force improved.

Except for the export sector, where the market obstacle was absent and skilled labor was imported from the advanced countries, the spread of new techniques throughout the economy depended upon a previous expansion of market opportunities and an improvement in the quality of the indigenous labor force. To the extent that the effects of export expansion created larger internal money markets and trained the local labor force, to that extent did new techniques spread throughout the economy.

Input Coefficients

The particular characteristics of the export industry used to describe its repercussions on other parts of the economy are the size and qualitative nature of the industry's labor, capital, and material input coefficients, and the importance of economies of scale in other industries supplying the export industry or dependent upon it as an input source. In emphasizing the magnitude of the coefficients, it is not assumed that they are fixed. Not only are groups of inputs generally less than perfect substitutes for each other in the production of any commodity, however, but the elasticity of substitution among inputs varies significantly from commodity to commodity. It is this relationship that serves as the basis for the analysis here.

Labor inputs.—Consider first the effect of different labor coefficients in the export industry upon an economy's development prospects. For underdeveloped countries specializing in mineral production, the labor coefficient in the export sector was relatively low. Furthermore, the skill component of the labor input was quite high. Despite the availability of cheap unskilled labor, it was not profitable to substitute it for skilled labor or for specialized capital equipment on a scale that would employ a large amount of the unskilled labor per unit value of output. As a result of the nature of this labor demand by the export industry, the money outlays for food and other simple consumer goods were not large. Skilled workers were recruited at high wage rates from the advanced countries. Although their wage bill was significant, only a small proportion of it went for these items because of the skilled workers' high income level. The locally hired, unskilled workers spent a higher fraction of their income for food and simple consumer goods, but there were too few of them to make a substantial contribution to the money market for these items. Yet such commodities were the ones in which the underdeveloped countries could most easily develop a comparative advantage with the aid of modern techniques. But the weak demand repercussion from the export sector prevented any large expansion in the industries producing these commodities.

In export industries where the number of workers employed per dollar of export output was high, for example, tea, tobacco, and coffee, demand effects from export expansion were more favorable. The larger number of workers employed, and the higher average propensity to consume food and simple consumer durables, created a larger increase in market demand for these commodities than where export activity was devoted to mineral production.

Besides influencing the demand for consumption goods, the nature and magnitude of the labor input in the export industry also affected the extent and type of the qualitative changes that occurred in the labor force. In this respect, mineral industries were more favorable to further growth than plantation crops. In the mineral industries there was a fairly large number of positions that varied in job content from semiskilled to highly skilled. It was cheaper at the start to import the labor needed to fill these jobs than to train local labor. But, as time passed, the indigenous workers became more stabilized and learned to perform their unskilled jobs more efficiently. This meant that the cost of training them for positions with a somewhat higher skill content decreased. It became more profitable to train local workers for the jobs than to continue using expensive foreign labor. Where monopolistic and discriminatory practices on the part of the imported laborers were prevented, local workers gradually were shifted into more skilled positions. A pool of skilled industrial laborers, who would work at rates significantly less than imported skilled labor, was created. This encouraged not only further export expansion but also the development of other industries requiring skilled labor. In particular, the new supply of skilled labor enabled local producers to compete more successfully with foreign firms for the small consumer-durables market that was created by the wage-earning export workers.

Unfortunately, the individuals who came from foreign countries to the mineral areas generally were successful in preventing the subsequent training of indigenous workers for their skilled positions. They organized into labor unions and thereby exerted considerable influence. They also exercised great power through government activities, for there were political repercussions, too, that resulted from the dualistic nature of economies specializing in mineral exports. In particular, the immigrants from the more advanced countries usually secured political control and exercised it in a manner that gave preferential economic treatment to themselves. Furthermore, after the export industry was well established, it was more difficult for the indigenous population to regain political control there than it was in the labor-intensive agricultural economies.

Nevertheless, even when advancement of local labor was blocked by monopolistic practices, there were still important development benefits derived from the presence of a group of skilled workers from the advanced countries. They often broke away from the export industry and established small firms to supply the export industry or the general consumption market. Their greater skills and larger supply of capital funds, in comparison with local unskilled labor, enabled them to take advantage of profit opportunities arising in these fields which the indigenous workers could not undertake, and which skilled workers in comparable jobs in advanced countries, who might be interested, were not likely to know about.

In most of the labor-intensive agricultural industries for export which were organized on a plantation basis, the proportion of skilled workers was relatively low and consisted mainly of managerial and technical workers. Because of their high degree of training, it was difficult to replace with local people those individuals who came from advanced countries to fill these jobs initially. By working in the export industry, the indigenous population thus did not acquire much in the way of general skills that could be readily adapted to manufacturing activity. They did acquire enough knowledge in many cases to establish their own small-scale unit in the agricultural export industry. But the production function for the commodity generally was such that without more training and much more capital, the local producers were unable to continue to raise their income levels.[2] They tended to remain poor, unskilled agricultural producers who employed backward methods of cultivation.

The small producers continued to grow most of their own foodstuffs with crude traditional methods. Owing to the seasonal nature of the labor requirements for the export crop, they found it more advantageous to utilize part of their land for food crops rather than to place it entirely into export production. This meant that the money demand for foodstuffs did not rise as much as might have been expected in the labor-intensive areas. The cash received from the export commodity was used largely to replace and augment the supply of consumer durables they formerly made for themselves. Even though this market demand consisted of rather simple consumer durables, the failure to develop industrial labor skills within the export sector enabled producers in foreign countries to retain the market for most of the items. Marketing activities connected with the purchase of these goods increased significantly within the economy, but manufacturing activities did not.

Capital inputs.—The composition and size of the capital coefficient in the export industry played a major role in shaping the pattern of growth within the underdeveloped areas. For some commodities, such as minerals, the most profitable factor combination tended to require large amounts of complex capital equipment. The production of this equipment in turn necessitated the use of relatively large amounts of skilled labor and other types of complex capital inputs. The advanced countries consequently possessed a cost advantage in producing this specialized capital equipment, and it was imported into the underdeveloped countries. On the other hand, when the capital needs of the export industry contained a large element of construction outlays, the chances for the creation of additional local industries were more favorable: transportation costs on such items as bricks, cement, and timber were high in relation to production costs; the commodities required less skilled labor then the equipment industry; small-sized units could produce nearly as efficiently as large productive concerns.

Material inputs.—The nature of the export industry's material inputs affected development prospects of other industries in much

---

[2] Baldwin, *op. cit.*, p. 170.

the same way as the export sector's demand for capital goods.[3] In many cases, the material inputs required did not fit the demand and supply conditions of the poor economy. Some of the necessary inputs were produced under conditions of significant economies of scale, and local production was not profitable because of the limited demand by the export industry. Similarly, certain inputs required relatively large amounts of skilled labor and therefore were uneconomic for local production. In many cases, natural resource conditions also were not favorable for the local production of some inputs.

The significance of the output of the export industry as an input for other industries was another important factor shaping the pattern of development. The initial export industries usually did not include many of the processing activities associated with the product's movement to final consumers, because of the relatively greater requirements for skilled labor and specialized equipment and material inputs involved in additional processing. Whether these "forward linkages" were in fact made later within the underdeveloped countries was influenced by the changes in demand and supply conditions created by the export industry. If a cheaper supply of skilled labor, as well as a supply of other goods and service inputs needed by the processing industries, was built up by the initial export industry, the possibilities for profitable production in these processing lines were enhanced. They were also improved if the final consumer goods that resulted from the export product were important consumption items in the budgets of the workers employed in the export industry. On the other hand, when the input requirements were quite different in the processing industry than the inputs created by the initial export industry; when the commodity did not lose much weight in further processing activities; and when the final goods produced from the product were not significant consumption items internally, then the chances of further forward production were poor.

Economies of Scale

A final factor to emphasize, in considering the impact of export development, is the nature of economies of scale in those indus-

---

[3] See Wassily W. Leontief, "The Structure of Development," *Scientific American*, CCIX (Sept., 1963), 148–154, for a general analysis of the differences in interindustry input-output flows between developed and underdeveloped economies.

tries that supplied the export industry as well as in those that utilized the export product as an input. For some export industries the magnitude of their demand for many material and capital equipment inputs was too small for the production unit that supplied such inputs to operate efficiently. The establishment of local firms to furnish these inputs, consequently, was not profitable. Again, it was the mineral industries that ranked unfavorably with respect to this factor. Specialized capital equipment and material inputs constituted a high proportion of their nonlabor inputs, and the production of these items usually was subject to considerable scale economies. Sometimes the scale factor worked against the development of additional processing activities within the mineral field. An efficient plant required larger inputs of the export product than a particular underdeveloped country could supply. Processing units were therefore located outside the underdeveloped country. The importance of economies of scale worked against further development in those countries producing labor-intensive agricultural products but not to the extent they did in the mineral-producing nations. A characteristic of labor-intensive industries seems to be that their capital and material inputs do not require large, complex productive units in order to achieve minimum unit costs.

Export industries for which the goods and services content of inputs were favorable to domestic production induced greater secondary development, and indirectly increased the possibilities for still further growth. For example, an export industry that induced the development of a complex railway system servicing a large part of the country increased the opportunities for further growth. The lower transport cost made it more feasible to establish other export industries, to develop industries directly supplying the export industry, or to create industries supplying commodities demanded by those employed in the export sector. The development of these industries in turn stimulated further growth. On the other hand, when the export industry was based, for example, upon the extraction of crude petroleum, the development impetus stemming from its transportation facilities was often negligible. Single-use pipelines were frequently constructed to transport most of the oil, and these facilities had little impact on the stimulation of other industries.

PLANTATION AND MINERAL ECONOMIES COMPARED

In an economy characterized by an efficient allocation of resources, many of the secondary effects associated with foreign investment in the export sector result merely in a reorganization of given resources according to changes in market demand and supply conditions. The output of some industries expands (or new industries arise), while the output of others declines. In measuring the increment in national product derived from export investment, the only secondary effects that should be counted under these circumstances are technological spillovers, that is, output or input changes in one industry that affect the physical output another industry can obtain from the physical inputs the latter industry uses. From a dynamic viewpoint, the labor-training effects and the repercussions caused by changes in the location of resources seem to be the most important spillovers.

The model employed here emphasizes that the development impetus resulting from these technological external effects varies significantly with the nature of the export industry established. But it goes further than this. It stresses the point that in an economy where resources are inefficiently allocated (which is the case in the typical underdeveloped country), income transfers associated with purely pecuniary external effects—that is, changes in an industry's profits owing solely to changes in its input or output prices which occur when another industry varies its output or inputs—tend to produce changes that bring about additional growth. Introducing an improved agricultural technique may involve, for example, the use of some "lumpy" capital good, yet the existence of an imperfect capital market prevents rural producers from borrowing the funds needed to purchase the capital good. If, however, the demand for certain agricultural products rises because of expansion in the export sector, the larger incomes received by some rural producers enable them to purchase the "lumpy" capital good and introduce the better productive method. Pecuniary spillovers also affect the magnitude of the inflows of skilled labor and capital funds from more advanced areas.

Another important pecuniary repercussion concerns the effect of a rise in income on producers' attitudes toward risk. Because their incomes are at such a low level, small producers in underdeveloped countries tend to possess a high degree of risk aversion, that is, they prefer a smaller expected (or average) income to a larger expected income if the range of possible outcomes is smaller in the former situation. Since the probability of incurring a disastrous loss is likely to be greater with new productive techniques than with well-established ones, producers do not introduce new techniques, even though the expected income is higher with the new methods. When the incomes of producers employing traditional methods increase because of favorable demand repercussions from another industry, they become more willing to introduce innovations that further increase national product.

From the demand side, the most favorable type of export industry is one requiring labor, capital, and material inputs that fit the existing relative factor conditions of the underdeveloped countries. From this point of view, such export products as tea, coffee, tobacco, or sisal are more favorable than oil, copper, or bauxite. The former group of commodities is more labor-intensive and requires less specialized capital equipment and raw-material inputs. A high proportion of the outlays associated with their production tends, consequently, to be spent internally, and the possibilities of a further spread of better techniques by means of an expansion of production in the money economy are improved.

Demand forces, however, are only one side of the total repercussions. Factor conditions within the underdeveloped countries are altered by the expansion and contraction of some productive lines and by the creation of entirely new industries. Outputs that become relatively cheaper as their supply increases, and are used as inputs for other industries, improve the possibilities for expansion in the other industries. To the extent that these pecuniary external economies lead to the utilization of better techniques, or to a more efficient use of existing resources, the shifts in production represent change leading to increases in the economy's national product.

The effects of export production on changing the quality of the labor force is another extremely important supply repercussion. The introduction of a higher state of technology into the export sector is an important step forward in the development process, but initiating a process of sustained growth requires more than this. A mechanism must be established whereby the indigenous labor force can acquire greater skills. This opens up the possibility of establishing new industries. Furthermore, since the use of many types of capital equipment requires additional skilled labor, the training of labor tends to improve profit prospects for investment in industries employing specialized equipment, and thereby encourages foreign investment. The development of an indigenous pool of skilled workers is important, too, for the creation of a group of vigorous, local entrepreneurs. These workers are more likely than unskilled workers to recognize profit opportunities and to possess the financial and technical means for exploiting them.

In terms of facilitating the training of skilled labor, the mineral industries are in a more favorable position than are the agricultural producers of export commodities working under a plantation system. But the low level of domestic demand generated by mineral industries tends to confine the demand for skilled labor to the mineral export industry itself. A small part of the population gains considerably from the creation of the mineral export industry, but development fails to affect the rest of the economy to any significant extent. The opposite situation tends to prevail for many agricultural exports. More favorable demand repercussions bring more people into the money economy, but the agricultural export sector does little in the way of improving the quality of the labor force.

These are the two positions that characterize much of the underdeveloped world. One set of export industries is well adapted to the existing labor endowment of these areas but does not provide much of an impetus for eliminating the backwardness of the labor force. Countries with these export industries become caught in a new, low-level equilibrium trap. The other type of export activity provides a ladder for further growth, but the impetus for additional development is confined only to a small part of the economy.

4

Factor Combinations
in the Copper Industry

The preceding chapter analyzed patterns of development both
when the initial growth impetus stems from mineral exports
and when it originates from labor-intensive, agricultural export
commodities. No attempt is made here to analyze historically
the development process in a labor-intensive export economy.[1]
The remaining chapters are devoted, instead, to examining
Northern Rhodesian growth in terms of that part of the theory
that pertains to development in an economy initially dominated
by mineral exports. This chapter discusses the general characteristics of the copper industry and considers the causes and effects
of changes in its labor and capital inputs over the years. Subsequent chapters trace the effects of Rhodesian copper development
on other inputs used by the copper industry, such as transportation services, electric power, food rations for African workers,
certain manufactured commodities, and government services.

GENERAL TECHNOLOGICAL CHARACTERISTICS

Three characteristics of copper production should be emphasized
in considering the effect of the industry's technology on factor
combinations. These are (1) a low aggregate labor coefficient in
which the skilled-labor component is comparatively large; (2) sig-

---

[1] It might be noted, however, that Malawi (formerly Nyasaland), where tea and
tobacco dominate the export structure, appears to fit this type of export economy.

nificant economies of scale; and (3) a moderately high capital coefficient.

Low Labor Coefficient

The number of employees per $1,000 of annual gross output (the labor coefficient) of various industries in Northern Rhodesia is presented in table 4-1. As the table indicates, copper mining

TABLE 4-1

LABOR COEFFICIENTS FOR SELECTED NORTHERN
RHODESIAN INDUSTRIES, 1959
(per $1,000)

Industry	Labor coefficient
Metal mining	.146
Grain mill products	.088
Other food manufacturing	.233
Alcohol, beer, soft drinks	.114
Textiles, wearing apparel, and footwear	.404
Manufacturers of wood and cork, except furniture	1.059
Transport equipment	.439
Other manufacturing	.412
Construction	.681
Electricity and water	.045
Rail transportation	.603
Maize and tobacco	1.300
Tea[a]	2.600

[a] This figure refers to Nyasaland. There is no tea industry in Northern Rhodesia.

SOURCES: *The Censuses of Production of the Federation of Rhodesia and Nyasaland, 1958–1959*, Federation of Rhodesia and Nyasaland, Central Statistical Office (Salisbury: Government Printer, 1961), pp. 44–47. Rail transportation computed from data in Rhodesia Railways, Annual Reports (Bulawayo); maize and tobacco computed from data in M. R. Colebrook, "Economic Factors in Farm Planning," *Rhodesia Agricultural Journal*, LVII (March–April, 1961), 107–110; and tea from the gross value of tea production in Nyasaland as reported in *Report on the Agricultural Production of Southern Rhodesia, Northern Rhodesia, and Nyasaland, 1961*, Federation of Rhodesia and Nyasaland, Central Statistical Office (Salisbury: Government Printer, 1961), p. 8, and an estimate of 30,000 employees in the Nyasaland tea industry.

(together with lead and zinc mining) is much less labor-intensive than such agricultural export crops as tobacco and, in Nyasaland, tea. Furthermore, even compared with the purely domestic sectors of the economy, copper mining and processing ranks as a small labor-user per unit value of output. Electric power and certain food and beverage industries are the only ones listed with lower labor coefficients.[2]

In addition to being a small-scale employer of labor in unit-value terms, the copper industry uses a high proportion of skilled to unskilled labor compared with most other industries in the economy. In underground operations a high degree of experience and judgment is important in executing the continuously changing pattern of day-to-day mining operations. For example, each new section of the ore body or footwall to be removed and then made safe presents somewhat different problems. Similarly, a large amount of skilled labor is required to operate and repair the complicated and expensive machinery used in underground and surface activities. An indication of the relative uses of skilled and unskilled labor in the copper industry in relation to other industries is given in table 4-2 where proportions of Europeans to total workers employed are compared. Since Europeans are hired for the skilled jobs and Africans for the unskilled, it is evident that the skill requirements for copper are very large in comparison with commodities such as maize, tobacco, or tea. Most secondary industries (but not tertiary industries) also use much less skilled labor than does copper mining. The high European proportions may in part be attributable to the restrictive conditions on African advancement imposed by the European union during World War II, but even in 1937, before this union existed, the copper industry had one of the highest proportions of European to African labor among all primary and secondary industries.[3]

---

[2] In the theory presented in the preceding chapter, the absolute size of the labor coefficient in the underdeveloped country's export sector was emphasized. Prices of capital goods and labor services were regarded as reasonably similar among the underdeveloped nations. The difference in labor coefficients among the export industries of these countries was considered to be dependent upon whether their natural resource endowment and their nearness to product markets were favorable to mineral exports or to exports of agricultural commodities such as tea, cotton, and coffee. At the much higher wage rates in relation to the prices of capital goods which prevail in developed countries, however, mineral industries such as copper also tend to rank as low labor-coefficient industries. In the United States, for example, food and tobacco products, the rental sector, and chemicals were the only industries, in a 41-industry breakdown of the American economy for 1947, which used less labor per unit value of output than nonferrous metals, and only the rental sector exceeds petroleum (Wassily W. Leontief, "Domestic Production and Foreign Trade: The American Capital Position Re-examined," *Proceedings of the American Philosophical Society*, XCVII (Sept., 1953), 334.

[3] Phyllis Deane, *The Measurement of Colonial National Incomes*, National Institute of Economic and Social Research, Occasional Paper, no. 12 (Cambridge: Cambridge University Press, 1948), pp. 26–29. In Katanga, where much greater efforts were made to advance Africans, about 8 percent of copper mine employees

TABLE 4-2

PERCENTAGE OF EUROPEAN EMPLOYEES IN LABOR FORCE OF
SELECTED NORTHERN RHODESIAN INDUSTRIES, 1961

Industry	Percent
Agriculture and forestry	1.6
Mining and quarrying	15.3
Food, drink, and tobacco	11.1
Textiles and clothing	1.8
Wood and furniture	3.5
Construction	6.8
Electricity and water	15.8
Commerce and finance	26.1
Rail transportation	31.3

SOURCE: "Preliminary Results of Federal Censuses of Population and of Employees: (1) Industrial and Racial Distribution of Employees," Federation of Rhodesia and Nyasaland, Central Statistical Office (Salisbury, 1962), p. 5.

Economies of Scale

Copper production is also subject to important economies of scale. In Northern Rhodesia, as elsewhere in the world, the amount of copper supplied by small productive units is insignificant in terms of the total supply of the metal.[4] The amount of capital required to develop new ore bodies and plant facilities within Northern Rhodesia during the last 10 years varied from $10 million to $50 million. In addition, a period of from 3 to 4 years elapsed before full-scale operations commenced. Other expansions of capacity throughout the world also involved large sums and a long gestation period.[5]

The use of such equipment as giant earth-moving machines for open-pit mines, elaborate mechanical loaders in underground operations, continuous conveyor belts for transporting the ore, huge crushing machines and large-capacity furnaces has so reduced unit costs for large-scale operations that today small pro-

still were Europeans in 1953 (F. Bézy, *Problèmes Structurels de l'Économie Congolaise* [Louvain: Institut de Recherches Économiques et Sociales, 1957], p. 144).

[4] In 1956, for example, three small mines produced only 584 tons of copper concentrate. *Annual Report for the Year, 1956,* Northern Rhodesia, Mines Department (Lusaka: Government Printer, 1957), p. 6. By 1961 there were no small copper mines operating.

[5] Helena M. Meyer, "Copper," in *Mineral Facts and Problems,* Bulletin no. 556, U.S. Department of the Interior, Bureau of Mines (Washington: Government Printing Office, 1956), pp. 229–231.

ductive units cannot compete in the world market. Before the establishment of a modern copper industry in Central Africa, Africans had for centuries produced small quantities of high-grade copper that was processed into wire ornaments, crude agricultural instruments, and currency units. But, as in the case of their iron and pottery-making activities, the native copper industry was destroyed soon after the introduction of trade and the resultant access to similar goods made under modern conditions. The cost of producing and marketing copper on such a scale—even with the near subsistence wage level—was so much higher than the cost under modern, large-scale conditions that African producers could not compete successfully.

High Capital Coefficient

The capital costs of developing new Rhodesian capacity—from mining through electrolytic refining—amounted in the mid-fifties to about $1,100 per short ton of copper.[6] Using $562 per short ton (the average price from 1956 to 1960) as the price of copper, the capital coefficient per $1,000 of output was, therefore, approximately $2,000. Unfortunately, it is difficult to obtain capital coefficients for other Rhodesian industries. The following are estimates for a few: electricity, $4,100; rail transportation, $3,100; maize farming, $2,400; cement, $3,100.[7] If, as seems likely, the ranking of capital coefficients by industry in Northern Rhodesia is similar to those in the United States,[8] it follows that the magnitude of the capital coefficients for most of the secondary industries listed in table 4–1 (on which there is no direct information) is less than copper's coefficient. Because of the moderately high capital coefficient for copper and its low labor coefficient, investment per worker is also high compared with other Rhode-

---

[6] Based upon the costs of establishing mining and concentrating operations at the Bancroft mine plus estimates of smelting and refining operations. The cost of European and African housing is not included (Annual Report, 1959, Bancroft Mines, and annual reports of the other Rhodesian mining companies during the fifties). In the United States it was estimated around 1956 that new mining, milling, and smelting capacity for copper cost $1,500 to $2,000 per short ton (Meyer, *op. cit.*, p. 229).

[7] *Second Report of the Secretary for Power Covering 1 July 1957 to 30 June 1958*, Federation of Rhodesia and Nyasaland (Salisbury: Government Printer, 1959), Appendix II; "Annual Report," 1950–1960, Rhodesia Railways (Bulawayo). Capital expenditure over this period was divided by the increase in railway revenue; *Legislative Council Debates* (Hansard nos. 60–62), June 29, 1951, Northern Rhodesia (Lusaka: Government Printer, 1951); M. R. Colebrook, "Economic Factors in Farm Planning," *Rhodesia Agricultural Journal*, LVII (March-April, 1961), 107–108.

[8] Leontief, *op. cit.*, p. 334.

sian industries. Electricity apparently is the only significant industry that is more capital-intensive.[9]

The composition of expenditures on capital items is another important aspect of an industry's capital-output picture. Detailed data are lacking for the Rhodesian mines, but a study of United States copper mining and milling reveals that labor costs comprise 45 percent of total capital costs; construction materials, 12 percent; and equipment costs, 43 percent.[10] In the development of the Bancroft mine, shaft-sinking and development expenditures were listed as £5.6 million, and building, machinery, plant, and shaft equipment costs as £13.6 million. A large share of shaft-sinking and development costs and a part of the other expenditures presumably represent labor costs, so that a figure of around 40 percent does not seem unreasonable as the share of labor cost in total capital outlays for the Rhodesian copper industry.

Effect on Development

The various technological characteristics of copper production outlined above determined the manner in which the industry affected economic development in Northern Rhodesia. There was no possibility, for example, of the industry expanding into a major world supplier from the simple, small-scale works operated by Africans. These producers were highly skilled and imaginative in terms of the technology of several hundred years ago, but backward and untrained in terms of the copper technology that dominated the world market in the late twenties. Furthermore, the gap between African and modern copper technology was too great for the Africans gradually to develop the industry themselves. To compete on the world market required the formation of large-scale productive units, based on large amounts of capital and a high degree of technological knowledge. These were requirements that the African was far from able to satisfy himself.

Not only was there no opportunity for the creation of a world-supplying copper industry based on African capital and talent, but small units operated by European immigrants were also ruled out on technological grounds. Unlike the gold industry of Southern Rhodesia, which was developed by large numbers of miners of moderate means, successful copper production in

---

[9] The nonferrous metals industry is also one of the more capital-intensive industries in the United States (*ibid.*).

[10] Sidney Sonenblum, "A Report on Capital Purchases by the Copper Mining and Milling Industry," U.S. Department of the Interior, Bureau of Mines, Inter-Industry Analysis Branch, Item no. 21 (Feb., 1953), pp. 12–13.

Northern Rhodesia required large, highly capitalized productive units.[11] The high costs of discovering potentially profitable ore bodies, and of undertaking the necessary large-scale development and construction work for producing the metal on a competitive basis, excluded the small productive unit. The outcome was that the industry, of necessity, was developed by large financial interests from abroad which could furnish the capital requirements and the technical skills needed to establish profitable production.

The concentration of high-grade copper deposits in a relatively small number of areas in the world, and the importance of scale economies in exploiting these deposits, created an oligopolistic world-market structure of copper. The Rhodesian industry, being a potentially large producer, necessarily became involved in this market system. The production policy of the dominant industry in Northern Rhodesia became closely connected to world-market conditions.

The relatively low labor coefficient that technological conditions impose upon the copper industry meant that the direct employment impact of the new industry was bound to be low in relation to its output in monetary terms. Substitution of labor for capital does occur in the industry under favorable changes in relative factor prices—and the history of the Rhodesian industry in this respect is analyzed in the next two sections—but from a general point of view the substitution possibilities for labor in absolute terms are comparatively small. Copper mining is not an industry that is attracted to an area mainly because of a plentiful supply of cheap labor—the dominant economic characteristic of the Rhodesian economy in the late twenties. Obviously the existence of cheap labor influences production decisions, but in Northern Rhodesia it was the richness of the copper deposits which played the major role in the development of the industry.

It was previously pointed out that, besides a relatively low overall labor content of copper output, the industry is characterized by a comparatively high requirement for skilled in relation to unskilled labor. Given Rhodesian labor conditions of the twenties, this led to large-scale importation of skilled labor from abroad (see next section).

Because of these various technological constraints, an industry

---

[11] In Southern Rhodesia in 1938 there were 1,548 gold mines (*Report of Commission of Enquiry into the Mining Industry of Southern Rhodesia,* Southern Rhodesia [Salisbury: Government Printer, 1945], p. 24).

was established in Northern Rhodesia which was well adapted to the plentiful supply of copper resources but not to the other relative factor conditions of the economy—an abundant supply of unskilled labor and a relatively small stock of capital. The latter factor conditions favor labor-intensive industries, whereas copper is a capital-intensive industry. It was necessary for those who developed the copper resources to import the capital and skilled labor needed for the establishment of a profitable copper industry. The direct impact on existing factor conditions other than natural resources was comparatively small.

Although the general technological features discussed above impose general constraints that hold the labor coefficient for copper to a low level in comparison with most agricultural export industries in underdeveloped countries, changes in the copper industry's labor coefficient which are significant in percentage terms do occur, as relative factor conditions and prices change during the development process. These shifts—together with the manner in which the labor-training mechanism associated with the establishment of a copper industry in an underdeveloped country operates—are important factors determining the more detailed nature of an economy's development pattern. The next two sections analyze the major changes in labor and capital utilization within the Rhodesian copper indusry from the late twenties until the late fifties. The problem of African advancement is then considered, and finally some general conclusions are drawn concerning how well the development impetus from the copper industry has been utilized.

THE USE OF AFRICAN LABOR IN THE EARLY YEARS

Initial Inefficiency of African Labor

It is hard to imagine a labor force less trained for employment in a modern, mechanized industry than the Africans hired by the copper companies in the late twenties. Such simple tools as shovels, picks, and wheelbarrows were unfamiliar to them.[12] Moreover, because much of the work in the village was done in spurts, they were ill-suited to the regular work habits demanded

---

[12] For example, at one time during the early days of the mines two new recruits were witnessed carrying a wheelbarrow filled with earth (C. F. Spearpoint, "The African Native and the Rhodesian Copper Mines," *African Affairs*, XXXVI [July, 1937], 4). The main tools used by Africans in their village activities were the short-handled hoe and the axe.

by a modern industrial enterprise.[13] Occurrences of several employees vanishing from work in the middle of the day and bring-
ing operations to a standstill were common, and the companies
soon learned to carry a reserve supply of labor to cope with such
occasions. The employment period spent at the mines by Africans
was also very short. During the harvest period from April to
June, and again at the planting season near the end of the year,
most workers returned to their villages and thereby caused a
seasonal labor shortage at the mines. [14] To solve the problem of
an adequate supply of labor, the companies in the late twenties
turned more and more toward the use of recruited labor.

Fear and superstition were additional obstacles to overcome in
assembling an effective labor force. One especially difficult task,
for example, was to persuade African employees to work underground. The compound manager at Roan Antelope remarked:
"Encouraging them to work underground was an almost insuper-
able task, . . . and . . . it was almost a nightly occurrence to
find the night shift gang standing dumbly defiant before a dis-
tracted European miner who was doing his best to get them to go
down. If one were too persistent in persuading people like this
to go down the shafts it was not uncommon to find that the following day most of them had deserted and completely van-
ished." [15] At Mufulira it was finally necessary to hire 200 workers
with previous underground experience from Southern Rhodesia.
This group seemed to allay the fears of the inexperienced Northern Rhodesian workers, and thenceforth the problem was less
troublesome. Difficulties in inducing workers to wear safety equipment and to report an injury or illness and then go to the hospital were other manifestations of fear and superstition on the
part of Africans.

The existence of many different languages among the Africans
further complicated labor problems.[16] Few Europeans spoke any
African language, and fewer Africans spoke English. As a result,
Kitchen Kaffir—an elementary and limited language combining

---

[13] Another early experience at one of the mines was the disappearance after
a week's work of an entire gang of African workers. After a search they were discovered fishing several miles up a nearby river. They felt that after working for
one week they were entitled to a few days off (*ibid.*, pp. 4–5).

[14] In 1928 the average labor turnover per month at Roan Antelope was 22 percent (*ibid.*, p. 53).

[15] *Ibid.*, p. 3.

[16] Spearpoint asserts that 90 percent of Roan's earlier troubles with African labor
was due to the language problem (*ibid.*, p. 15).

Zulu (70 percent), English (24 percent), and Afrikaans (6 percent)—became the accepted medium of communication.[17]

Because of these backward characteristics, the African worker was regarded as suitable only for the most rudimentary tasks. Although the African's real wage was less than one-twentieth of the European worker's, the cost of training him, in relation to the length of time he was likely to remain in employment, was sufficiently high that the European worker proved to be less expensive for jobs requiring almost any significant degree of skill.[18] The chairman of the Rhodesian Selection Trust Group summarized his early attitude toward African labor by stating: "It is our intention to use mechanical appliances as far as possible, both in our plant and in the mine, and so reduce to a minimum the native labor required." [19] As an illustration of this general policy, the Roan Antelope mine announced in 1930 that an electrically-powered hoist and slides had been put into successful operation and had materially reduced the amount of African labor required for lashing.[20]

Dual Wage Structure

The majority of European labor was recruited in South Africa, although it was necessary to hire specialists from the United Kingdom and the United States. The market rate for European employees was determined by alternative opportunities abroad, whereas that for African labor was set by wage rates in the Katanga and Southern Rhodesian mines. This in itself created a very large differential between the wages of African and European workers. But, in addition, it was necessary to pay Europeans even more than they had been earning in order to induce them to migrate to Northern Rhodesia. Malaria, blackwater fever, the appearance of an occasional lion, as well as rudimentary medical, educational, and recreational facilities, and the like, were disad-

[17] D. T. Cole, "Fanagalo and the Bantu Languages in South Africa," *African Studies*, XII (March, 1953), 1–9. The total vocabulary is under 2,000 words.

[18] In 1929, for example, the starting money wage for African surface workers was 6d. per day, and the daily cost of the food supplies for these workers (using a 1932 estimate) was about 8d. The total of 14d. (about 28¢) compares with 1933 daily earnings of 28s. ($6.82) for a European artisan.

[19] *Financial Times* (London), Nov. 26, 1929, Chester Beatty's statement to stockholders. The Anglo-American group also stated that it was "likely the mines will be mechanised as far as possible" in order to overcome a possible shortage of native labor (*Mining Developments in Northern Rhodesia*, Rhodesian Anglo-American [London, 1929] p. 62).

[20] "Progress Report," Roan Antelope Copper Mines (London, March 31, 1930).

vantages to living in the Copperbelt that could only be offset by a substantial payment above the going wage rate in the more developed countries. The typical artisan's wage rate in Great Britain during the early thirties, for example, was less than half that paid to the European artisan in Northern Rhodesia. From the beginning, therefore, a dual wage structure arose in Northern Rhodesia, with a differential arising between skilled and unskilled labor which was greater than in the developed economies.

Supply of Labor

Just as Roan Antelope, Mufulira, Rhokana, and Nchanga were coming into production, the Great Depression struck the copper industry. Mufulira and Nchanga closed down and Roan and Rhokana barely managed to stay in operation. A 1931 labor force of 13,948 Africans and 2,221 Europeans was reduced to 5,831 Africans and 959 Europeans by 1932.[21] The surplus of European labor was handled by reducing hours of work per employee, while the excess African workers were discharged and given travel rations to tide them over until they returned to their villages.

Even before the slump in copper production, however, fundamental changes were occurring with regard to the nature of the African labor force. One of the these was a marked shift of the supply curve of African labor to the right. Until 1930 the supply of African labor was barely adequate. The basic rates of 10s. per ticket of 30 shifts for surface labor and 15s. for underground workers were increased to 17s. 6d. and 30s., respectively, by 1929, but labor still tended to be somewhat short, especially at planting and harvesting times.

By 1931 the comparative shortage of labor disappeared. A "swarm" effect, similar to that described by J. A. Schumpeter with regard to entrepreneurial activity, seemed to occur with regard to labor.[22] Workers returning to their villages must have assured less venturesome individuals that the mines really were not as bad as they had feared. As a result, more and more workers offered themselves for employment, not just through recruitment agencies but at the mines themselves. In late 1930, Mufulira, for example, instructed its recruiting agency not to send any more workers, and by 1931 less than 30 percent (as compared with

[21] *Report of the Commission Appointed To Enquire into the Financial and Economic Position of Northern Rhodesia,* Colonial, no. 145, Great Britain, Colonial Office (London: H.M.S.O., 1938), p. 356, hereafter referred to as the *Pim Report.*

[22] J. A. Schumpeter *The Theory of Economic Development* (New York: Oxford University Press, 1961), pp. 228–230.

about 60 percent in 1930) of Roan Antelope's labor was recruited.[23] The centralized recruitment agency established by the mines in 1930 was abolished in 1932. This shift to voluntary labor resulted in a substantial decrease in labor costs, as it required between £3 and £4 to bring an African worker from his village and send him back after his contract term (6 tickets of 30 days each before 1930 and 12 such tickets thereafter) was completed.[24]

From 1931 until near the end of the decade, the mines had no difficulty securing sufficient African labor. The beginning wage rates actually were cut in 1932 to 12s. 6d. and 22s. 6d. per ticket for surface and underground labor, respectively (and remained at these levels until 1940),[25] but the supply of labor still remained more than adequate. What in the late twenties had been a wage rate barely sufficient to attract the desired numbers became, in the thirties, even with a reduction in wages, a rate that produced conditions of excess labor supply. In 1935, for example, at Nkana 20,034 Africans applied for employment and only 6,723, or 33.5 percent, were accepted.[26] At Ndola, at this time, there was an average of 1,000 seekers of work to be found at any time in the African compounds of the town.[27] Similarly, the mine manager at Mufulira reported that there usually were 200 to 300 Africans looking for work every day.[28] Yet on the basis of a 10 percent turnover per month,[29] and an African force of about 1,900, only 190 jobs were available at Mufulira during an entire month.[30]

[23] "Progress Report," Mufulira Copper Mines (Mufulira, Sept. 30, 1930); Spearpoint, *op. cit.*, p. 36.

[24] E. A. G. Robinson, "The Economic Problem," in *Modern Industry and the African*, ed. J. Merle Davis (London: Macmillan, 1933), p. 161.

[25] Although the basic rate was not changed, a bonus of one shilling a month after 18 months of service was introduced in 1935. In addition, bonuses for good behavior and general efficiency and for wearing safety clothing were put into effect during the thirties.

[26] J. L. Keith and Lt. Col. Hon. A. Stephenson, *Report of the Sub-Committee of the Native Industrial Labour Advisory Board*, Northern Rhodesia (Lusaka: Government Printer, 1936), p. 4.

[27] *Ibid.*

[28] *Evidence Taken by the Commission Appointed To Enquire into the Disturbances in the Copperbelt, Northern Rhodesia, July-September 1935*, Northern Rhodesia (Lusaka: Government Printer, 1936), I, 374, hereafter referred to as the *Russell Commission*.

[29] *Ibid.*

[30] Labor was so cheap and plentiful that the mines carried a reserve of workers who were provided with free rations and were ready to be used at a moment's notice. An interesting procedure developed in deciding which applicants to accept. All were given medical examinations with the standard of acceptance being raised and lowered depending upon labor needs of the mines at the particular

It is not clear why the mining companies did not respond by deliberately reducing wages still more. Apparently they believed that the ability to pick only the most physically fit workers and to replace an unsatisfactory worker immediately were worth the extra cost above what would have attracted a sufficient number of average quality workers.[31] A reduction in real wages did occur, however, between the late thirties and 1947 (table 4–3) .

The mines also apparently allowed the quality of some of their fringe benefits to deteriorate during the thirties. Housing facilities, for example, were less satisfactory near the end of the decade than at the beginning, particularly for single men. A commission in 1940 complained of overcrowding at Anglo-American's Nkana and Kitwe compounds where six persons were assigned to each hut.[32] Almost no attempts were made to provide educational facilities for the children of the rising proportion of married employees.[33] Nonmonetary benefits were, nevertheless, considerable in relation to wage payments. The average service wage, that is, food, hospital care, welfare, and recreation, for Africans at Roan Antelope in the early thirties was 137 percent of the monetary wage, and at Rhokana it was 96 percent.[34]

Labor Efficiency

Besides an increase in the supply of African labor during the early thirties, there was a substantial increase in the efficiency of this labor. The observation that there had been a marked improvement in the efficiency of African labor began to appear in the reports of the mining companies in the early thirties.[35] By 1933 it was asserted that the efficiency of underground workers had increased 100 percent over the late twenties.[36] A significant part of this improvement was associated with the greater use of married workers. Mine managers discovered that, by providing

time (Major G. St. J. Orde Browne, *Labour Conditions in Northern Rhodesia,* Colonial, no. 150, Great Britain, Colonial Office [London: H.M.S.O., 1938], p. 29; Keith and Stephenson, *op. cit.,* p. 4).

[31] *Russell Commission,* p. 273.

[32] *Report of the Commission Appointed To Inquire into the Disturbances in the Copperbelt, Northern Rhodesia, July 1940,* Northern Rhodesia (Lusaka: Government Printer, 1941), p. 14, hereafter referred to as the *Forster Commission, 1940.*

[33] Charles W. Coulter, "The Sociological Problem," in *Modern Industry and the African,* ed. J. Merle Davis (London: Macmillan, 1933), pp. 69–70; Browne, *op. cit.*

[34] Coulter, *op. cit.,* p. 65.

[35] *Financial Times* (London), Dec. 9, 1930, statement to stockholders by Chester Beatty; "Progress Report," Mufulira Copper Mines (Mufulira, June, 1931).

[36] *Russell Commission,* p. 386.

TABLE 4-3

AFRICAN AND EUROPEAN WAGES, NORTHERN RHODESIAN COPPER MINES, 1935–1960
(all wages in pounds per year)

Year	African				European		Ratio of European real wage to African real wage
	Money wage[a]	Value of food[b]	Total of money wage and value of food	Real wage[c]	Money wage[d]	Real wage[e]	
1935	10	10	20	21	f	f	f
1936	14	10	24	25	f	f	f
1937	12	8	20	21	431	444	21
1938	12	11	23	23	f	f	f
1939	13	11	24	24	431	431	18
1940	13	11	24	17	431	375	22
1941	15	11	26	21	431	436	21
1942	17	11	28	22	462	412	19
1943	18	14	32	22	462	385	18
1944	19	14	33	21	462	373	18
1945	19	14	33	19	462	364	19
1946	20	15	35	20	462	350	18
1947	20	18	38	19	539	388	20
1948	30	17	47	23	562	385	21
1949	33	19	52	25	562	377	15
1950	36	21	57	27	562	365	14
1951	43	25	68	31	716	443	14
1952	50	27	77	33	855	501	15
1953	74	30	104	43	1,040	588	14
1954	76	31	107	43	1,040	566	13
1955	80	33	113	43	1,040	548	13
1956	82	20	102	38	1,040	531	14
1957	121	8	129	48	1,040	510	11
1958	133	1	134	47	1,143	545	11
1959	138	1	139	49	1,176	555	11
1960	140	1	141	49	1,281	590	12

[a] Figures for 1935–1954 were based on average surface-wage rates; figures for 1955–1960 based on weighted average wage rates excluding staff employees. SOURCES: *Annual Report of the Department of Labour, 1935–1954*, Northern Rhodesia, Ministry of Labour and Mines (Lusaka, Government Printer); *Year Book*, 1955–1960, Northern Rhodesia Chamber of Mines (Kitwe, Rhodesian Printers).

[b] Value of food (African rations) for 1935–1945 computed by taking the cost of a ration in 1952 (£27) as a base and tying the cost of food to the maize price, because maize is the main component of the food ration. It is assumed that the content of the food ration remained unchanged so that the value of food fluctuated with maize prices. For 1946–1951 the same method was used, but Southern Rhodesian maize prices were used. For 1952–1960 the actual cost of rations was used. SOURCES: *Final Report of the Commission of Inquiry into the Cost of Living*, Northern Rhodesia (Lusaka: Government Printer, 1950); *Report of the Secretary for Native Affairs and Chief Native Commissioner for the Year 1959*, Southern Rhodesia (Salisbury: Government Printer, 1960); *Year Book*, 1955–1960, Northern Rhodesia Chamber of Mines.

[c] To compute real wages of African workers, the following price indexes were used: 1935–1939 based on South African retail price index for food, fuel, light, rent, and sundries, weighted average of 9 principal urban areas (1938 equals 100). SOURCE: *Final Report of the Commission of Inquiry into the Cost of Living;* 1939–1954 based on Euro-

TABLE 4-3 (Continued)

pean cost-of-living index (1939 equals 100); 1955–1960 based on African urban cost-of-living index (1939 equals 100). SOURCE: *Annual Report of the Mines Department,* 1955–1960, Northern Rhodesia, Ministry of Labour and Mines (Lusaka, Government Printer).

The three indexes were combined as follows. The base of all indexes was changed to 1939 equals 100. African urban cost-of-living allowances, based on list of articles bought by a man, wife, and one child, were as follows: £6 in 1939, £11 17s. 2d. in 1947, and £20 2s. 2d. in 1952. The combined cost-of-living index was adjusted to these budget studies. The year 1939 was taken as a base, and 1947 and 1952 served as other reference points. The fluctuations in cost of living between the reference points follow those of the combined cost-of-living index. SOURCE: budget studies from *Report of the Commission Appointed To Review the Salary Structure, Remuneration and Terms of the Civil Service of Northern Rhodesia,* Northern Rhodesia (Lusaka: Government Printer, 1952), Part II, p. 69.

    [d] European wages were computed from shift rates for surface artisans. Data for the years 1937 and 1939 were furnished by Roan Antelope Copper Mines, Luanshya; 1940–1960 furnished by Northern Rhodesia Chamber of Mines, Kitwe.

    [e] To compute European real wages, the European consumer price index and the South African retail price index (adjusted to 1939 equals 100) were used.

    [f] Data not available.

special housing facilities for married workers and their families, they could attract more of these workers and thereby sharply reduce turnover rates.[37] At Rhokana, for example, married men remained in employment at the beginning of the thirties an average of 12.9 months, while single men stayed only 8.6 months.[38] By 1935 more than 50 percent (as compared with 20 percent in 1928) of the workers at Roan Antelope were married, and turnover rates fell from around 20 percent to 10 percent per month.[39] Family life also resulted in better-fed, healthier workers. Single men apparently neglected to cook their rations properly, or only utilized part of them, and their health and stamina suffered in relation to married workers.[40] The increase in the average length of employment at the mines was not just attributable to use of a larger proportion of married workers. Both single and married workers lengthened the time they spent on any one job. At Rhokana, for example, by 1946, the length of time that departing married and single workers had spent on the job was increased to 27.9 months and 13.2 months, respectively.[41] As African workers remained at the mines longer, additional training efforts be-

---

[37] Spearpoint, *op. cit.,* p. 54.

[38] Coulter, *op. cit.,* p. 61 n.

[39] The number of married employees who had their families with them is not known, but unquestionably the proportion of married men with their families was also much higher than in the late twenties.

[40] Spearpoint, *op. cit.,* p. 28.

[41] *Annual Report for the Year 1951,* Northern Rhodesia, Labour and Mines Department (Lusaka: Government Printer, 1952), p. 20.

came profitable, and this training improved efficiency still further.

Demand for Labor

The use of relatively more African workers became profitable for the mines, not only because of the remarkable increase in their efficiency but also because of the relative increase in European wages. European wage rates were not reduced in the early thirties, as were African rates. Furthermore, in 1937, when the European trade union was formed, a cash-bonus plan based upon the price of copper was instituted for European workers.[42] This bonus arrangement and the pension and benefit schemes put into effect at the same time increased European wages in relation to African labor costs. By 1940 the ratio of European to African earnings was 34 to 1 compared with 28 to 1 in 1937 (table 4-4).

The result of this shift in the real costs of African versus European labor during the 1930's and early 1940's was a drop in the ratio of European to African laborers. Table 4–5 presents these ratios for all mines in Northern Rhodesia and also separately for Roan Antelope—a mine company that built no additional processing facilities, for example, an electrolytic refinery, during the years covered in the table. Whereas in the late twenties the African's unreliability made it desirable to minimize his use despite his low absolute wage, his increased efficiency in the thirties meant that it was profitable to substitute him for European labor. Such jobs as driving trucks, operating drilling equipment, working with explosives (under supervision) and operating underground locomotives increasingly were turned over to Africans. Europeans were used only as supervisors and where some special skill was necessary.

At first the European workers did not resist the relatively greater use of African labor. Employment was expanding absolutely as the industry came out of the depression, and the jobs of the existing European labor force were not in jeopardy. Labor substitution took the form of separating unskilled-labor tasks from skilled jobs rather than turning skilled tasks over to African employees. The European union agreed to "the dilution of labor"

---

[42] In 1947 the scheme was altered so that it would be based upon industry profits rather than the price of copper. African workers did not participate in a profit-sharing bonus system until 1951.

TABLE 4-4

TOTAL AVERAGE MONEY AND REAL EARNINGS OF AFRICAN AND EUROPEAN
EMPLOYEES, NORTHERN RHODESIAN COPPER MINES, 1937–1960
(all earnings in pounds per year)

| Year | Europeans | | Africans | | |
	Total average money earnings[a]	Total average real earnings[b]	Total average money earnings[c]	Total average real earnings[d]	Ratio of European to African real earnings
1937	564	581	20	21	28
1940	606	588	24	17	34
1949	1,056	708	52	25	28
1950	1,068	693	61	28	25
1951	1,275	787	78	35	22
1952	1,500	877	86	37	24
1953	1,782	1,007	124	51	20
1954	1,734	942	123	49	19
1955	1,943	1,023	134	52	20
1956	2,295	1,171	166	61	19
1957	1,910	936	189	69	14
1958	1,699[e]	809[e]	200	71	11
1959	1,868	881	218	76	12
1960	2,160	995	258	89	11

[a] Total money earnings for Europeans: 1937 furnished by Roan Antelope Copper Mines, Luanshya; 1940 and 1949 from D. T. Jack, *Report of the Board of Inquiry To Consider the Proposed 40-Hour Week in the Copper Mining Industry of Northern Rhodesia*, Northern Rhodesia (Lusaka: Government Printer, 1950); 1950–1960 from *Year Book*, 1955–1960, Northern Rhodesia Chamber of Mines (Kitwe, Rhodesian Printers).

[b] To compute European real wages, the European consumer price index and the South African retail price index (adjusted to 1939 equals 100) were used.

[c] Total money earnings for Africans include wages (weekday shifts and Sunday and special shifts), overtime payments, efficiency awards, task bonuses, safety bonuses, paid company-holiday bonus shifts, travel allowances or holiday bonuses, cost-of-living allowance, prosperity bonuses, and cost of food provided. SOURCE: Figures for 1937, 1940 and 1949 from third column in table 4-3; figures from 1950–1960 from *Year Book*, 1955–1960.

[d] The price index used to deflate total money earnings for Africans is the same as that described in table 4-3, note c.

[e] Wages affected by strike.

during the war, but insisted upon a return to prewar practices with regard to working conditions at the end of the conflict.[43]

The substitution of African labor for some machinery appears

---

[43] The extent of dilution that actually occurred during the war period was negligible (*Report of Board of Inquiry Appointed To Inquire into the Advancement of Africans in the Copper Mining Industry in Northern Rhodesia*, Northern Rhodesia [Lusaka: Government Printer, 1954], p. 7, hereafter referred to as the *Forster Commission, 1954*.

TABLE 4-5

European Employees as a Percent of African Employees
in the Mining Industry of Northern Rhodesia, 1931–1961
(percentages)

Year	All mines	Roan Antelope Copper Mines
1931	14.4	20.4
1933	13.1	18.8
1935	11.4	12.1
1937	9.1	14.2
1939	10.9	12.3
1941	9.5	11.0
1943	9.4	10.3
1945	9.9	9.9
1947	11.3	12.2
1949	11.8	13.1
1950	11.9	13.1
1951	13.0	13.8
1952	13.3	15.1
1953	13.0	15.2
1954	13.3	15.9
1955	16.5	16.5
1956	15.7	17.3
1957	15.6	18.1
1958	17.7	18.7
1959	17.9	20.1
1960	17.6	19.9
1961	18.4	—

Sources: All mines, including large and small mines producing
mineral products other than copper: Annual Reports, 1931–1961,
Northern Rhodesia, Mines Department (Lusaka, Government
Printer). Roan Antelope Copper Mines: employment data supplied by the company.

to be another development that began to take place in the thirties. No longer does one find remarks in company reports stating
that machinery is being introduced to replace African laborers,
or asserting that the mines are the last word in terms of modern
equipment. By 1958 the general manager at Rhokana noted that
the Northern Rhodesian mines were ten years behind the times
in mechanization.[44] Despite all the technological improvements in
mechanical devices for handling materials, the mines found it
cheaper in many cases to continue to use labor-intensive meth-

[44] Rhokana Corporation, press release, June, 1958, copy in the files of Rhodesia
House, London.

ods. Even today, with much higher African wages and the consequent mechanization that has occurred, it is frequently less expensive to maintain older productive methods than to introduce the latest mechanical devices. The greatest scope for mechanization underground, for example, exists in the process of sublevel lashing, that is, the handling of broken rock from a passageway blasted out preparatory to mining a section of the ore body. On the Copperbelt this activity still is performed by hand labor using shovels and wheelbarrows. Elsewhere it is done by mechanical loaders that load into track-mounted trucks or power-driven trackless equipment.[45]

Recent technological developments in the drilling of blast holes provide another illustration of the greater profitability of more labor-intensive methods over highly mechanical techniques. Current practice in developed industrial countries is to use 3 or 4 heavy drilling machines mounted on mobile carriages. In Rhodesia light machines mounted on pneumatic legs or pushers are employed. The latter equipment is operated by Africans, whereas the former method would require a European operator and European personnel to service the equipment. Since the wages of skilled Europeans are much higher than those for unskilled African labor, it is not worthwhile to introduce the heavier equipment.[46]

Another area of work where older methods are employed, although to a lesser and lesser extent in recent years, concerns the movement of materials on the surface. Bulldozers, forklift trucks, conveyor loaders, motorized carts, and mobile cranes are in extensive use in Europe and the United States, but in many cases still are not worthwhile on the Copperbelt.[47]

---

[45] One mechanical loader in Northern Rhodesia handling 250 tons per day and working 6 days a week would cost (in 1959) $54 per day including spares, maintenance, and amortization. This is equivalent to the cost of 39 laborers. In the United States the daily cost for the equipment would be $60, or an amount equivalent to the cost of less than 4 laborers. The loader can do the work of about 10 workers, so that it is highly profitable in the United States but a dead loss on the Copperbelt (D. Young, "The Future of Mechanization in Our Mines, Paper no. 1," and A. W. Schumann, "The Future of Mechanization in Our Mines, Paper no. 3," speeches delivered at Rhodesian Selection Trust Symposium, Lusaka, Sept. 25, 26, 1959).

[46] Young, *op. cit.*, pp. 3–4.

[47] P. B. Mattushek, "The Future of Mechanization in Our Mines, Paper no. 2," speech delivered at Rhodesian Selection Trust Symposium, Lusaka, Sept. 25, 26, 1959, p. 7.

Summary

The most significant point that emerges from this survey of the use of African labor in the copper mines from the late twenties until the end of World War II is the considerable improvement in the efficiency of African labor, and consequently the relatively greater utilization of such labor. This experience illustrates one of the most important relationships in the development process, namely, the qualitative changes that occur in a labor force simply because of the use of labor in a new industry. The copper industry, to repeat, is not one in which the labor coefficient is high compared with many agricultural export commodities. The employment of relatively more unskilled labor does occur, however, when labor costs fall relative to those for skilled labor and capital goods, and this change in employment can be significant in percentage terms.

In the late twenties Africans were reluctant to work in the copper mines and most inefficient when they did. It was then economical to minimize their use in the mines. But, by the act of working in the industry, they acquired more skills and became more willing to work in urban areas. These changes resulted in a significantly greater use of African workers during the latter part of the thirties and early forties. Indeed, by the late thirties African labor conditions became tight. After a 5s. increase in minimum wages (per 30 working days), the supply of African labor promptly improved.[48] Although the copper industry's labor force still was composed of two very different types of workers, progress was made during the thirties in extending the impact of the industry on African employment and in raising levels of industrial skills.

POSTWAR CHANGES IN THE LABOR SUPPLY

The ratio of European to African employees reversed its trend after the war and began to rise (table 4-5). By 1960 the ratio at Roan Antelope actually had returned to its level of the early

---

[48] This increase, which amounted to a rise of 40 percent in the minimum wage for surface employees, occurred as a result of a strike of African employees during which rioting broke out and 17 Africans were killed. The companies awarded 2s. 6d. during the strike as a cost-of-living bonus, and an additional 2s. 6d. was granted on the recommendation of the commission investigating the disturbances (*Forster Commission, 1940*), p. 29.

thirties. In addition to this shift in the employment figures for the two groups of workers, there was a sharp postwar decline in the overall number of workers used per ton of copper produced. Between 1932 and 1946 the number of employees at Roan Antelope per ton of copper produced fell only from 1.93 to 1.84. From 1946 to 1960 the reduction was from 1.84 to .095.[49] In analyzing these two changes, three factors are discussed: the introduction of new productive methods since the war; the shift in the relative cost of European versus African labor; and (in the next section) the issue of African advancement.

New Productive Developments and Processes

During the thirties as well as the war years, no major new technique was introduced in the Rhodesian copper industry. A steady stream of minor, productivity-increasing improvements were put into operation, but no outstanding innovation, particularly one that significantly altered the proportion of European to African workers, was adopted. By the end of the war, however, a backlog of new methods, which had not been adopted previously because of wartime shortages, had accumulated. One of the most important of the new types of equipment developed was the tungsten-carbide drill, which was introduced into the Copperbelt mines about 1950. Before this innovation, the tip of the ordinary drill was made of forged steel, which had an average drill life of about 42 inches. The tungsten-carbide–tipped drill, on the other hand, possesses a drilling life of about 35 feet.[50] Not only did this new drill increase underground productivity, but it cut the size of a European miner's gang of African workers from 16 to 12. Fewer workers were needed to carry new drills to replace the ones wearing out. Besides the direct effect of this to increase the European-African employment ratio, the proportionate decrease in the numbers of both Europeans and Africans employed underground acted to increase the ratio of Europeans to Africans in the industry as a whole, since this ratio is higher for surface than underground operations. Another drilling improvement pioneered and introduced by Rhokana about 1946 was the use of high-speed diamond drills for drilling long blast holes. This allowed larger amounts of the ore body to be undercut at one time, gave a better

---

[49] Based on reports and records of Roan Antelope Copper Mines, Luanshya.

[50] L. S. Cole, "Hard Metal: The New Rock Drilling Medium," *Optima*, II (June, 1952), 20.

fragmentation of the ore, and reduced the cost of secondary blasting.[51]

Still another important improvement in underground operations was the perfection of continuous and block-caving methods of mining. These techniques are employed where the ore body is thick and does not dip too steeply. The principle is to undercut and weaken the ore body so that the ore is crushed by the weight of the collapsing ore body and the overlying rocks. It eliminates the need to blast all the ore out of the ore body, as is the case with sublevel stoping. Both Anglo-American and Rhodesian Selection Trust shifted increasingly to these methods after the war. The development of open-pit mining at Nchanga in 1955 also resulted in a very large increase in the average productivity of labor. The ratio of Europeans to Africans was approximately the same as if the ore were mined by underground methods, but, as this ratio was lower than for the entire operation, the reduction in the number of workers involved in mining acted to increase the total European to African ratio.[52]

There were no spectacular technological improvements in surface operations. Continuous casting operations were perfected, but these processes were not adopted on the Copperbelt because of the cost of power. Except for this new process, the basic concentrating, smelting, and refining techniques were the same as in the thirties. There were, however, many small improvements introducd, especially in the handling of materials.

On the basis of conversations with engineers in the Rhodesian copper industry, it appears that the net effect of postwar technological progress was to raise the European to African employment ratio. But such a conclusion can be only very tentative until a more careful study is made.

Changes in the relative importance of different production processes in the industry must also be included in accounting for the postwar upward trend in the ratio of European to African employment. In the thirties and forties, for example, the mines

---

[51] "Annual Report," 1946, Nchanga Consolidated Copper Mines, Salisbury.

[52] H. E. Nelems, "Open Pit Mining at Nchanga," *Optima*, V (March, 1955), 6–14. To produce 150,000 tons of ore per month by underground mining would have required 220 Europeans and 1,800 Africans. With open-pit mining only 40 Europeans and 400 Africans were necessary. For a discussion of other improvements in mining, see Sir Ronald L. Prain, "The Development of the Copper Industry," in *Royal School of Mines, University of London,* Special University Lectures, No. 3 (London: Portsoken Press, Nov., 1957).

undertook most of their construction programs themselves. Later a sizable amount of construction work was undertaken as contract work by newly formed firms on the Copperbelt. Because the construction industry uses a high proportion of African workers, the exclusion of many construction programs from the employment activities of the mines raised the overall proportion of Europeans to Africans. Similarly, the introduction of electrolytic refining on the Copperbelt acted in the same way. The ratio of Europeans to Africans is higher in this process than the average ratio from mining operations through the smelting process, and the total ratio for the entire operation has therefore been increased.

Increased Earnings

Although technological progress and shifts in the relative importance of various processes are significant factors in accounting for the decline in the general labor coefficient, and also for the growing relative importance of European workers, an analysis of these matters is far from complete without considering the effects of wage changes. African and European earnings increased considerably after the end of the war (tables 4-3, 4-4). Whereas equipment costs rose about 100 percent between 1947 and 1958,[53] African and European earnings rose 284 percent and 61 percent respectively, between 1949 and 1958.

The supply of European workers was more than adequate during this period except for a few years shortly after the end of World War II. The European union was nevertheless very successful in raising steadily the wage rates of its members. A bonus arrangement, based (since 1947) on industry profits, also was an important cause of increased earnings. Between 1949 and 1960 these bonus payments averaged 58 percent of basic wages.

Industry officials, it is interesting to note, frequently extol the advantages of this system. They point out that it introduces an additional variable element into their cost structure and thereby aids in mitigating the fluctuations in profit levels. An examina-

---

[53] The increase in equipment cost is based on O. B. Bennett, "The Improvement in Plant Practice and Labour Utilisation at Rhokana Corporation," *Journal of the South African Institute of Mining and Metallurgy* (May and Sept., 1958), p. 9. The end year used to compute the rise in European earnings was 1959 rather than 1958 because of the abnormally low figure for 1958. An even larger spread in the rise in costs occurred in labor costs per shift, that is, wages plus oncosts. Between 1948 and 1958 these costs rose 470 percent for African labor and only 60 percent for European labor (*ibid.*, p. 10).

tion of the wage experience of the copper companies, between sterling devaluation in 1949 and the collapse of copper prices in 1956, raises doubts about whether the system actually was a success from a more general company viewpoint. The very sharp increase in copper prices between these years (nearly 150 percent) obviously was not generally anticipated and consequently resulted in much larger profits than were expected. Because of these much higher profits, European earnings rose 117 percent in the mining industry but only 87 percent in all other industries.[54] This suggests that neither total earnings nor basic wage rates in the copper industry would have increased to the extent they did without the bonus system. Part of the large African wage increases awarded by government arbitrators also may be attributable to the rapid rise in European earnings. A final drawback of the bonus system from the copper companies' viewpoint is the difficulty of cutting earnings sharply when profits decline substantially. Workers treat the bonus as part of their normal wages after a period of high bonuses and strongly resist any cut in their income as a result of declining profits. A case in point occurred in 1958 after copper prices and profits had dropped sharply in 1957. Workers in the industry were successful in obtaining a consolidation of 10 percent of the bonus into their basic wage rate.

Even more remarkable than the substantial increase in European earnings was the rapid rise in African real earnings after the war. These earnings rose 300 percent between 1945 and 1960 as compared with an actual decrease of 21 percent between 1930 and 1945.[55] This postwar development increased wages to a level considerably above that necessary to hold the existing work-force level, and also brought about a substantial amount of factor substitution against African labor. Except for two brief periods, the condition of the labor market between about 1932 and 1953 is probably best described as one in which a moderate excess supply of African labor existed. A relative shortage of labor appeared in the late thirties, but a wage increase in 1940 quickly eased

---

[54] Mining data from table 4-4. Earnings in all other industries cover the period 1945 (rather than 1949) to 1956. Data for 1945 from Phyllis Deane, *Colonial Social Accounting* (Cambridge: Cambridge University Press, 1953), p. 243; *National Accounts of the Federation of Rhodesia and Nyasaland, 1954–1959*, Federation of Rhodesia and Nyasaland, Central Statistical Office (Salisbury: Government Printer, 1960), p. 74.

[55] Total average real earnings for Africans in mining from 1930 to 1934 were: 1930; £24.0; 1931, £23.1; 1932, £25.5; 1933, £20.4; 1934, £23.1. They were computed in the same way as the figures given in table 4-4.

this condition, and also proved sufficient to attract the large labor force needed during the war. After the impetus given to copper production by the sterling devaluation of 1949 and by the Korean War, excess demand conditions for African labor again began to appear in 1949, 1950, and 1951.[56] African wages were tied to a cost-of-living index in 1950, and a wage increase plus a profit-sharing plan was negotiated in 1951, but labor conditions still remained somewhat tight. Then, in January, 1953, C. W. Guillebaud, an arbitrator appointed under the Industrial Conciliation Ordinance, awarded a 77 percent increase in the starting rate of surface employees and a 63 percent increase in the starting rate of underground workers.[57] The basis of this very large award, as the arbitrator candidly stated, was not a shortage of African labor. Instead, Guillebaud stressed the great discrepancy between European and African earnings and the ability of the companies to pay the increase out of their high profits. He pointed out that the average basic wage for European surface workers was £89 per month, and that for African employees only £4 2s. 7d. The latter group received free rations, housing, and water valued at £3 2s. 7d. per month, but Europeans, in addition to their basic wage, were getting a copper bonus that amounted to 75 percent of their basic rate.[58] This meant that the average real earnings of Europeans (even neglecting their subsidized housing and other facilities) were about 20 times greater than those for Africans.

African wages continued to rise significantly after 1953 mainly because of the efforts of the African Mineworkers Trade Union.[59] This organization was formed in 1949, but did not become very powerful until the mid-fifties. During the thirties a system of consultation between the mining companies and a group of tribal

---

[56] See, for example, "Annual Report," 1950, 1951, Roan Antelope Copper Mines (Luanshya). At one time in 1950 African labor strength at the Broken Hill lead and zinc mine was 500 short of the mine's immediate requirements (D. T. Jack, *Report of the Board of Inquiry To Consider the Proposed 40-Hour Week in the Copper Mining Industry of Northern Rhodesia*, Northern Rhodesia [Lusaka: Government Printer, 1950], p. 22).

[57] "Report and Award of the Arbitrator, C. W. Guillebaud, Esq., C.B.E.," Jan., 1953, esp. pp. 10–12, hereafter referred to as the "Guillebaud Award." Also published in the *Northern Rhodesia Government Gazette* Jan. 9, 1953.

[58] *Ibid.*, pp. 10–11.

[59] Besides ordinary increments in the basic rate, earnings increased owing to the consolidation into the basic wage rate of the cost-of-living allowance and the efficiency awards, and to a change in the bonus system, making the African bonus arrangement comparable with the European system. The issuance of free rations was gradually discontinued between 1950 and 1956 and monetary payment substitued in their place.

elders existed at some of the mines. This developed in 1942 and 1943 into a general system of tribal representatives who were elected by the workers on a tribal basis. But in 1951 the arrangement was abandoned after a vote by the workers.

The wage awards of 1951 and especially 1953, however, marked a definite turning point in the attitude of management toward African labor. The substantial rise in African wages at these times caused management to initiate a far-reaching program of mechanization and rationalization designed to reduce the relative importance of Africa labor.[60] The extent of the change in the use of African labor is indicated by the fact that if the same ratio of African workers to output prevailed in 1959 as in 1949, African employment would have been 69,000 in 1959 instead of 35,000. The European labor coefficient also declined, but less rapidly. For example, at Roan Antelope copper output rose 23 percent between 1951 and 1960, whereas African employment dropped 33 percent and European employment remained constant. The narrowing of the differential between the costs of European and African labor began to reverse a trend that had continued for a third of a century.

The cutback of African labor was accomplished in two ways. First, mechanical equipment was substituted for hand labor. The greater use of forklift trucks and, in some places, mechanical ore-loaders are prominent examples of this substitution. As was remarked by one labor specialist at the mines, this type of mechanization resulted in the replacement of unskilled African labor by semiskilled African labor rather than by European workers. A second manner of reducing African employment was merely to cut the number of workers performing a particular task without using more capital equipment or substantially reorganizing the work pattern. This involved, of course, more work for the remaining employees. African workers apparently accepted this increase in their work standard without any noticeable complaint. It would appear that their work ability had been increasing gradually since the thirties, but European supervisors were treating the African as if he were the same as he was in the thirties. A job that required 10 laborers in earlier years could now be accomplished with (say) 7 workers. Supervisors did not fully realize this

---

[60] For a careful analysis of the new cost relationships and their possible effect on African employment, see "The Utilisation of African Labour, Cost Trends, Policy and Programme To Meet the Situation," Rhokana Corporation (Nkana, Dec. 6, 1956).

(nor probably, when wages were low, was it profitable to ascertain this fact and bring about a change) until they were pressed to search for ways to reduce costs because of the sudden, substantial increase in wages. The greater training acquired by longer service, and the realization that jobs in the mines were now much harder to obtain, were other factors accounting for the ease by which the work standard was raised.

The substantial amount of capital substitution for labor, a sharp drop in the labor turnover ratio (the number of leavers per month or per year divided by average daily employment), and the desire by more Africans to work in the Copperbelt as wages increased and employment conditions improved, all worked together to make excess labor-supply conditions progressively worse on the Copperbelt during the last half of the fifties. Significant excess-supply conditions prevailed between 1954 and 1957, and thereafter the situation became even more serious. For example, at Rhokana the number of Africans offering themselves for employment per month jumped from 1,500 in 1956 to 6,000 in 1961.[61] Reports from the government's Department of Labour also stress the seriousness of the unemployment problem after 1957.[62]

AFRICAN ADVANCEMENT

Before the increases in wages in the early fifties, the African advancement issue was not a major problem on the Copperbelt.[63] Management thought it was not profitable to invest the sums necessary to train skilled African employees, because they would not remain long enough for the expenditures to be worthwhile. The turnover of European workers was also high, but these workers were already trained, and, even though they had to be paid much more, it was profitable to use them for most jobs requiring considerable skill. The rise in African wages and the drop in African turnover rates (from about 60 percent annually in the forties to around 35 percent by 1955) completely changed this view. It became evident around 1953 that it was profitable to train Africans and substitute them for skilled European workers.

[61] Based on conversations with members of the African Personnel Department at Rhokana Corporation. The number actually hired per month averaged only about 250 in 1956 and 200 in 1961, respectively.

[62] Annual Reports, 1957–1961, Northern Rhodesia, Department of Labour (Lusaka, Government Printer).

[63] "African Advancement," Roan Antelope Copper Mines (Dec., 1960), p. 1.

Unfortunately the mining companies had been maneuvered into an unfavorable position by the European union on this matter. European employees became fearful of African advancement around 1940. Although they agreed to some advancement during the war years, they made it subject to the condition that prewar conditions of employment be restored after hostilities ceased. The union then pressed for what in effect was an indefinite continuation of this employment arrangement, and in 1945 European workers succeeded in inserting the following clause into their labor contract: "DILUTION OF LABOUR. The Company agrees that work of the class or grade that is being performed or job that is being filled, by an employee at the time of the signing of this Agreement shall not be given to persons to whom the terms and conditions of the Agreement do not apply." [64]

Under another clause the companies recognized "the union as representing the daily paid European employees to whom its [the contract's] terms and conditions are applicable," and African advancement was effectively blocked.[65] The copper companies were fully aware of the implications of both the wartime and postwar contracts. They point out that in 1940 and at subsequent contract negotiations, pressure was brought by the British government to avoid a strike at any cost.[66] The postwar pressure was applied because of the need not only to meet the greatly increased demand for copper but also to help the balance of payments difficulties of the sterling area. In addition to these factors, the high profits being earned in the industry, and the apparent lack of significant numbers of suitable candidates for advancement, acted to make the mines reluctant to force a strike on the issue.[67]

In 1953 bulk buying by the British government ceased, and the London Metal Exchange reopened. The mines promptly gave

---

[64] *Agreement between Northern Rhodesia Mine Workers Union and Mufulira Copper Mines, Ltd., Nchanga Consolidated Copper Mines, Ltd. . . .* (Ndola: Rhodesian Printers, 1956), pp. 37–38.

[65] "Annual Report," 1954, Mufulira Copper Mines (Mufulira). The union offered to delete the word "European" but the companies objected, as they were unwilling to let Africans come under the control of the European union (*Forster Commission, 1954*).

[66] See, for example, Sir Ronald L. Prain, "The Problem of African Advancement on the Copperbelt of Northern Rhodesia," *African Affairs*, LIII (April, 1954), 91–102.

[67] The mines at this stage still held views similar to the following statement made in 1929: "It seems unlikely that the native will, for many generations at least, be able to compete with Europeans in work that entails more than the very minimum of real responsibility" (*Mining Developments in Northern Rhodesia*, p. 17).

six months' notice to the European Mineworkers Union of cancelling their agreement because of the clauses preventing Africans from being given jobs previously held by Europeans. By this time it was perfectly obvious that African advancement was in the best interests of the mining companies. For example, even in 1959, after some advancement of Africans had already taken place, one copper executive estimated that a reduction in costs of £6 per ton of copper (thereby raising profits about 10 percent) would occur under a program of a comparatively moderate degree of advancement. With a more extensive program, especially with respect to the routine servicing of mechanized equipment, costs would be cut much more.[68] The mines also came to regard African advancement as "good politics." It would lessen the possibility of nationalization, if and when an African government came into power.[69]

The proper position for the Europeans to take on the issue of African advancement was quite obvious. They had nothing against the promotion of Africans—provided that the principle of equal pay for equal work was followed, and also that the sons of European workers were ensured of employment opportunities. This policy, of course, would in effect eliminate the desire by the companies to advance African workers.[70]

The mines found themselves in a most difficult position. For many years it was necessary to attract skilled labor from the more developed countries. This meant that the companies were required to pay these workers the wage for this type of labor abroad plus an additional sum to attract workers to an underdeveloped country. In 1959 one executive estimated the expatriation allowance to be 40s. per shift for daily-paid European employees.[71] At the same time that a very high wage was necessary to attract Europeans, a much lower wage was sufficient to secure all

[68] E. C. Bromwich, "Problems of Arresting Cost Increases in Our Mines," speech delivered at Rhodesian Selection Trust Symposium, Lusaka, Sept. 25, 26, 1959, p. 14.

[69] The mines also justified their relatively higher than average wage rates for Africans on the grounds that, if the government nationalized the copper industry, it would be forced to pay its other government employees these same high wages. The great additional cost involved—so the argument goes—would make any government hesitate about nationalization (*ibid.*, p. 3).

[70] It is interesting to note that the European Mineworkers Union advocated nationalization. The union did not wish "alien interests in the Federation" to handle the problems of African advancement (*Rhodesia Herald* [Salisbury], Aug. 22, 1959).

[71] Bromwich, *op. cit.*, p. 13. Their basic wage rate varied from about 60 to 80 shillings per shift at this time.

the African labor necessary. As long as there were two noncompeting groups, there was no problem. But when the African became properly qualified candidate for advancement, the question of what wage to pay him in his more skilled job became a bitter issue. It was obvious that the wage level necessary to attract intelligent, hard-working, and stable African workers could be far below that being paid Europeans for the same job. The Rhodesian mines had only to look across the border at the Katanga mines where, for example, the ratio of Europeans to Africans was 1 to 25 in the concentrating plant and 1 to 42 in the electrolytic tank houses, as compared with to 1 to 8 and 1 to 13, respectively, in Northern Rhodesia, to see the possibilities for a tremendous increase in profits through African advancement.[72] But, African workers could not be advanced sufficiently rapidly to prevent a long shutdown, if the European workers went on strike over the wage issue. Furthermore, the Europeans were needed to train the Africans.

The outcome of the long negotiations between the European miners and the companies was a compromise. In 1955, after an impartial commission had made recommendations concerning African advancement, about 30 employment categories were turned over to Africans.[73] Some of these involved a one for one replacement of a European by an African; others were "fragmented" jobs, that is, more than one African now performed a task previously accomplished by one European. The wage rate paid those Africans who were promoted was higher than their previous level but still much lower than the rate that had been paid Europeans for these jobs. Between 1955 and 1960 about 1,000 Africans, or slightly less than 3 percent of the average African labor force, were advanced into the new positions.[74]

In late 1960 the European union accepted a further set of proposals for African advancement—ones that were designed to provide a final solution to the problem. The same procedure as followed in 1955 was adopted. Approximately 35 jobs were to be opened up to Africans on a man to man basis, and 20 new jobs, representing parts of tasks formerly done by Europeans, were to

---

[72] "Report of a Visit to the Belgian Congo by Copper Company Executives," Dec., 1952, copy in the American Metal Climax Company library, New York.

[73] *Forster Commission, 1954.*

[74] "African Advancement Proposals," Northern Rhodesia Mine Workers' Union (Chingola Printers, Oct. 4, 1960).

be created.[75] It was estimated that 350 Europeans would be replaced by Africans.[76] The companies agreed, though, that any
European displaced by an African would continue to be employed at terms at least as favorable as those he would have enjoyed had the removal not taken place. In addition, the establishment of a training program for the more specialized mining jobs,
which gave preference to the sons of employees, was part of the
proposal.

In theory, all positions were to be open to Africans on a competitive basis with Europeans. Only for the approximately 55 jobs
covered by the agreement, however, were wage rates to be adjusted. For these the African wage scale, plus an amount to compensate (in African terms) for the increased skill requirement,
was to be used. By doing this the highest paid African job would
equal the lowest paid European job. In other words, the gap between European and African wage scales was bridged under the
proposal. The wage rate for all other jobs held by Europeans was
to remain the same. As only 350 Europeans were likely to be replaced by the new wage scale applicable to the 55 jobs, it meant
that for the positions held by more than 95 percent of the European employees, the principle of equal pay for equal work would
prevail. Because of the superior education and training back-
ground of the Europeans, it was not likely that many Africans
would successfully compete for these jobs.

The African union was not consulted during the negotiations
from which the advancement proposals emerged. It was brought
into the picture only when rates of pay for the new intermediate
jobs were to be determined. As is not surprising, little progress
was made in these wage discussions, because the African union
raised the whole issue of African advancement and also pressed
for a very large wage increase. The negotiations finally broke
down and a strike became imminent. In response to this threat,
the governor appointed a commission to inquire into the breakdown of negotiations as well as into general wage and working
conditions in the industry. The commission chose to interpret the
governor's instructions narrowly and largely confined its inquiry
to the specific matters raised in prior negotiations. Furthermore,
the commission purposely did not make specific recommendations
on these matters. It concluded that a lack of adequate communication and understanding between the parties involved was the

---

[75] *Ibid.*, pp. 8–14.
[76] *Ibid.*, p. 14.

major cause of breakdown. The commission recommended certain changes in consulting and negotiating procedure, and urged the companies and the African and European unions to work out the advancement problem themselves.[77]

CONCLUSIONS

It has been pointed out that in terms of employment opportunities, the period from the late twenties through World War II was a relatively favorable one for African workers in the copper industry. Although the production function for copper seriously restricted the possibilities for large-scale employment of Africans in an industry of that size (even with the low wage rates), the gradual improvement in the quality of African labor induced management to increase progressively the use of African workers over the period. The prospects for a gradual elimination of the dualistic wage structure, which was established initially for sound economic reasons, also seemed to be favorable.

Since the war, however, this situation has changed drastically. African and European wages have been raised by monopolistic actions to levels considerably above the rates necessary to attract the numbers actually employed. The consequences of this wage policy have been the creation of unemployment conditions in the Copperbelt towns, especially among Africans, and the widespread substitution of machines for men in the industry. Jobs that otherwise would have opened up and been filled by workers migrating from the rural areas have not become available. The result is that more people are forced to remain in the subsistence sector than if industrial wage rates were set by the forces of a free-market system. Those who do come to the towns in hope of securing one of the high-paying jobs are faced with a long waiting period before they obtain one of these positions. Conditions of excess labor supply on the Copperbelt are far more serious than anything that prevailed in the thirties. At Roan Antelope in 1961 an average of 20 Africans applied for each job available.[78] Unless workers are lucky enough to obtain high-wage jobs soon after they arrive from the rural areas, they either return to their vil-

---

[77] *Report of the Commission Appointed To Inquire into the Mining Industry in Northern Rhodesia,* Northern Rhodesia (Lusaka: Government Printer, 1962), p. 20.

[78] "Human Problems at Roan Antelope," Roan Antelope Copper Mines (Luanshya, Jan., 1961), p. 3.

lages without obtaining work or find employment in nonunion-
ized service industries not regulated by the government, where
wage rates are depressed to an artificially low level. The serious
social, political, and economic problems that arise because of the
presence of a large group of unemployed people in the urban
areas are obvious.

Some writers contend that the increase in wage rates actually
has acted to stimulate domestic industry and employment by
leading to a rise in spending within the economy.[79] The reason
given for this view is that the reduction in employment, in response to the wage increment, has been proportionately less than
the increase in wage rates. The wage bill of the mine workers
(particularly the African workers) has therefore increased. Total
revenue earned by the industry and, in particular, profits have
tended to decrease—these writers would agree—but a large share
of profits is sent abroad. The loss in the amount of profits spent
internally by the companies is more than made up by the larger
wage bill, most of which is spent internally.

There is no question but that the above result is theoretically
possible. But there are a number of considerations that suggest
that it did not hold in the Rhodesian case. On the basis of technical opinion in the industry, at least half the reduction, between
1949 and 1959, in the number of African workers employed per
ton of copper produced was in response to the artificially high
wage rates set in the industry. This means that perhaps between
50,000 and 55,000 Africans would have been employed at the
1959 output level instead of 35,000, if wages had not been artificially raised. Using previous supply response experience to labor
demands in the industry and in the economy as a whole, a con-
servative estimate of the increase that would have occurred in
real wages under free-market conditions is 50 percent. Under these
assumptions, this implies that the 1959 African wage bill at the
1959 output level would have been about 2.5 times as large as
the 1949 wage bill under free-market conditions. Since real earnings per worker were in fact about 2.7 times greater in 1959 than
in 1949, and African employment was about 1.1 times larger, the
actual African real-wage bill in 1959 was about 2.9 times larger
than in 1949.

These estimates are, at best, educated guesses. Thus far, however, they support the view that wage policy in the economy

---

[79] J. G. Scott, "Memorandum Submitted to the Commission of Inquiry at the
Request of the African Mineworkers' Union, May 23, 1962" (Kitwe), p. 17.

may have increased the African wage bill. There are several additional factors that must be taken into account. If wage rates had not increased as much as they did, copper production unquestionably would have been greater in 1959 than it actually was. The number of Africans employed directly in the industry (and thus the wage bill) would then have been more than the 50,000–55,000 estimated above. Furthermore, employment in those internal industries that supply materials and plant facilities to the copper industry would have been larger. The larger employment impact of the greater copper output that would have existed under free-market conditions must also take into account the effects associated with the larger local taxes paid by the companies, and the large internal expenditures made out of their higher profits. Still another factor to remember is that, even if the African wage did not decrease under the monopolistic wage policy followed, the distribution of the same wage bill among fewer workers, that is, a higher income per worker, means that the total expenditure out of this wage bill on imported goods tends to be larger.

The most unfavorable repercussion of the high-wage policy on internal spending concerns its impact on the growth of other industries. The copper industry is the wage leader in the unionized part of the economy. Union and government pressures cause a higher copper wage scale to spread (though at a discount) to the railways, the government, and secondary industry in general. Whereas African wages are only 18 percent of operating costs in the copper industry, they are 40 percent of operating costs in the rest of the manufacturing and construction industries. This means that a given percentage increase in wage costs raises total costs more in these other industries, and thus causes a relatively greater reduction in output and employment. In addition, most of the secondary industries in the economy face severe competition from imports. When they are forced to raise their prices because of an increase in their wage costs, they are likely to lose a substantial volume of sales to foreign producers. African employment, consequently, tends to be sharply reduced in these industries in response to wage increases. There are probably a number of import-competing lines of goods which have never been established within Northern Rhodesia because of the high-wage policy in the country.

When these elements are all taken into account, the argument supporting wage increases on the grounds of stimulating domestic demand seems incorrect. Instead, it is much more likely that total wages of Africans in the industrial sector have been reduced significantly as a result of the artificially high wage policy.

A small group of Europeans and urban Africans, who possess monopolistic labor power, have gained, at the expense of the masses of Africans in the rural areas and in the low-paying service industries in urban areas. The latter group does not have the economic or political power to prevent the massive misallocation of labor resources which is being frozen into the economy. The real economic conflict is not between European and African workers but between those workers in the key industrial sectors of the economy and the rest of the people. The highly unequal distribution of income, which began for solid economic reasons, is being perpetuated to the detriment of the entire country.

5

The African Worker

INTRODUCTION

The one characteristic of African labor in Central Africa that has without doubt attracted the most attention and comment for the past 35 years has been the instability of African workers in urban employment. Africans have not accepted employment in the towns and then become permanently urbanized. Instead, most of them return periodically to the rural economy throughout their working life and finally retire there. Moreover, they do not bring all their dependents with them on their employment trips to the urban areas.

During the late twenties and early thirties the flow of labor to and from the copper mines was mainly on a seasonal basis. From April to June, when crops in the rural economy were being harvested, and again near the end of the year at planting time, there was a mass outflow of labor from the mines. The average period of native employment in the industry at this time was only about 6 months.[1] By the 1940's the seasonal nature of the two-way flow between the villages and towns had become much less pronounced, but the African worker was still far from stabilized. Although the turnover rate in the copper industry had fallen from around 20 percent per month in the late twenties to 5 per-

[1] C. F. Spearpoint, "The African Native and the Rhodesian Copper Mines," *African Affairs*, XXXVI (July, 1937), 53; *Report of the Commission Appointed To Enquire into the Financial and Economic Position of Northern Rhodesia*, Colonial, no. 145, Great Britain, Colonial Office (London: H.M.S.O., 1938), p. 357, hereafter referred to as the *Pim Report*.

cent per month in 1941,[2] the average period of employment for those leaving the mines in 1947 was only 15 months.[3] Many of these workers, however, did not return directly to the rural areas after they left a particular job. Godfrey Wilson found, in his 1940 study of the African population in Broken Hill, that the average period each job lasted was 16 months, whereas the average period between visits home was 40 months.[4]

The trend toward stabilization continued in the 1950's. Monthly turnover rates for Africans in copper mining declined to an average of 2.6 percent for the years 1956 to 1959,[5] and the average period of employment for those leaving the mines had risen to approximately 2 years by 1959.[6] Whereas, in 1937, 71 percent of the African labor engaged in the copper mines had been employed for less than 2 years, the same figure for 1959 was 39 percent.[7] Merran McCulloch also found, in his 1952 study of Livingstone, that the average period between visits home was 6 years.[8]

Additional information on the extent of African urbanization in the Copperbelt, collected by J. Clyde Mitchell, is presented in table 5-1. The results of D. G. Bettison's 1957 study of Lusaka's African population relating to the length of time spent in town are given in table 5-2. In both Mitchell's and Bettison's studies, the longer period spent in town by those residing in

---

[2] The 20 percent figure is for Roan Antelope (Spearpoint, *op. cit.*), whereas the 5 percent figure is for the entire industry (*Year Book*, 1955, Northern Rhodesia Chamber of Mines [Kitwe, Rhodesian Printers], pp. 91, 95).

[3] *Annual Report for the Year 1951*, Northern Rhodesia, Labour and Mines Department (Lusaka: Government Printer, 1952), p. 20.

[4] Godfrey Wilson, *An Essay on the Economics of Detribalization in Northern Rhodesia*, Rhodes-Livingstone Papers, no. 5 (Livingstone: Rhodes-Livingstone Institute, 1941), Part I, p. 41.

[5] Annual Reports, 1956–1959, Northern Rhodesia, Department of Labour (Lusaka, Government Printer).

[6] *Year Book*, 1959, p. 47. Other evidence indicating that the length of the time spent in employment was lengthened since the 1930's is presented by W. Watson, *Tribal Cohesion in a Money Economy* (Manchester: Manchester University Press, 1958). In a study of the Mambwe people of Northern Rhodesia made in 1952 and 1953, Watson found that in the over-40 age group of males, 90 percent of the employment trips to the Copperbelt and other Northern Rhodesian towns were for two years or less. The comparable figure for the under-40 age group was 65 percent (p. 66). For an analysis of migration in southern Tanganyika, see P. H. Gulliver, *Labour Migration in a Rural Economy*, East African Studies, no. 6 (Kampala: East African Institute of Social Research, 1955).

[7] *Pim Report*, p. 357; *Year Book*, 1959, p. 48.

[8] Merran McCulloch, *A Social Survey of the African Population of Livingstone*, Rhodes-Livingstone Papers, no. 26 (Manchester: Manchester University Press, 1956), p. 56.

TABLE 5-1

URBANIZATION CLASSIFICATION OF AFRICAN MEN, 1951

Category	Amount of their time spent in town since first leaving village	Roan Antelope Mine township (percentage)	Other Luanshya townships (percentage)
Peasant visitors	Less than ⅓	37.0	31.3
Migrant laborers	Between ⅓ and ⅔	36.3	24.1
Temporarily urbanized	More than ⅔	19.2	20.2
Permanently urbanized	Born and bred in town	7.5	24.4
Total		100.0	100.0

SOURCE: J. Clyde Mitchell, *African Urbanization in Ndola and Luanshya*, Rhodes-Livingstone Communication, no. 6 (Lusaka: Rhodes-Livingstone Institute, 1954), p. 17.

municipal townships compared with private industrial townships brings out the "job-hopping" nature of African employment within the towns. To remain in a private industrial township one must maintain employment with the particular firm that owns the township. In municipal townships, however, a worker can change employers and still retain his residence.

Although data clearly indicate that Africans are spending longer periods in an urban environment, there still remains a close two-way dependency relationship between urban and rural Africans. The age structure of the urban and rural population brings out this relationship very clearly. The attraction of the town for men of working age is apparent from table 5-3. In urban

TABLE 5-2

TOTAL NUMBER OF YEARS SPENT IN LUSAKA BY AVERAGE AFRICAN MALE IN DIFFERENT AGE GROUPS, 1957

Age group	Those residing in municipal townships[a]	Those residing in private industrial townships
20.1–25	3.6	1.2
25.1–30	4.2	2.5
30.1–35	6.3	3.6
35.1–40	6.8	3.6
40.1–50	8.5	6.5
50.1 and over	8.7	—

[a] Matero and Chilenje townships.
SOURCE: David G. Bettison, *Numerical Data on African Dwellers in Lusaka, Northern Rhodesia*, Rhodes-Livingstone Communications, no. 16 (Lusaka: Rhodes-Livingstone Institute, 1959), p. 78.

TABLE 5-3

ESTIMATED PROPORTIONS OF AFRICAN POPULATION IN AGE
AND SEX CATEGORIES, NORTHERN RHODESIA, 1955
(in percentages)

Age groups	Urban		Rural		Total	
	Male	Female	Male	Female	Male	Female
0–4	9.5	9.8	7.6	8.0	7.9	8.2
5–9	3.8	5.6	6.5	7.1	6.1	6.9
10–14	3.2	2.6	5.2	6.6	4.9	6.1
15–19	2.7	4.8	4.1	5.4	3.9	5.3
20–24	6.3	7.1	3.2	4.8	3.6	5.1
25–29	7.6	5.7	2.7	4.0	3.4	4.2
30–34	8.6	4.3	2.4	3.6	3.2	3.7
35–39	6.9	2.1	2.1	3.0	2.8	2.9
40–44	3.7	1.2	2.1	2.6	2.3	2.4
45–49	1.5	.4	1.7	2.2	1.7	2.0
50–54	1.1	.2	1.7	2.1	1.6	1.8
55–59	.2	.0	1.6	1.7	1.4	1.5
60–64	.1	.0	1.5	1.5	1.3	1.3
65–69	.0	.0	1.2	1.1	1.0	1.0
70–74	.0	.0	.8	.8	.7	.7
75 and over	.0	.0	.5	.5	.5	.5
Total	56.2	43.8	44.9	55.0	46.3	53.6
1955 population	247,000		1,569,000		1,816,000	

SOURCE: J. C. Mitchell, "Demographic Appendix" in *Social Relations in Central African Industry*, eds. D. Mathews and R. Apthorpe, Twelfth Conference Proceedings of the Rhodes-Livingstone Institute for Social Research (Lusaka, 1958), p. 10.

areas 37.3 percent of the population consists of males between 15 and 50, whereas the corresponding percentage for rural areas is only 18.3 percent. Although many workers bring their wives, there is still a preponderance of men in the towns. Between the 15–50 age group there are 140 men for every 100 women in the towns. The rural ratio is just the reverse of this, that is, 100 men to 140 women. The extent of the denudement of men from the traditional rural economy is even greater than this table shows, since it does not include those working on European farms or in small towns. In 1959, for example, 55 percent of the taxable males in the territory were at work for wages.[9]

The role of the rural economy in caring for the young and

[9] *Annual Report of the Department of Labour for the Year 1959*, Northern Rhodesia, Ministry of Labour and Mines (Lusaka: Government Printer, 1960), p. 72.

aged also is evident from table 5-3. Very young children usually
are kept with their mothers in the towns. Thus, in the urban
areas, for every child between 0–4 years of age, there are 1.33
women between 15 and 50 years of age, while in the rural areas
there are 1.64 women between 15 and 50 for each child of this
age. In contrast with these figures, the ratio of children between
5 and 15 to women between 15 and 50 is 1:1.74 in town and
1:1.01 in the rural areas. In other words, when children no
longer require the personal care of their mothers, they often are
sent back to the village economy.[10] The rural economy is also a
place where older men and their wives can retire and—unlike in
the town—still contribute to the economy. Only 1.6 percent of
the urban population is over 50 years of age. In the rural area
15 percent of the population is in this category. Still another
social service performed in the village environment is the care
of the physically handicapped. A study of the physically handicapped among African families in Broken Hill showed that half
the handicapped members of these families were living in the
rural area.[11]

In addition to the continuous flow of people between the urban
and rural sectors, there is a significant movement of goods from
the towns to the country. Returning migrants do not come back
empty-handed. They bring cash and commodities with them into
the rural economy, part of which they distribute to those who are
maintaining the rural economy. Another stream of money and
commodities is sent by those still in town who remain for longer
periods.[12] Wilson found in his study of Broken Hill that 35 per-

---

[10] J. Clyde Mitchell (*African Urbanization in Ndola and Luanshya*, Rhodes-
Livingstone Communication, no. 6 [Lusaka: Rhodes-Livingstone Institute, 1954],
pp. 6, 7) found in his Copperbelt study that 96 percent of the male children 0–4
years of age, whose mothers lived in town, resided with their mothers, but only
63 percent of the male children 10–14 years of age did so. He also found, however,
that a number of children in the 10–14 age group were children of relatives of
Copperbelt families. They had been sent into town for educational purposes.

[11] W. Clifford, *Physical Handicap amongst Africans in Broken Hill*, Social Welfare Research Monograph, no. 2, Northern Rhodesia (Lusaka: Government Printer,
1960), p. 6.

[12] One writer has commented concerning this flow of goods and money as follows: "At present the 'profligate wage earner' who sends presents to his distant
relations in the country or allows his wife's second cousin to 'batten on him' in the
town is in fact cementing the kin group and paying his social security contribution just as surely as if he were licking a stamp and sticking it on a card each
month" (H. Fosbrooke, "Effect of Economic Change on African Society," in "Economic Development in Northern Rhodesia," Study Conference, no. 2, sponsored
by the United Northern Rhodesia Association [Lusaka, Oct., 1958], p. 70, copy in
library of Rhodesian Selection Trust, Salisbury).

cent of the annual cash earnings of the African male population was transferred to the rural economy.[13] Of the share that was personally transferred to rural areas, a third was in cash and two-thirds in goods.[14]

THE TARGET-WORKER HYPOTHESIS

Nature of the Hypothesis and General Evidence Pertaining to It

A widely accepted assertion concerning the behavior of migrant labor in underdeveloped countries is that a higher wage rate decreases rather than increases an individual migrant's supply of labor.[15] Indeed, in Africa where the migratory system is still very important, it is frequently claimed that the typical employee is a "target" worker. When migrants come to town it has been said that "they have a definite sum in view, and that they hope to earn that amount and then go home again. The sooner that can be done, therefore, the quicker the worker's return to his village. . . . This accounts for the statement frequently made that the offer of a higher wage means less work and not more." [16]

A literal interpretation of this statement implies a particular type of negatively sloped labor-supply curve. Specifically, if one assumes the worker spends a fixed sum per month for his own support in town, then his supply of labor (in months) per urban employment trip is equal to his target sum, divided by an amount equal to his monthly wage, less his monthly self-support allowance.[17] Most writers who use the term "target worker" do not place such a strict interpretation upon it. Instead, they seem to mean simply that an individual migrant's supply curve of labor to urban areas is backward bending. It is this more inclusive interpretation of the term which will be discussed below.

There are ample testifiers to the existence of a backward-bending supply curve for the typical African worker. A good example is the following statement made by a group of European business men.

---

[13] Wilson, *op. cit.*, p. 43.

[14] *Ibid.*, p. 44.

[15] For a survey of the literature discussing this view, see E. J. Berg, "Backward-Sloping Labor Supply Functions in Dual Economics: The Africa Case," *Quarterly Journal of Economics*, LXXV (Aug., 1961), 468–492.

[16] Major G. St. J. Orde Browne, *Labour Conditions in East Africa*, Colonial, no. 193, Great Britain, Colonial Office (London: H.M.S.O., 1946), p. 5.

[17] For example, if the amount used for self-support was zero, the supply curve would be a rectangular hyperbola of negative slope, that is, of unitary elasticity.

He [the African] is born into a position within that group which he takes for granted. It never occurs to him that he may attain a higher position, which means that he has a very restricted range of wants. For his monetary wants, probably not much more than tax and bride price, he comes to the urban areas. There he does not look for a very great deal and the more easily and quickly he can satisfy these wants, the better. Big money does not interest him as it leaves him with two alternatives upon his return to the community; either he will be exploited by his relatives or he can set himself up on a higher standard of living which will make him unpopular and cause him to lose his social position in the community. The rural migrant worker who intends to go back is therefore not only much less responsive to normal incentives than the detribalised man, but is also mainly responsible for the large turnover so evident in African labour.[18]

The International Labour Office boldly asserted—without disclosing the source of its information—that in Northern Rhodesia "54.7 percent of the males are said to be target workers." [19] Government officials and copper-company executives also have described Africans as target workers.[20] As recently as 1960 the general manager of one of the mines explained an increase in the African turnover rates on the basis of an increase in bonus payments.[21]

Occasionally, statements are made which seem to imply the belief that the aggregate labor-supply curve in urban areas as well as individual supply curves are backward bending. For example, Sir Ronald Prain, chairman of the Rhodesian Selection Trust Group, in discussing African labor problems, stated: "Higher individual earnings may well reduce rather than increase

---

[18] "Report of the Committee Appointed To Inquire into the High Cost of Building in the Territory, 1951," Northern Rhodesia (1951), p. 72, copy in the Colonial Office Library, London.

[19] *African Labour Survey*, International Labour Office (Geneva, 1958), p. 142.

[20] T. B. Kelley, "Paternalism versus Greater Responsibility and Independence in Relation to African Life on the Copper Mines, Paper no. 1," speech delivered at Rhodesian Selection Trust Symposium, Lusaka, Sept. 25, 26, 1959, p. 6; *Annual Report for the Year 1951*, Northern Rhodesia, Labour and Mines Department, p. 20.

[21] "Annual Report," 1960, Rhodesian Selection Trust (Salisbury), p. 53. It is interesting to note how the other two mines in the Rhodesian Selection Trust Group, Mufulira and Roan Antelope, explain their higher 1960 African turnover rate. The Mufulira manager claims it was "due to a higher rate of resignations among short service Africans resigning to return to Nyasaland and also to a greater number of employees retiring on pension or with long service bonuses" (*ibid.*, p. 37); the Roan Antelope manager merely states that it is "due to an increase in the retirement rate of long-service men" ("Annual Report," 1960, Roan Antelope Copper Mines [Salisbury], p. 24).

the supply of labour." [22] A similar remark was made by C. W. Guillebaud in his famous arbitration award.[23]

Even the views of Africans themselves seem to confirm the hypothesis that large numbers are target workers. Table 5-4 pre-

TABLE 5-4

ATTITUDES OF AFRICAN WORKERS TO TOWN LIFE, 1951, 1952
(in percentages)

Category	Roan Antelope Mine township[a]	Other Luanshya townships[a]	Livingstone township[b]
Labor migrants			
Will return home as soon as possible	6.0	3.3	—
Working so as to go home soon	28.3	38.4	—
Will return home as soon as wealthy	24.2	15.1	—
Subtotal	58.5	56.8	39.0
Temporarily stabilized			
Will return home at some future date	18.1	15.5	—
Will stay but keep contact with village	2.7	12.6	—
Will return home on retirement	14.4	5.7	—
Subtotal	35.2	33.8	50.8
Permanently stabilized			
Thinks will always be on Copperbelt	5.5	6.1	—
Born and bred in town: "It is as if it were my village"	.8	3.3	—
Subtotal	6.3	9.4	10.1
Total	100.0	100.0	99.9

[a] J. Clyde Mitchell, *African Urbanization in Ndola and Luanshya*, Rhodes-Livingstone Communication, no. 6 (Lusaka: Rhodes-Livingstone Institute, 1954), p. 19. This survey was made in 1951.

[b] Merran McCulloch, *A Social Survey of the African Population of Livingstone*, Rhodes-Livingstone Papers, no. 26 (Manchester: Manchester University Press, 1956), p. 58. This survey was made in 1952. Percentages are given only for the three subtotals.

sents the results of Mitchell's opinion survey in the 1951 Copper-belt study as well as those of McCulloch's 1952 survey of Living-stone. The category termed "labor migrants" by Mitchell and McCulloch closely corresponds to the concept of the target worker. Between 40 and 60 percent of the workers in these studies appear to fall into this behavior pattern.

[22] R. L. Prain, "Statement to Stockholders," in "Annual Report," 1951, Rhodesian Selection Trust (Salisbury).

[23] "Report and Award of the Arbitrator, C. W. Guillebaud, Esq., C.B.E.," Jan., 1953, p. 8, hereafter referred to as the "Guillebaud Award"; also published in *Northern Rhodesia Government Gazette* Jan. 9, 1953.

Whether individual labor-supply curves are in fact backward bending in underdeveloped countries, such as Northern Rhodesia, is an important economic question to answer. The prospects for African advancement into more skilled jobs, for example, are closely related to this matter. The high cost to employees of job training compared to the time the average worker spends on a particular job has been an important factor limiting the extent of advancement. If, at the higher wage rates associated with more skilled jobs, workers respond by devoting still less time to urban areas, then advancement schemes tend to dwindle. Negatively sloped individual curves also tend to make the aggregate labor-supply curve for urban areas more inelastic.[24] As a result it becomes more costly to obtain a given increment in urban industrial development—an objective that has high priority in many development plans.

The minimum-wage question is another matter affected by the slope of individual labor-supply curves. Often minimum-wage legislation is proposed in underdeveloped nations as a device for raising the living standards of those who work in the monetary sector. Some recommend such legislation even though they recognize that the total amount of labor employed in the urban sector will decline, and possibly also the total wage bill. If workers have a fixed money-income target, setting the minimum wage above the free-market rate will not increase that part of their living standard derived from the goods and services purchased with money income. Their income earned in the subsistence sector will rise, because they will spend more time in the rural sector, but the "distribution" argument for minimum wages loses much of its force.

Factors Affecting an Individual's Labor Supply to Urban Areas

The nature of the slope of the typical worker's labor-supply curve can be analyzed by considering each individual to be faced with the problem of determining a migration plan over his time horizon, for example, his working lifetime. In allocating his time he must decide such matters as the total time to spend in the urban sector, the average duration of his urban employment trips, and the amount of time to devote to different jobs during an urban trip. Economic theory suggests that these decisions de-

---

[24] The entrance of additional workers in the urban labor market at higher wage rates can make, of course, the aggregate supply-curve positively sloped even though each individual's labor-supply curve is negatively sloped.

pend upon an individual's preferences for the goods and services (including leisure) available in rural and urban areas, the ratio of real-earnings in the two areas, and the costs of transporting goods and people between towns and rural villages.

Individual preferences.—If the period under consideration is comparatively short, economists usually assume that preference functions do not change. Such an assumption is not appropriate for the nearly 40-year period covered in this study. Alternatively, it may be assumed that a rural person's attitudes toward working in urban areas is a function of his knowledge about urban living, and the extent of his participation in such life. Changes in the types of the commodities and services available in rural versus urban areas can also affect migration patterns significantly. Improvement of urban education and medical facilities, the construction by urban employers of family housing units for their workers, better long-term leave arrangements, and improved opportunities for advancement to more skilled jobs are illustrations of changes that are likely to increase the length of urban employment.

Rural and urban real earnings.—Consider next the possible relationship between a migrant's supply of urban labor and the ratio of his rural to his urban earning rate. A rise in his urban wage rate compared to his agricultural productivity increases the migrant's opportunity cost of not engaging in urban employment. If his real income is held constant when this change in the earnings ratio occurs, he will substitute urban employment for both rural living and urban leisure. In other words, economic theory suggests that the substitution effect associated with a rise in wages increases the time spent by the typical migrant in urban employment. There is also an income effect associated with a wage increase. Because of the higher wage per unit of time worked, it is possible for an individual to work less and still earn a larger aggregate income. If not working on an urban job is a "superior commodity," the income effect operates to reduce the amount of urban labor. Since the substitution and income components work in opposite directions, one cannot state what the net effect of a wage increase will be on the total amount of time spent in rural areas, or on the time spent in town between jobs during an urban trip of a given length. It is even possible for the individual's "consumption" of rural and urban leisure to move in opposite directions, although one would expect these activities to be highly competitive "commodities" and their consumption to change in the same direction.

When urban wages rise, the average duration of urban-employment trips also may increase or decrease. As far as the wage component is concerned, the opportunity cost of residing in the rural sector for a given period of time rises in the same proportion whether this time is spent consecutively or broken up with urban employment trips. But, since transportation costs become a larger proportion of the total opportunity costs when more frequent trips are made (keeping the aggregate time spent in the rural area constant), an increase in wages increases the opportunity costs of a given number of shorter, more frequent rural trips proportionately less than a given number of longer but fewer visits to the rural area. The substitution component, therefore, favors a decrease in the average duration of employment trips. The income effect also works in this direction if, when his income rises, a person prefers to substitute shorter, more frequent rural visits for fewer but longer trips. If, however, the urban wage structure at a given level is such that the longer an individual remains in town the more he is paid, then a reduction in the average length of urban employment trips (without any change in the total time spent in urban areas or in the wage level) reduces any tendency to substitute shorter, more frequent trips for fewer but longer ones, in response to the income effect associated with a rise in the wage level. Since a migrant also may prefer longer but fewer visits to his village, there is on balance no economic reason for expecting the average length of urban employment trips to change in a particular direction.

Employment conditions.—In the preceding chapter it was pointed out that urban unemployment began to emerge as a serious problem around the mid-fifties. When the amount of excess labor grows, an individual worker must spend more time searching for a job. A given wage rate does not, therefore, adequately reflect the change in the individual's earning per unit of time during which he offers himself for employment. In periods when excess-demand conditions for labor develop, the same point holds, except that in this case earnings per unit of time spent in employment or seeking work are increased. In addition to these effects, which can be analyzed in the same manner as wage changes, a rise in the unemployment rate acts to reduce earnings more the greater the number of job changes made by an individual over a given time period. Therefore, when the unemployment rate rises, an individual will tend to reduce the extent of his job hopping per urban employment trip as well as to increase the average length of his employment trips. Opposite results occur when labor-supply conditions tighten for employers.

If market forces are permitted to operate freely in determining wages, periods of rising wages will be associated with tight labor conditions. If turnover rates rise during these periods, it might be interpreted as support of the target-worker hypothesis, whereas in fact the rise may be caused entirely by the differential changes in earnings for the various job patterns just discussed. On the other hand, a lowering of work standards by employers, and thus an accompanying reduction in the number of employees discharged as unsatisfactory, could counter any tendency for turnover rates to rise in prosperous times. In the copper industry, where, even in the late fifties, about one-quarter of the leavers were discharged because they were unsatisfactory workers, this factor may be significant.[25]

When wage rates are changed on the basis of factors quite unrelated to free-market demand and supply forces, a tightening labor situation and increasing wages need not go together. On the contrary, a wage rise may lower turnover rates by causing a greater degree of unemployment. Employers, however, may respond to the greater excess-supply conditions by firing workers more readily. Without additional knowledge, it is impossible to disentangle these two opposing worker and employer responses from actual turnover data.

Transportation costs.—The last variable in the suggested supply function of labor is transportation costs. One can be certain that a decrease in these costs will increase an individual's purchases of transportation services, but this still does not imply any simple conclusion about migration changes. It is possible, for example, in areas not too distant from agricultural markets, that an individual responds to lower transportation charges by shifting from urban employment to commercial agriculture. Outside these areas, however, the likely response pattern of a labor migrant is to take his first employment trip at an earlier age, decrease the average lengths of his trips, and possibly spend more total time in urban areas.

Summary.—Although the preceding economic analysis is useful in suggesting possible relationships, it does not provide any basis

[25] *Year Book,* 1959, p. 47.

for expecting either positively or negatively sloped labor-supply curves for African migrants. Either hypothesis appears plausible. The results of prior investigations by economists are not very helpful, mainly because there have been so few,[26] and because the analysts have been seriously hampered by poor data. The view most widely accepted by professional economists seems to be that most Africans, until recently, were target workers. Even today the labor-supply curve of many employees is thought to be backward bending.[27]

As far as Northern Rhodesia is concerned, the various studies cited earlier in this chapter (see nn. 1–8) reveal that the typical migrant of the fifties, compared with the thirties, spent a longer part of his working life in urban employment, remained away from his village longer per urban trip, and also worked for a longer continuous period on each urban job. Since real wages for African workers increased substantially between these years, one might conclude that the various supply functions were positively sloped. But the observed changes may have been the result, over that time, of a shift to the right in a negatively sloped labor-supply curve, which was caused by a preference shift in favor of urban living and of the commodities that could be purchased with urban earnings. Or, perhaps the greater willingness to work in urban areas can be accounted for by an improvement in urban working and living conditions compared with those in the rural economy. Still another set of factors that may "explain" the data are shifts in the composition of the labor force. For example, the typical African worker of the fifties is more likely to be married than the earlier migrant. If married workers always remained on a job longer than single employees, the observed changes in turnover rates may be related entirely to a shift in the composition of the labor force.

An Analysis of Data for the Copper Industry

Fortunately, there are data covering copper-company employees which permit analysis of the labor-supply response of the average migrant more precisely. The main data available are annual turnover rates for African employees (number of workers leaving the various mines during a year/average daily attendance of these

---

[26] See W. Elkan, *An African Labour Force*, East African Studies, no. 7 (Kampala: East African Institute of Social Research, 1956), an early outstanding study of the supply behavior of the labor force employed by a particular firm.

[27] Berg, *op. cit.*, pp. 486–487.

mines $\times$ 100) since the early thirties. In addition, series of data covering dropout rates (the proportion of employees leaving within [say] one year of the date they are hired) and the average employment period of leavers are available for some of the copper companies.

Turnover rates.—Changes in turnover rates (or in dropout rates) reflect changes in the average length of continuous employment service with respect to a *particular* employer rather than urban employers as a group. It is possible for workers to remain on each job longer and still decrease the total time they spend in urban areas over their lifetime, diminish the average length of their employment trips, and even reduce the total time worked (nonconsecutively) during an employment trip of a given duration. These are all separate supply concepts, and there is no logical reason for each to change in the same direction. African workers who voluntarily or involuntarily leave a particular job seem to search immediately for another job, unless they return to their villages, so that it is highly likely that remaining longer on any job reduces the total nonworking time that a migrant spends in town on an employment trip of a given length. As noted, there are also good subjective reasons for expecting a change in the total nonworking time spent in urban areas to be positively correlated with the total time spent in rural areas. Nevertheless, the following analysis relates in a strict sense only to the noninterrupted flow of labor services to one employer.

Factors affecting turnover rates.—Ideally, a ratio of real-earnings in the copper industry and alternative employments, especially subsistence agriculture, should be correlated with turnover rates. Unfortunately, productivity figures in the subsistence areas (from which most of the migrants came) are impossible to obtain. Unquestionably, there was some upward trend in productivity in subsistence agriculture between 1930 and 1960 (a rough guess would be that it doubled), but it clearly was small in relation to the real-wage increase in the copper industry. Failure to modify real-earnings in the copper industry to take account of this modest rise in rural productivity does not seem, therefore, to be a serious matter. A more important consequence of using only copper earnings is the inability to take into account short-run changes in rural productivity. The amplitude of changes in rural output per man can be quite large and can significantly affect turnover rates. For example, in exceptionally bad harvest years, employees who normally would return to their villages are likely to remain at their jobs until conditions improve in the rural areas. Using earnings in the copper industry alone to measure changes in the level of urban wages in general may also introduce some inaccuracy into the analysis, but not to any appreciable extent. For example, the ratio of average mining earnings to average earnings in all industries between 1938 and 1959 did not change.[28] Short-run variations in this ratio also do not appear to be a particularly serious problem.

Since the extent of excess-supply (or demand) conditions in the labor market may affect turnover rates, it would help to have an index of unemployment conditions for the period covered in the analysis. Unfortunately, it is unlikely that an adequate index can be constructed. From descriptions in company reports, and in annual reports of the government's Labour Department, a rough idea of labor conditions during the period can be obtained, but the data are not sufficiently precise to form the basis of an unemployment index usable in multiple correlation analysis. The descriptions of labor-market conditions suggest that from 1930 to 1960 there were three periods when turnover rates and an unemployment index would have changed in a closely related manner. In the first two, 1939–1941 and 1949–1951, comparatively tight labor conditions existed. Wages in these years were still determined mainly by free-market forces, and one would expect wages in these two periods to have risen. If the turnover rate also rose in these years, it could have been owing entirely to the better employment opportunities rather than to the existence of backward-bending labor-supply curves. The third period extends from about 1954 to 1960. Wage rates in these years, particularly after 1958, were considerably above the levels required to eliminate industrial unemployment. If, as argued in the preceding chapter, the increase in African wages from 1953 onward was an important cause of this unemployment, one would expect high wages and high unemployment in this period to go together. If workers increased the time they spent on a particular job in this period, it

---

[28] This ratio was 2:0 in 1938, 1:9 in 1945, 1:8 in 1954, and again 2:0 in 1959 (Phyllis Deane, *The Measurement of Colonial National Incomes,* National Institute of Economic and Social Research, Occasional Paper, no. 12 [Cambridge: Cambridge University Press, 1948], p. 29; and *Colonial Social Accounting* [Cambridge: Cambridge University Press, 1953], p. 251; *National Accounts of the Federation of Rhodesia and Nyasaland, 1954–1959,* Federation of Rhodesia and Nyasaland, Central Statistical Office [Salisbury: Government Printer, 1960], p. 76).

could be because of the greater difficulty of obtaining new jobs rather than of the existence of a positively sloped labor-supply curve.

Except for the years 1939–1941, 1949–1951, and 1954–1960, the period 1930–1960 was one in which conditions of moderate excess labor supply generally prevailed. By running some correlation calculations that include the years when labor conditions changed significantly and others that cover periods of stable labor conditions, an effort will be made to ascertain the effect of changes in these conditions.

Studies by the copper companies suggest that at least two changes in the composition of the labor force help to explain changes in turnover rates between 1930 and 1960: shifts in the proportion of (1) workers who are married, and (2) employees engaged in underground work. The mines have known for many years that married workers remain on the job much longer than single workers. Similarly, they have found that underground workers leave sooner after being hired than surface employees. A third compositional factor sometimes suggested as an important cause of turnover-rate changes is a shift in the tribal origins of the labor force. There are no continuous data on this matter, but it is possible to rearrange some 1935 figures on tribal origin into data listing the provinces from which the workers came, and then to compare these figures with turnover rates in more recent years according to the provincial origins of the workers.[29] If the same turnover rates by province existed in 1935 as in the period 1956–1959, the turnover rate in 1935 for the entire group of provinces would have been 30 percent. The actual figure for the 1956–1959 period was 32 percent. The structural change in the origins of the labor force, therefore, acted to raise the turnover rate slightly between these years. But it seems too small to be a very important explanatory variable.

A fourth factor in the composition of the labor force that may affect turnover rates is length of service. For example, if a larger fraction of workers with short service records leave during a given period than those with longer service records, an increase in the labor force will increase the turnover rate because of the

---

[29] *Evidence Taken by the Commission Appointed To Enquire into the Disturbances in the Copperbelt, Northern Rhodesia, July-September 1935,* Northern Rhodesia (Lusaka: Government Printer, 1936), II, 649; *Year Book,* 1956–1959, tables 27 and 30.

shortening of the service age of the labor force. Fortunately, it is possible to obtain direct evidence on length of service. Figure 2 plots the manner in which dropout rates have changed over time and with length of service. The first few years of employment are the ones in which dropout rates are the highest. One interesting feature of the graph is that the dropout curves fan out as the years of service increase. Since 1936, yearly dropout rates have decreased relatively more for longer service employees than for shorter service workers. Although the graph indicates that the relationship between the service age of the labor force and turn-over rates is quite complex, nevertheless the level of employment in the copper industry is used in the correlation analysis to attempt to isolate short-run changes in turnover rates owing to changes in the service age of the labor force. The analysis of this relationship is confined to the postwar period, where the absolute trend factor in employment levels is not too significant.

The most difficult variable to quantify is the change in the average migrant's attitudes toward rural versus urban living. Several proxy variables suggest themselves but the simplest one to use is time itself. Specifically, each year—beginning with 1930— is numbered serially,[30] and this set of numbers then is used as an independent variable in the correlation analysis. With this pro-cedure, a straight-line trend is introduced as an "explanatory" variable in the turnover-rate analysis. The effect of changes in the comparative array of goods and services from which a migrant can choose is also included in this time factor, since there appears to have been a steady relative improvement in urban conditions. Another factor affecting the pattern of migration that this time variable covers in the statistical analysis is the gradual improvement in transportation conditions between rural and urban areas.

Correlation analysis.—The main results of the correlation analysis of the different variables discussed above are presented in table 5-5. On the basis of regression equations 1 and 3, which cover all the years from 1931 to 1960 for which data are available, it appears that African mine workers reduce the length of time they remain on a job when real earnings rise. These equations also indicate a highly significant (negative) relation between the proportion of married workers employed in the copper

---

[30] The number with which to begin does not make any difference in determining the significance of this variable.

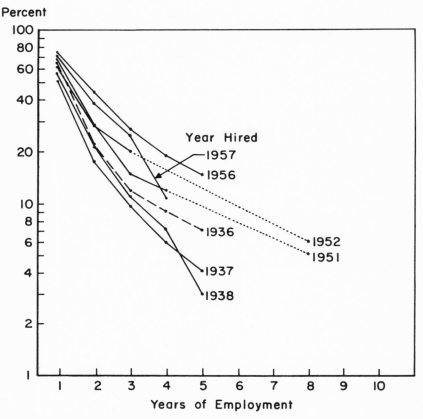

FIG. 2. Percent of African workers remaining in employment after specified number of years at the Rhokana Corporation.

Source: Data for 1936, 1937, and 1938 were taken from A. Lynn Saffery, *A Report on Some Aspects of African Living Conditions on the Copperbelt of Northern Rhodesia* (Lusaka: Government Printer, 1943), pp. 80–81. Data for 1951, 1952, 1956, and 1957 were computed from information furnished me by the Rhokana Corporation, Ltd., concerning the number of workers hired each year and the yearly service distribution of the labor force as of December 31.

industry and turnover rates. The time variable (equation 3) is negatively correlated with turnover rates, but the relation is not a significant one.

Further analysis of real earnings and turnover rates suggests, however, that the supply of labor by individuals to particular employers is not backward-bending, and that real earnings are not a significant factor in accounting for the historical change in turnover rates. The fact that there is little connection between real earnings and length of service becomes apparent when successive differences among the variables are correlated (equation 2).[31] The proportion of workers who are married still remains very significant, but real earnings do not. Dividing the entire period into subperiods also casts doubt on the target-worker hypothesis. From the early thirties until the late forties, for example, the regression coefficient relating real earnings and the turnover rate is not significant (equation 4). The same conclusion holds if one analyzes the thirties alone or runs the series only up to the mid-forties. Analyzing just the period 1947–1960 (equation 5) also seems to support the conclusion that there is no significant connection between real earnings and turnover rates. In this case, however, multicollinearity is a very serious problem, and little significance can be attached to the regression coefficients.[32] The multicollinearity problem also exists when the proportion of workers employed underground is introduced into this time period as an additional independent variable (equation 6). Fortunately, in this case, the use of first differences removes the multicollinearity problem. It shows that real earnings during the period were not correlated in any way with turnover rates (equation 7).

The reason why the regression coefficient for real earnings is positive and significant in equations 1 and 3 is the existence of a strong relationship between real earnings and turnover rates around 1950. When the time span covered in equation 4 is extended up to 1952, the coefficient for earnings becomes significantly positive. Thereafter, the relationship is not clear-cut. Adding the years 1955–1957 reduces the size and significance of the

[31] There is some multicollinearity between the explanatory variables of equation 1, as the simple correlation coefficient of .8 between real earnings and percent married indicates. Taking the first difference reduces the correlation coefficient between these two variables to only .06.

[32] The simple correlation coefficients between the proportion married and total earnings, between the proportion married and time, and between total earnings and time are all at least .98.

TABLE 5-5

Equation number	Equation	Multiple correlation coefficient	Number of observations
1	$TR = 204.9 - 2.98M + .45RE$ $[-11.8]^a \quad [3.1]^a$	.96	24
2	$\Delta TR = 1.1 - 1.93\Delta M + .27\Delta RE$ $[-4.24]^a \quad [.71]$	.73	20
3	$TR = 210.26 - 2.63M + .47RE - .53T$ $[-6.30]^a \quad [3.21]^a \quad [-1.05]$	.96	24
4	$TR = 278.1 - 2.26M - 1.27RE - 1.74T$ $[-4.7]^a \quad [-.77] \quad [-2.00]^b$	.96	15
5	$TR = 200.2 - 3.09M + .35RE + .34T$ $[-2.2]^b \quad [.6] \quad [.1]$	.96	11
6	$TR = 109.9 - 1.16M - .19RE + .3U/S$ $[-1.05] \quad [-.46] \quad [.58]$	.93	15
7	$\Delta TR = 2.7 - 2.04\Delta M + .00\Delta RE + .7\Delta U/S$ $[-1.81]^c \quad [.01) \quad [1.02]$	.62	12
8	$MD = 15.4 + .36RE$ $[3.78]^a$	.75	13
9	$SD = 7.6 + .08RE$ $[2.63]^b$	.62	13
10	$SD = 33.7 - .00S + .14RE + .09T$ $[-2.9]^a \quad [.7] \quad [.1]$	.77	15
11	$MD = 34.2 - .00S + .24RE + 1.5T$ $[-2.1]^b \quad [.3] \quad [.4]$	.71	15

regression coefficient, but 1959–1960 again raises these magnitudes. One suspects that the positive relationship between real earnings and turnover rates reflected the behavior of workers toward particular jobs as employment conditions in the labor market changed, rather than the urban-rural migration pattern of Africans. Specifically, the tight labor conditions between 1949 and 1951 gave African workers many more opportunities than ever before of obtaining higher wages and better working conditions by shifting from one urban employer to another. The period was characterized by competitive bidding for employees of the type one expects to observe in a market economy when the demand for labor increases during prosperous periods. Rising turnover rates and rising wages go together under these circumstances. This relationship was sufficiently strong around 1950 to dominate the sign and significance of the regression coefficient between real earnings and turnover rates for the entire period of available

TABLE 5-5 (Continued)

SYMBOLS

Dependent variables	Independent variables	Other definitions
TR Annual turnover rate (percent)	M Percentage of workers married (annual average)	[ ] t values
ΔTR Change in annual turnover rate	ΔM Change in percentage of workers married	a Coefficient significant to the 99 percent level
MD Number of tickets (30 working days each) worked by married employees leaving employment service during the year	S Number of workers in service (annual average)	b Coefficient significant to the 95 percent level
SD Number of tickets worked by single employees leaving employment service during the year	RE Annual total real earnings (in pounds)	c Coefficient significant to the 90 percent level
	ΔRE Change in annual total real earnings	
	U/S Percentage of workers employed underground (annual average)	
	ΔU/S Change in percentage of workers employed underground	
	T Time (1930 = 30; 1931 = 31, and so on)	

SOURCES: Annual turnover rate: 1930–1934, calculated from data given in C. F. Spearpoint, "The African Native and the Rhodesian Copper Mines," *African Affairs*, XXXVI (July, 1937), 53; 1935, calculated from information in *Report of Chairman of the National Industrial Labour Advisory Board*, Northern Rhodesia (Lusaka: Government Printer, 1936); 1936, based on *Report of the Commission Appointed To Enquire into the Financial and Economic Position of Northern Rhodesia*, Colonial, no. 145, Great Britain, Colonial Office (London: H.M.S.O., 1938), Appendix V; 1937–1940, calculated from material supplied privately by Roan Antelope Copper Mines, Rhokana Corporation, and Mufulira Copper Mines; 1941–1960: average number of African workers in service, 1941–1948, from Annual Reports, 1941–1948, Northern Rhodesia, Mines Department (Lusaka: Government Printer), and 1949–1960 from *Year Book*, 1955–1960, Northern Rhodesia Chamber of Mines (Kitwe: Rhodesian Printers); number of African workers leaving service, 1941–1960, from *Year Book*, 1955–1960.

Number of tickets worked by married and single employees (figures pertain to the Rhokana Corporation): 1939 from A. Lynn Saffery, *A Report on Some Aspects of African Living Conditions on the Copperbelt of Northern Rhodesia*, Northern Rhodesia (Lusaka: Government Printer, 1943), 1946–1951, Annual Reports, Northern Rhodesia, Labour and Mines Department (Lusaka: Government Printer); 1952–1960, calculated from data privately supplied by the Rhokana Corporation.

Percentage of workers married: 1931–1938 from Annual Report, 1937, Northern Rhodesia, Department of Lands, Mines and Surveys (Lusaka: Government Printer), Part IV; 1942–1952 from Annual Reports, Northern Rhodesia, Mines Department; 1953–1960 from Annual Reports, Northern Rhodesia, Department of Labour (Lusaka: Government Printer).

Annual real earnings: 1930–1934, see p. 97, n. 55; 1935–1949, see table 4-3, African real wage column; 1950–1960, see table 4-4.

Number of workers in service and proportion of these employed underground: *Year Book*.

data. The relationship between real earnings and turnover rates throughout the rest of the period analyzed was ambiguous in terms of sign and not statistically significant.

The final group of equations in table 5-5 relates the employment period of discharged married and single workers, separately, to the various other factors that may affect service length.[33] These equations are especially interesting, because they remove the influence of marital status—the most significant variable in the analysis thus far—on the service period of migrants. Simple correlation analysis between real earnings and service length of the two groups of dischargees (equations 8 and 9) supports the positively sloped labor-supply curve hypothesis. But, when such variables as total employment and time are added, the regression coefficient for real earnings is no longer significant.

Summary.—The hypothesis receiving the strongest support in the preceding correlation analysis is that married workers (who are probably older than unmarried ones) remain on a particular job longer than single workers. This is confirmed by the turnover analysis and also directly by the discharge data on married versus single workers. The other independent variables examined show no clear-cut relationship with length of employment service. In the thirties and forties, there is some evidence that the time factor worked to lower the turnover rate, but the relationship was not a strong one. The regression coefficient for the proportion of underground employees, although usually possessing the positive or negative sign predicted in the theoretical analysis, also was not generally statistically significant. The relationship in which there was most interest, that between real earnings and length of service, also was not significant. Factors other than real earnings were more important in causing changes in length of service in the copper industry over the period analyzed. The data do leave much to be desired, particularly in the thirties and early forties, but until additional, more discriminating data are obtained, this is the only conclusion possible.

An important question raised by the significant relationship between length of service and marital status is what accounts for the increase in the proportion of married workers employed by the mines. From the early thirties at least to the early fifties, the mines could not obtain all the married workers they desired.

---

[33] An equation showing the results of correlating dropout rates with various dependent variables is not given because of the very bad multicollinearity problem in this analysis.

They therefore encouraged workers to bring their wives to town and built housing facilities for married workers. To what extent this encouraged workers to return to the mines after they had married, and to what extent relatively more married workers migrated to the urban areas simply because of a shift in their preferences for urban living, are hard to determine. Probably both factors were important. By the fifties, however, the extent to which the companies were prepared to provide comfortable living facilities was undoubtedly the main determinant of the number of married workers who migrated to town. The level of earnings may have had some long-run influence on the willingness of married individuals to migrate, but the lack of any correlation between annual changes in real earnings and annual changes in the proportion of married employees seems to rule out wages as a significant short-run determinant of the share of married workers.

Incentive wage systems.—Another supply response that is important to development concerns the short-run behavior of workers when an incentive wage system is introduced. The most widely used incentive device in Central and South Africa is the task system, which sets a particular daily task to be done, such as clearing a specific underground area of rock or drilling a certain number of feet, and permits workers to go home as soon as the task is completed. In the mining industry, as elsewhere, there is evidence that workers who are given this option accomplish in less than a day work that formerly took one day. Indeed, often the employer increases the task per worker (frequently by reducing the number of employees in the group), and still the workers reach their daily output goal in less than 8 hours. Another incentive device employed in some departments of the copper companies is a piece-rate system based upon a fixed working day.[34] Data covering the results of the piece-rate incentive arrangement are not as extensive as with the task system, but what is available indicates that when it is used each worker greatly increases both his daily output and real earnings.[35] A third type of bonus system with which the mines have experimented is a modification of the task system. After completing their task, workers can either go

---

[34] Departments engaged in repair activities, for example sharpening drills, often use this system. These shops must be kept open the full working day to handle emergency repairs.

[35] The number of employees in the shops using this system invariably was reduced, since the usual repairs could be accomplished in a much shorter period.

home or undertake another group task at a higher rate of pay. In general, the African mine workers have preferred the leisure option. The instances where the workers did work longer hours seemed to involve very small groups of workers and European supervisors who were highly respected by the workers.

African Urbanization

A wider issue than the manner in which African workers respond to a change in wage levels is why so few Africans have become permanently urbanized. Periodic employment trips to the urban areas and eventual retirement in the village environment still form the typical migratory pattern in Rhodesia. Why do not Africans reside permanently in their villages or else move once and for all into the town areas?

Causes of Labor Migration

The anthropologists who have exhaustively investigated the causes of labor migration in Central and East Africa almost all agree that Africans seek employment in urban areas mainly because of economic reasons.[36] Both "pull" and "push" forces operate on the migrant. In the early days "push" factors, especially the necessity of earning sufficient funds to pay the native tax, were no doubt much more important than they are today. The tax on all adult males during the 1920's varied between 5s. and 10s. per year in Northern Rhodesia. The opportunities for earning this sum within the village setting were very meager then, and a trip to the towns or to the European agricultural areas was almost a necessity. As a matter of fact, the imposition of the tax was a convenient way for the Europeans to recruit the labor they desired.[37] At the same time, the appeal of European-produced goods that could be purchased with money also served as a powerful stimulus to migration. The young men soon learned that by working in the towns they could reach the wealth and income

---

[36] J. Clyde Mitchell, "Migrant Labour in Africa South of the Sahara: The Causes of Labour Migration," *Inter-African Labour Institute Bulletin,* VI (Jan. 1, 1959), summarizes most of these studies. See also W. Watson, "Migrant Labour in Africa South of the Sahara: Migrant Labour and Detribalization," *Inter-African Labour Institute Bulletin,* VI (March 1, 1959), 8–33; H. A. Fosbrooke, "Social Security as a Felt Want in East and Central Africa," *Inter-African Labour Institute Bulletin,* VI (May 1, 1959), 8–57; W. Elkan, "The Persistence of Migrant Labour," *Inter-African Labour Institute Bulletin,* VI (Sept. 1, 1959), 36–43.

[37] L. H. Gann, *The Birth of a Plural Society* (Manchester: Manchester University Press, 1958), pp. 76–91.

position of the older married men in a much shorter period than if they remained in the village milieu. For example, if he worked for money wages in town, a young man could more quickly raise the cash and commodities needed to obtain a wife[38] and establish his social-security position in the village by gifts to relatives and the tribal chief.

An exception to this behavior pattern does exist in the few African areas near the railway. As is discussed at length in chapter 6, commercial agriculture is important in these regions, and the extent of migration from there to urban areas is much less than from most other regions. This is clearly evident from a comparison of the proportion of taxable males working for wages in the Southern Province (where most of the African commercial maize production is concentrated) with the rest of the country (table 5-6). One group of investigators who studied an important

TABLE 5-6

PERCENTAGE OF TAXABLE AFRICAN MALES AT WORK
FOR WAGES, BY PROVINCE, 1962

Province	Percent
Western	56
Northern	62
Central	62
Eastern	61
Southern	43
North-Western	51
Barotseland	44
Luapula	58

SOURCE: *Annual Report of the Department of Labour*, 1962, Northern Rhodesia, Ministry of Labour and Mines (Lusaka, Government Printer), p. 79.

tribe living along the line of rail found that, contrary to the general pattern in Northern Rhodesia, the proportion of time spent in urban employment by the individual African actually declined as the commercial market for maize expanded.[39]

Other factors than the market outlet for agricultural com-

[38] A wife, because of her agricultural labors, was an important capital asset to a man (see chap. 6). It is not at all surprising, therefore, that the man pays for a wife.

[39] W. Allan *et al.*, *Land Holding and Land Usage among the Plateau Tonga of Mazabuka District*, Rhodes-Livingstone Papers, no. 14 (London: Oxford University Press, 1948), pp. 160–163.

modities affect the proportion of males who seek wage employment: the level of subsistence income and the nearness of employment opportunities are two other major economic factors. On the basis of the distance factor alone, one would expect to find a high proportion at work for wages in the Western, Central, and Southern provinces, because the railroad, along which the main employment opportunities exist, passes through these provinces. As far as the level of subsistence income is concerned, the Northern, Eastern, Luapula, and North-Western provinces are low compared with the Central Province and Barotseland.[40] Apparently the comparative isolation of Barotseland from labor markets, coupled with the high level of its subsistence economy, accounts for the low proportion of work-seekers from this area. The poverty of the Northern, Eastern, Luapula, and North-Western provinces seems to be the main reason why so many males from these provinces leave their villages and migrate to the line-of-rail area. The nearness of the labor markets apparently accounts for the high figures for the central and western areas. Moreover, despite some opportunities for cash agriculture in these provinces, the amount of fertile land for such production is much less than in the southern provinces.[41]

Permanent versus Temporary Urbanization

A lack of commercial agricultural opportunities and a strong desire to earn at least some cash explain why Africans sought urban employment, but do not explain why they accepted this employment only on a temporary basis. This question involves an analysis of the comparative attractiveness both to Africans and European employers of permanent versus temporary African urbanization.

Consider first the permanent urbanization alternative during the period before World War II. If an individual moved to town permanently and brought his wife, children, and other family dependents with him, he would have to support the group entirely from his own wages. In the town, there were few opportunities for income-producing activities for women and children, except

---

[40] Deane, *Colonial Social Accounting,* pp. 262–267. The diet study discussed in chapter 2 also suggests this ranking.

[41] For an extensive discussion of the relationship between agricultural income and wage employment, see William J. Barber, *The Economy of British Central Africa* (Stanford: Stanford University Press, 1961), chap. 4.

the cultivation of a small patch of maize.[42] The same conditions held for men over 45 or 50.[43] On the basis of Mitchell's estimated age and sex structure of Northern Rhodesia's population (table 5-3), there are nearly 4 dependents in this group for every man between 15 and 50.[44]

In 1938 the average annual full-time earnings (real and in kind) of African workers in nonagricultural wage employment was £18.[45] Using Mitchell's dependency-group data, this gives a per capita income of £3.6 for the members of the family of an African who brings his dependents to town. This per capita income was not as large as could be earned by residing in the rural economy. The level of subsistence income is extremely difficult to ascertain with any accuracy, but on a basis comparable with recent more exhaustive studies of the subsistence sector,[46] per capita subsistence income around 1938 was at least £4.

Besides the absence of a significant per capita income difference in favor of urban living, there were several other factors operating against permanent urbanization. One of these was the higher costs of living in an urban environment. Because of social pressure from European employers and conspicuous consumption pressure from fellow employees, urban workers spent relatively greater sums of food, clothing, and household appliances than they normally spent in their villages. It is always difficult to decide in such cases just what consumption expenditures should be considered as costs that must be incurred by an individual in order to earn his income. By setting up certain "necessary" expenditures, however, two careful investigators claimed that the African urban worker during the early forties was not receiving a sufficient income to maintain a "reasonable minimum" stand-

---

[42] Single women are prevented by law from seeking work on the Copperbelt in Northern Rhodesia (Watson, "Migrant Labour in African South of the Sahara," p. 20).

[43] In the thirties mine officials believed that the productivity ability of an African worker declined after 10 years of service (*Evidence Taken by the Commission Appointed To Enquire into the Disturbances in the Copperbelt, Northern Rhodesia, July-September 1935*, I, 459).

[44] Wilson, *op. cit.*, p. 36, also states that if the 7,500 men working in Broken Hill in 1940 had brought a normal number of women, children, and old and infirm people, the African population in Broken Hill would have been 40,000. The actual numbers were 3,500 women and 4,000 children.

[45] Deane, *The Measurement of Colonial National Incomes*, p. 29.

[46] *National Accounts of the Federation of Rhodesia and Nyasaland, 1954–1959*, p. 64.

ard of living.[47] Africans moving their families permanently into an urban community also may regard the move as causing a loss in noneconomic welfare. The traditional close relations among a kinship group are highly valued by Africans, and a move to a town environment eliminates many cherished ties. New sets of behavior rules and regulations, as well as considerable social discrimination by Europeans, reinforced the undesirable aspects of urban life. Compared with rural work, urban employment was also less pleasant for Africans. In contrast with rural activity they were tied down to regular hours, constant supervision, and—especially in mining—unpleasant, arduous, and dangerous work.

The mines and the government did not encourage African workers to bring their families into town to live permanently. The government's attitude was conditioned by its experience with the depression of the early thirties. Providing financial assistance to the European sector at that time put a great strain on the resources of the government. On the other hand, the costs of providing aid to African workers who lost their jobs was minimal, as they were then simply sent back to the subsistence sector. Officials have since been fearful of the burden that the government would have to assume, if both Europeans and Africans could not find alternative urban employment when the unstable copper industry suffered a recession. The built-in unemployment insurance system in the African sector, and the ability of the rural economy to absorb labor, long have been considerations that make the government hesitate about promoting African urbanization.[48] The copper mines and other urban employers also used this argument. The manner by which the government and the mines discouraged permanent urbanization was simple. They did not provide the housing, education, medical, and social facilities that

---

[47] A. Lynn Saffery (*A Report on Some Aspects of African Living Conditions on the Copperbelt of Northern Rhodesia*, Northern Rhodesia [Lusaka: Government Printer, 1943]) estimates (p. 10) the amount of monthly expenditure necessary to maintain a reasonable minimum standard for a worker, his wife, and two children to be as follows: food, £4 10s. 8d.; housing, 5s.; clothing and covering, 19s. 1d.; furniture and kitchen equipment, 4s. 9d.; fuel and light, 2s. 2d.; tax, 1s. 3d.; miscellaneous, 8s. 8d.; total, £6 11s. 7d. The average monthly family income (cash and in kind) he placed (p. 13) at: cash income £2 1s.; food, £2 4s. 7d.; rent, 5s.; other sources, 4s.; total, £4 14s. 7d. R. J. B. Moore ("Native Wages and Standard of Living in Northern Rhodesia," *African Studies*, I [June, 1942], 145), argues that an urban worker needs a minimum of 35s. per month in contrast to the Copperbelt starting rate (at the time he wrote) of 27s. 6d. for underground, and 17s. 6d. for surface employment.

[48] *Legislative Council Debates* (Hansard), Dec. 12, 1940, Northern Rhodesia (Lusaka: Government Printer, 1940), pp. 282–283.

would make a worker wish to bring his entire family to an urban area on a permanent basis.[49] To cap this, all sorts of rules limiting freedom of movement were imposed upon the African population.

Consider next the alternative of short employment trips to the towns in contrast to permanent urban residence. During the thirties the real income that a family could earn if the husband split his time between the town and village was substantially greater than it could earn by residing in either place permanently. For example, on the basis of the 1938 figures (£18 annual urban wage for a man and £4 per capita subsistence income), a family could earn £27, or £5.4 per person, if the head of the household left his family and worked in town 6 months of each year.[50] The crucial assumption in these calculations is, of course, that the per capita income of the man's dependents is unaffected by his absence. Although this per capita income fell somewhat, it did not fall significantly in the thirties, as long as the man was at home during the planting season and prepared new gardens every few years.[51] The women traditionally undertook most of the remaining agricultural activities, so that the absence of the men during the rest of the year did not seriously curtail output. The agricultural system gradually was modified to permit a significant proportion (around 60 percent) of the men in a village to be in town for trips averaging about 2 years, without the incomes of those remaining in the villages being much lower than before.

Even though a family enjoyed income advantages if the man undertook periodic urban labor trips, it suffered a serious loss of welfare because of family separation. In order to ease the restrictive effects on the flow of urban migrants that this family separation caused, the mining companies built housing facilities for

---

[49] Since the urban areas were Crown Lands, Africans could not just move into them and build their own villages. They were permitted to reside in towns only by permission of the European population and under conditions specified by this population.

[50] The man would earn £9 in town for 6 months and £2 during the other 6 months in his village. Adding to this the £4 per person for each of his 4 dependents gives an annual figure of £27. For a comparison of rural and urban income-earning opportunities in Southern Rhodesia in 1960, see R. W. M. Johnson, *The Economics of Subsistence*, Technical Paper in Agricultural Economics, no. 1 (Salisbury: University College of Rhodesia and Nyasaland, 1963), pp. 8–10.

[51] See below, pp. 168–170, for a discussion of the effects of migration on rural productivity and nn. 97 and 99 in the next chapter for literature on the division of labor in the rural sector.

married men and encouraged them to bring their wives on their
employment trips. But, as noted, the copper companies did not
wish workers to bring their entire family nor to retire in the
urban areas. They feared that if permanent urbanization occurred, not only would they be confronted with serious African
labor problems in recession periods but they would also be forced
to spend much larger sums for housing and social services. Sir
Ronald Prain, chairman of Rhodesian Selection Trust, described
the prospect of these additional costs as "frightening." [52] In 1946
the mining companies formalized their previous position by stating that "detribalization and urbanization should not be encouraged in any manner" but rather "stabilization" of African
labor should be sought.[53] The term labor stabilization meant to
the companies "long service in one type of employment." "Urbanization," on the other hand, implied a "severance from rural
ties combined with a tendency to settle down for ever as a town
dweller." [54] By seeking stabilization without urbanization the
mines hoped to obtain the advantages of low turnover rates and
well-trained workers, without the disadvantages associated with
the costs of permanent African urbanization.

As the mining companies and municipal authorities improved
the living facilities for married employees, and as urban wages
rose relative to rural subsistence income, a growing number of
Africans began to choose permanent urban residence. By 1951,
for example, 6 percent of the workers at Roan Antelope planned
to live their entire lives in town (table 5-4). The same factors
that brought about longer urban trips apparently also led to more
permanent urbanization. In an effort to achieve the first condition
without paying the costs of the second, the mining companies introduced some rather ingenious fringe-benefit schemes. For example, workers are permitted to take long leaves without losing
their jobs, and since 1954, they actually have been able to take
leave without pay. The pension scheme (employees with 20 years
of service were paid £48 upon reaching the age of 50 with payments for additional service up to £72 per year) is also used to
promote a return to the villages. As one mine executive candidly
stated: "The pension scheme, in conjunction with leave travel
allowances offers an incentive to the African to maintain his ties

[52] Sir Ronald L. Prain, "The Stabilization of Labour in the Rhodesian Copper
Belt," *African Affairs,* LV (Oct., 1956), 308.
[53] *Ibid.,* p. 307.
[54] *Ibid.,* p. 306.

with—and eventually return to—his home district when he reaches pensionable age. The pension is of an amount that will permit him to live comfortably within a rural economy, but will discourage him from remaining in the town where living costs are much higher. The scheme has achieved its objectives (i.e., stabilization rather than urbanization) as very few Africans have elected to collect their pensions in urban areas." [55]

Conclusion

The conclusion that seems warranted with respect to urbanization closely resembles that reached with regard to length of service. During the thirties and forties most Africans did not seriously consider permanent town residence. Their preferences for rural life and the obstacles put in the way of town residence eliminated permanent urbanization as a significant choice in their minds. In recent years, though, some permanent urbanization has occurred despite the barriers operating against it. The impression deepens that in the absence of active efforts of employers and government authorities against it, permanent urbanization would now take place on an extensive scale.

---

[55] Kelley, *op. cit.*, p. 5.

6

The Market for Agricultural Products

THE GROWTH OF MARKET-ORIENTED AGRICULTURE

Until fairly recently much of the food consumed by African wage earners could be regarded as an industrial input much like such items as fuel and transport services. This is because European employers, as part of their wage payments, directly provided their African workers with foodstuffs. The practice was not given up until the mid-fifties, when the copper companies and other large producers began substituting money payments for rations. But up to this time there was a very direct and simple relationship between the development of the internal market for maize and meat (the two main components of the scale of African rations) and growth in the rest of the economy.

The mining industry provided the main growth impetus to Northern Rhodesia's agriculture, as it did to other sectors of the economy. Before the late 1920's, it was the copper industry of Katanga Province in the Congo that furnished this stimulus. In 1926 41 percent of the marketed maize[1] and 30 percent of the marketed livestock[2] were sold to the Katanga mines. The other main agricultural outlet was the lead and zinc mine at Broken Hill. By the time the Northern Rhodesian copper mines began full-scale production in 1930, the internal market for these com-

---

[1] Annual Report, 1926, Northern Rhodesia, Department of Agriculture, p. 11.

[2] Annual Report, 1926, Northern Rhodesia, Department of Veterinary Services, p. 22; S. Milligan, *Report on the Present Position of the Agricultural Industry and the Necessity, or Otherwise, of Encouraging Further European Settlement in Agricultural Areas*, Northern Rhodesia (Livingstone: Government Printer, 1931), p. 27, hereafter referred to as the *Milligan Report*.

modities had expanded to nearly threefold its former size. Domestic consumption of maize rose from 106,000 bags in 1928 to 300,000 bags in 1930.[3] Cattle purchases by the mines likewise increased from 5,000 to 18,000 head between 1926 and 1930.[4] The economy quickly turned from a net exporter to a net importer of maize and cattle.

Since the early thirties the Northern Rhodesian copper industry has continued to provide the major market outlet for cattle and maize. In 1937 the mines purchased 80 percent of the beef consumed in the territory,[5] and even in 1959 the mining areas consumed 50 percent of the total livestock slaughtered for commercial markets.[6] Similarly, just before the mines discontinued issuing rations to their African employees, they purchased about 25 percent of the total maize sold internally.[7]

Northern Rhodesian farmers attempted to cultivate a succession of other commodities besides maize and livestock, in particular, cotton, coffee, wheat, groundnuts, citrus fruits, and tobacco. Of these commodities, only tobacco remains a significant agricultural product. Moreover, it is the only important domestically produced commodity that does not owe its development directly or indirectly to the mining industry. The industry developed initially as a result of a tariff imposed by South Africa on unmanufactured tobacco purchased outside the South African Customs Union. The fact that Northern Rhodesia was within this customs union encouraged the search for suitable tobacco lands, and the area around Fort Jameson, consequently, was developed under the auspices of the United Tobacco Company.[8] Imperial preference further stimulated the industry, and by 1928 exports amounted to about £100,000.[9] Output along the line of rail re-

---

[3] *Report of the Maize Sub-Committee of the Northern Rhodesia Agricultural Advisory Board,* Northern Rhodesia (Lusaka: Government Printer, 1935), p. 3.

[4] *Memorandum on the Economics of the Cattle Industry in Northern Rhodesia,* Northern Rhodesia, Department of Animal Health (Livingstone: Government Printer, 1935), p. 17.

[5] *Report of the Commission Appointed To Enquire into the Financial and Economic Position of Northern Rhodesia,* Colonial, no. 145, Great Britain, Colonial Office (London: H.M.S.O., 1938), p. 253, hereafter referred to as the *Pim Report.*

[6] *Annual Report for the Year 1959,* Northern Rhodesia, Ministry of Land and Natural Resources, Department of Veterinary and Tsetse Control Services (Lusaka: Government Printer, 1960), p. 19.

[7] *Annual Report, 1951–1952,* Northern Rhodesia, Maize Control Board (Lusaka, Government Printer).

[8] *Pim Report,* p. 215.

[9] *Blue Book for the Year Ended 31 December 1928,* no. 5, Northern Rhodesia (Livingstone: Government Printer, 1929), Section T.

mained small until the middle forties when the high price of tobacco, coupled with technical improvements in tobacco growing, stimulated a large expansion in this area. By 1960 the value of the tobacco crop reached £1.9 million. Of the 14.8 million pounds sold, the Fort Jameson area contributed only 2 million pounds.[10]

— Transportation problems, together with unfavorable soil and climatic conditions, were major factors limiting the growth of other agricultural exports. The distance to any seaport is more than 1,000 miles, and even then the major international markets are far away. Profitable agriculture on an export basis requires high-value commodities in relation to weight. Except for tobacco, no suitable crops were found. Soil and weather conditions, together with plant diseases, caused frustrating failures for every attempt to discover alternative lines of production. Maize is now exported overseas, but only because the industry is subsidized.[11]

Even domestic production of maize owes much of its existence to the fortunate fact that the railroad built from Livingstone to Broken Hill happened to pass through the best agricultural lands in the country. Imports of maize from Southern Rhodesia and the Union of South Africa would have been far more important if the line of rail did not transverse this area. Except for this thin strip of land (approximately 20 miles on each side of the railroad) there is no other large, single area in Northern Rhodesia that possesses soils of high fertility.[12] Since this region and the much smaller area of fertile land around Fort Jameson are the main centers of European agriculture, the possibility of commercial farming by Africans on a scale similar to European agriculture is severely limited merely from a resource point of view. The Department of Agriculture estimated that, excluding Barotseland and land required for game reserves, forest conservation, and

---

[10] The tobacco industry around Fort Jameson declined drastically owing to an aversion on the part of buyers to the quality of the leaf grown there (J. C. Collins, "Review of Research on Flue-Cured Virginia Tobacco in Northern Rhodesia," in *Agricultural Bulletin*, no. 12, Northern Rhodesia [Lusaka: Government Printer, 1956], p. 41).

[11] For example, the net price of maize exported to the United Kingdom in 1958, after deducting freight and insurance charges, was 32s., whereas the government-guaranteed producer price for that year was 40s. (*Report of the Grain Marketing Board and Memorandum on Grain Marketing in Northern and Southern Rhodesia during the Period Ended 30th June, 1958,* Federation of Rhodesia and Nyasaland, Grain Marketing Board [Salisbury, n.d.], pp. 7, 54, 55).

[12] C. G. Trapnell, J. D. Martin, and W. Allen, *Vegetation: Soil Map of Northern Rhodesia,* Northern Rhodesia (Lusaka: Government Printer, 1950), esp. p. 19.

economic forestry, only 7 percent of the Native Reserves and Native Trust Land can be termed "good" for agricultural crops. In addition, only 27 percent of this soil is termed "cultivable." [13] The fact that these reserves and trust land constitute 94 percent of the entire area of Northern Rhodesia serves to reemphasize the lack of fertile agricultural land in the country.

By 1958 there were about 1,200 European farmers in Northern Rhodesia who employed 45,000 Africans and farmed 5 million acres,[14] an average of more than 4,000 acres each. Approximately 80 percent of this land was in the railway belt, and the rest mainly in the Eastern Province around Fort Jameson. Around 5 percent of European-occupied land was under crop or lying fallow in the mid-fifties.[15] The remainder was used for cattle grazing or else was too poor to be utilized at all. Virginia tobacco, maize, livestock, and dairy products are the major agricultural commodities marketed by European farmers. The total value of European agricultural production in 1960 was £6.2 million. The maize and tobacco crops were worth £2.1 million and £1.9 million, respectively, whereas the value of livestock slaughtered and of dairy products was £.7 million and £.6 million, respectively.[16]

Roughly 340,000 African families, with access to an area of 173 million acres, are engaged in agricultural activities.[17] Maize is by far their most important crop marketed in the monetary sector. In 1960, 50 percent of the £1.8 million worth of the African agricultural produce marketed was derived from this one commodity.[18] Sales of cattle and groundnuts were the only other important sources of cash income and amounted to £.3 million each. High hopes exist for a substantial increase in the production of Turkish and burley tobacco, but in 1959 the market value of these products was only £11,000. There is, however, one other important rural industry carried on by Africans, namely, fishing.

[13] J. Hadfield, "Aspects of the African Agrarian Economy in Northern Rhodesia," in *Agricultural Bulletin*, no. 17, Northern Rhodesia (Lusaka: Government Printer, n.d.), pp. 2–3.

[14] C. W. Lynn, "Agricultural Development," in "Economic Development in Northern Rhodesia," Study Conference, no. 2, sponsored by the United Northern Rhodesia Association (Salisbury, Oct., 1958), p. 47.

[15] L. G. Troup, *Report of a Commission of Inquiry into the Future of the European Farming Industry of Northern Rhodesia,* Northern Rhodesia (Lusaka: Government Printer, 1954), p. 4.

[16] *Report on the Agricultural Production of Southern Rhodesia, Northern Rhodesia, and Myasaland, 1960,* Federation of Rhodesia and Nyasaland, Central Statistical Office (Salisbury: Government Printer, 1961), p. 8.

[17] Lynn, *op. cit.,* p. 47.

[18] *Ibid.,* p. 8.

The total market value of fish production, half of which is marketed, was estimated to be £2.6 million in 1959.[19]

In chapter 3 the point was made that the introduction of cash markets into a subsistence economy stimulates the adoption of better agricultural techniques by subsistence cultivators. Although the size of the cash market for foodstuffs created by a new, export-oriented mining industry is limited by the relatively low labor coefficient for minerals, this repercussion does rank as one of the most favorable domestic effects of a mining industry, especially when account is taken of the possibilities of supplying the industry's other derived demands from internal production. On the basis of the theory outlined in that chapter, one expects, therefore, to find historically in Northern Rhodesia a gradual introduction by African producers of better productive methods after they enter the money economy.

GOVERNMENT POLICY

The main theme of this chapter is that to some extent this prediction was realized, but its fulfillment was thwarted seriously by government policies. The agricultural policy for most of the period covered was designed to benefit European settlers. African farmers were largely ignored or discriminated against when their interests conflicted with those of the European population. Furthermore, those few agricultural measures specifically directed toward helping African farmers were often poorly conceived and ineffective.[20] Three main government policies are analyzed in support of these conclusions: the land policy adopted by the government; the measures enacted to control grain prices; and the steps taken to influence cattle prices. In evaluating these measures it also is contended that contrary to the claims of many Europeans, African farmers responded positively to price incentives and to feasible opportunities to utilize improved techniques.

Land Policy

The encouragement of European settlement.—Until 1924 Northern Rhodesia was administered by the British South Africa Company. This chartered company, by means of a series of treaties in the 1890's with native chiefs, secured land rights over the entire

---

[19] *Report of the Rural Economic Development Working Party,* Northern Rhodesia (Lusaka: Government Printer, 1961), p. 65.

[20] This point is developed further in chapter 8.

territory except Barotseland.[21] It thereby possessed the authority to alienate any land outside Barotseland to European settlers, and Africans occupying the land were obliged to move. As compensation for such loss of land, the Northern Rhodesia Order in Council of 1911 stated that the company "shall from time to time assign to the natives inhabiting Northern Rhodesia land sufficient for their occupation, whether as tribes or portions of tribes, and suitable for their agricultural and pastoral requirements, including in all cases a fair and equitable proportion of springs or permanent water." [22]

The main objective of the company, of course, was to earn a profit for its shareholders, and the best way of accomplishing this seemed to be to encourage the development of the country's mineral resources. Agricultural development was viewed mainly as an important ancillary activity. The establishment in the economy of an agricultural sector, capable of supplying low-cost maize and meat, they believed, would attract new mining activity as well as increase existing mineral output, and thereby provide more royalties for the company. The company owned the railway, so agricultural development also would yield additional revenue from the expanded use of transport services.

Two alternative approaches for developing commercial agriculture were possible. The company could rely upon the African population to supply agricultural products, or it could encourage the immigration of European farmers. The outlook for native production seemed extremely unfavorable in the early years. The railway was constructed through a sparsely populated region, and there were not immediately available large settlements of Africans whose agricultural output might be tapped.[23] Existing African agricultural practices before the twenties seemed at best capable of producing only a small surplus of cereals above customary consumption levels, and even this amount could not be counted

---

[21] The treaty between the British South Africa Company and Lewanika, the Barotse Paramount Chief, excluded European settlement and prospecting from Barotse proper in return for the granting of these rights to the company over the rest of North-Western Rhodesia. It is questionable whether the treaties signed with other native chiefs actually covered the entire territory. The British government, however, sanctioned the company's mineral rights as extending over all the territory, except Barotseland (L. H. Gann, *The Birth of a Plural Society* [Manchester: Manchester University Press, 1958], pp. 55–59).

[22] *North Charterland Concession Inquiry Report to the Governor of Northern Rhodesia by the Commissioner, Mr. Justice Maugham*, Colonial, no. 73, Great Britain, Colonial Office (London: H.M.S.O., 1932), p. 96.

[23] Edward Clegg, *Race and Politics* (London: Oxford University Press, 1960), p. 31.

upon regularly. Yet the mines demanded a comparatively large, regular supply in order to provide food for the African workers. Attempts to stimulate modern agricultural techniques among the natives were not tried. There was a more attractive alternative. This was to import European settlers who possessed the skills and capital necessary for modern agricultural practices. The company proceeded despite initial Colonial Office opposition to encourage European settlement.[24]

There can be little doubt that in the early years, this alternative produced the larger, commercial agricultural output. The company succeeded handsomely in attracting immigrants possessing substantial capital,[25] and by 1921 there were 714 Europeans engaged in agriculture.[26] The new settlers did not find many Africans occupying the land granted them. Those who were encountered were mostly compensated, and they resettled on other land.[27]

Government policy toward Africans.—The government's responsibility toward Africans merely extended, as the 1911 Order in Council states, to maintaining the status quo of native agricultural production. Thus, after the investigations leading up to the establishment of native reserves in 1928–29, the procedure followed was to determine the number of acres used at the time by a particular tribe for agricultural purposes, and then to assign to this tribe an area sufficient to satisfy those current requirements. Two of the three commissions appointed to recommend reserve areas issued general instructions to consider future economic development and population growth, but when actually establishing the size of the reserves they made little provision for land requirements under modern agricultural methods. The reserves in the Abercorn and Fort Jameson districts were enlarged in 1938 and 1941, respectively, but this action was taken because of population pressures in the regions. The objective was still to maintain African agricultural income at its existing level rather than to provide sufficient land to farm successfully

[24] Gann, *op. cit.*, pp. 137–138.

[25] In 1920, for example, the average capital of the families accepted for settlement in the country was £3,775 per head of family (*Directors' Report and Accounts for the Year Ended 31 March 1920*, British South Africa Company [London, 1921], p. 19).

[26] *Report on the Census of Population, 1951*, Northern Rhodesia (Lusaka: Government Printer, 1954), p. 21. This number includes both men and women.

[27] Gann, *op. cit.*, pp. 145–146. He mentions that the compensation rate was between £1 and £2 per hut and 10 s. per acre of cultivated land.

under modern techniques. Moreover, it was generally believed that, because African agriculture did not "require" the type of fertile soil and access to transportation facilities "essential" for European agriculture, and because the Africans periodically moved their villages anyway, a program of resettlement would not work undue hardship on these people. The following remark by the secretary for Native Affairs, informing a tribal chief that he must soon move his people elsewhere, typifies the government's attitude: "You are very close to the railway. Now the railway is necessary to the white farmer but the natives do not make use of it, nor do they feel the want of it." [28] Similarly, the assertion in 1930 by the elected European representatives to the legislative Council that "the British Empire is primarily concerned with the furtherance of the interests of British subjects of British race and only thereafter with other British subjects, protected races, and the nationals of other countries, in that order," [29] represents an extreme expression of this view; but even the official representatives of the Crown believed that only by European immigration could the market demand from the mines for foodstuffs be satisfied from domestic production.[30]

The African population was even expected to bear its full share of the costs of government, and native taxes were set at a level designed to cover the full cost of maintaining law and order and administering justice in the native areas. The British South Africa Company could hardly have been expected to adopt any other policy, given its obligation to its stockholders. Taxing the European population in order to meet the administrative costs in African areas would have discouraged European immigration. Another advantage of taxing the Africans, which was not overlooked, was the effect it was thought to have in forcing Africans to seek employment in the urban areas in order to obtain the funds needed to pay the tax. When the company relinquished its administrative control over the country in 1924, the new government followed the same policy on native taxation. In 1930, the chief secretary was able to state that "the natives of this Territory pay for every service that Government provides for them, and

---

[28] F. V. Worthington, "Proposed Native Reserves," Northern Rhodesia (1913), Appendix I, p. 7, copy in the National Archives of Rhodesia and Nyasaland.
[29] *Correspondence with Regard to Native Policy in Northern Rhodesia,* Cmd. 3731, Great Britain (London: H.M.S.O., 1930), p. 3.
[30] Based on conversations with civil servants familiar with this period.

that if there is any balance it is rather in favour of the Government." [31]

Despite being obliged to finance the costs of European administration and in some cases being required to move to new areas, the African population still was regarded by Europeans as benefiting enormously from European colonization. The establishment of a stable government, able to put an end to the slave trade and tribal warfare, was in itself considered to be a great advance. In addition, the employment opportunities on European farms and in urban areas, as well as the opportunity to adopt Western ways, were thought to be important benefits for the African.[32]

At one stage in Northern Rhodesia's history the British government did issue a statement implying a vastly different policy toward the African population. The Passfield Memorandum of 1930 reemphasized the policy incorporated in the Kenya White Paper of July, 1923, namely, "that the interests of the African natives must be paramount, and that if, and when, those interests and the interests of the immigrant races should conflict, the former should prevail." [33] The response of the European settlers in Northern Rhodesia to this statement was vehemently negative. It was typified by such assertions as: "To subordinate the interests of civilized Britons to the development of alien races, whose capability of substantial further advancement has not been demonstrated, appears to be contrary to natural law." [34] The colonial secretary briskly dismissed the request of the Europeans for a hearing on the Passfield policy, but a parliamentary joint select committee soon announced that the doctrine meant "no more than that the interests of the overwhelming majority of the indigenous population should not be subordinated to those of a minority belonging to another race, however important in itself." [35] The "no more" phrase and the emphasis upon the interests of only "the overwhelming majority of the indigenous popula-

[31] *Legislative Council Debates* (no. 11), Second Session, Third Council, 7th March–1st April 1930, Northern Rhodesia (Livingstone: Government Printer, 1930), p. 123.

[32] "Charter of the British South Africa Company and Conditions on Extending the Field of the Operations of the British South Africa Company to the North of the Zambezi," reprinted in *North Charterland Concession Inquiry: Report to the Governor of Northern Rhodesia by the Commissioner, Mr. Justice Maugham,* p. 4.

[33] *Memorandum on Native Policy in East Africa,* Cmd. 3573, Great Britain (London: H.M.S.O., 1930), p. 3.

[34] *Correspondence with Regard to Native Policy in Northern Rhodesia,* p. 5.

[35] J. W. Davidson, *The Northern Rhodesian Legislative Council* (London: Faber and Faber, 1948), p. 72.

tion" considerably weakened the doctrine, and it was never interpreted as requiring significant changes in the then existing policy. The governor still was able to state after the Passfield Memorandum: "The policy of the Government is one of providing for the Natives sufficient land to enable them to develop a full Native life in their own areas; sufficient land to meet the inevitable expansion of the populations settled thereon and sufficient to enable the Government with a quiet conscience to release to European settlement other areas suitable for the purpose." [36]

By the mid-thirties the land of the territory was divided roughly into three categories.[37] Areas reserved specially for Africans totaled 71 million acres and comprised Barotseland (37 million acres) and the native reserves (34 million acres). Land already alienated to Europeans consisted of 5.5 million acres, held by two companies, and of more than 3 million acres in farms. The remaining areas came to about 105 million acres, of which 11 million were forest and game reserves and 94 millions were unallocated. The Pim Commission in 1937 recommended that these areas be made native trust land, and in 1947 this recommendation was made into law. Northern Rhodesia, therefore, is now divided into crown land (5.6 percent of the territory), native reserves (18.9 percent of the total land area), the Barotseland protectorate (16 percent), and native trust land (59.5 percent). The crown land is at present entirely held by Europeans, although theoretically Africans can also use this land.[38] According to the Order in Council, native trust land is "administered and controlled by the Governor for the use or common benefit, direct or indirect, of the natives of Northern Rhodesia." [39] Non-Africans are permitted access to this area only under special conditions, such as the development of rural townships and public utilities.

Although Africans were ill-prepared to seize the initial market opportunities created by mining expansion, the entrance of European settlers along the railway line caused an unexpected revolution in African agriculture nearby. Africans began to expand the size of their cultivated gardens and to set aside the hoe for

---

[36] Clegg, *op. cit.*, pp. 66–67.
[37] Richard Gray, *The Two Nations* (London: Oxford University Press, 1960), p. 85.
[38] Despite the equal access law to Crown Land, no African has ever secured a farm on such land (*Report: Appendix VI—Survey of Developments Since 1953*, Great Britain, Advisory Commission on the Review of the Constitution of the Federation of Rhodesia and Nyasaland, Cmd. 1149 [London: H.M.S.O., 1960], p. 241, hereafter referred to as the *Monckton Report*).
[39] *Ibid.*, p. 39.

the European plow. By 1927 they sold 30,000 bags of maize to traders[40] compared with a negligible quantity in the early twenties. They also began to dominate the cattle trade.[41]

Rather than welcoming this response, the government viewed it with concern. By this time the number of European farmers was sufficiently large to exercise a dominating influence on agricultural policy, and obviously, these farmers were not interested in lowering the price of agricultural products to the mines. Instead, they wanted sufficient land for further expansion and high prices for their output. As a means of attaining their land objective, in 1928 native reserves were established in the railway area, and the process of moving Africans into these areas was begun.[42] The effects of the measure were to lesson existing African market competition,[43] and, more important, by reserving for European settlement a strip extending in most areas about 20 miles on each side of the railway, to limit severely potential African competition in commercial markets.

Maize and Livestock Controls

The Maize Control Ordinance of 1936.—Even the severe limitation imposed by the small amount of land available to Africans near the railway was not sufficient, by itself, to remove the possibility of sizable African participation in the maize market. With the development of the Northern Rhodesian copper mines and the resultant greatly enlarged markets, African as well as European production expanded sharply. But, African sales rose more rapidly. In 1930 African producers sold about 30,000 bags to traders, but by 1935 the figure had risen to 100,000. European output available for sale increased only from 168,000 bags to 211,00 bags between these years.[44]

The rise in the African's market share did not cause undue

---

[40] *Annual Report for the Year 1928,* Northern Rhodesia, Department of Agriculture (Livingstone: Government Printer, 1929), p. 6. A bag of maize weighs 200 pounds.

[41] By 1930, half the marketed cattle came from native sources (*Milligan Report,* p. 19).

[42] At the same time native reserves were gazetted in the Fort Jameson and Abercorn areas, where there also was a problem of Europeans and Africans desiring to use the same land.

[43] For example, the removal of natives from land near the lead and zinc mines at Broken Hill and near the Roan Antelope copper mine in the Ndola District resulted in the loss of existing markets (*Pim Report,* p. 67; and *Annual Report upon Native Affairs, 1933,* Northern Rhodesia [Livingstone: Government Printer, 1934], p. 12).

[44] *Report of the Maize Sub-Committee* . . . , p. 3.

alarm among European settlers, as long as domestic production was insufficient to meet the internal demand at the prevailing prices. After the sharp retrenchment in the copper industry in 1932, however, the situation altered drastically. European farmers feared that they would be driven off their farms by African competition. Even before the slump a pessimistic report was submitted to the government concerning further expansion possibilities for European agriculture. This report estimated that with a price of 9s. per bag of maize (it fell to 6s. in 1932) a farmer on a 500-acre unit would require a yield of 8 bags per acre to earn £300 per year.[45] In 1931 the average European yield per acre was only 4.5 bags. Another committee estimated that the yield per acre of two-thirds of the growers (who supplied only 20 percent of the European market output) did not exceed 5 bags between 1931 and 1935.[46]

If the weakness of European agriculture was recognized, so also was the growth potential of African maize production. In his 1931 report, the Director of Agriculture justified the lack of systematic agricultural assistance to Africans in the railway belt with the following remark: "If the whole of this market were taken by the native (as it might well be, with the exception of a very few commodities, should deliberate attempts be made to foster the production of crops for this purpose) the European population would be rapidly driven off the land, and it is hard to see how the individual native would greatly be benefited, for his share of the proceeds would be infinitesimal."[47] The absurdity of this argument merely attests to the fears of the European farmer.

As a result of these concerns, the Maize Control Ordinance of 1936 was enacted.[48] This ordinance established the Maize Control Board and gave it the power to purchase and sell all maize at fixed prices. The market was separated into an internal pool and an export pool. The purpose of the division was to set the domestic price above the international price and then dump any surplus above internal sales on the export market.[49] African

---

[45] *Milligan Report*, p. 13.

[46] *Report of the Maize Sub-Committee* . . . , p. 6.

[47] *Annual Report for the Year 1931*, Northern Rhodesia, Department of Agriculture, p. 16.

[48] *Laws of Northern Rhodesia*, Northern Rhodesia (Lusaka: Government Printer, 1948), Vol. III, chap. 98.

[49] The existence of protective devices enabled the board to set the internal price above the international price.

producers were allocated one-quarter of the internal pool and Europeans three-quarters. In the event the deliveries of either group fell short of its domestic quota, the other group was permitted to supply and to receive credit for the unfilled part of the quota. Subject to that provision, any production on the part of either group in excess of its assigned quotas was to be thrown into the international market, and the proceeds of such export sales were to be divided according to the amount by which each group exceeded its internal quotas.

The measure was a typical device for price stabilization under conditions of a declining market. Like all such measures, it penalized those producers whose market share was expanding. The Northern Rhodesian copper companies were in a similar position with respect to the international copper cartel. Unlike African farmers, however, the copper companies could (and did) refuse to accept their allotted quota.

The African internal quota was determined by computing, for the years 1933–1935, the average ratio of native grain sold to private traders to the sum of this amount plus European sales.[50] As the *Pim Report* noted, this procedure did not represent fairly either the amounts available for sale by each group or the amounts actually sold internally. The North-Western Rhodesia Farmers Cooperative Society, which controlled 80 percent of the European-produced maize, possessed facilities for exporting maize, whereas the traders in native maize did not. As a result, the quantity of African grain actually bought by traders "did not represent the surplus of native grain available for sale, as in the absence of facilities for export the traders could not buy more than they could hope to sell in the local market."[51] In addition, "if the comparison is to be based on the sales in the local market the grain exported should be deducted from the total amount of grain produced. In 1932–33 exports amounted to 70,100 bags, all of it European grain, out of 247,000 bags produced by European growers."[52]

The committee that drafted the maize ordinance even argued that the 25 percent native quota would help African producers. It was claimed that the Africans, in their attempts to imitate European techniques, were neglecting to follow the measures necessary for maintaining soil fertility, and a rapid deterioration of the

---

[50] *Report of the Maize Sub-Committee* . . . , p. 22.
[51] *Pim Report,* p. 227.
[52] *Ibid.,* p. 228.

land in the native reserves was therefore taking place. Output had expanded considerably, "but, if present methods persist, production will almost certainly diminish in the course of years. Before this happens, however, native competition will have gone far in eliminating the European maize grower and the Territory as a whole will not have gained in the process. . . . The native has already acquired a substantial share of the internal market, probably as much or more than he could supply in perpetuity if he persisted in his present methods, but not more than could safely be supplied if he ceased to produce maize regardless of damage to the land." [53] The committee concluded, therefore, that by holding down the profitability of African production, the African would be restrained from expanding his acreage by means of improvident productive methods, and thus ultimately be spared from a much lower level of income.

The Cattle Control Board.—Another restrictive agricultural measure adopted by the Northern Rhodesian government was the Cattle Marketing and Control Ordinance of 1937.[54] As was the case with maize, the internal market for cattle declined sharply in the early thirties while the African share of this market increased: in 1928, the native market share was 50 percent, in 1936, 67 percent. The fact that the Congo market had been captured by Southern Rhodesia in the late twenties weakened even more the position of the European farmer.[55] The reason that Southern Rhodesia did not also secure a large part of the Northern Rhodesian market was that before 1930 disease restrictions limited livestock imports from Southern Rhodesia. Soon thereafter a gentlemen's agreement was reached whereby imports into Northern Rhodesia were restricted.

As early as 1931 an attempt was made, on a voluntary basis, to maintain livestock prices, but this did not prove successful. Sales at prices below the agreed levels were common. Finally, in 1937 a Cattle Control Board was established, under government auspices, and was given the power to fix minimum prices below which livestock sales were illegal. Furthermore, the board in effect was permitted to regulate imports and exports of cattle. The main purpose of the ordinance was, of course, to prevent the destruction by competition of a significant part of the Euro-

---

[53] *Report of the Maize Sub-Committee* . . . , p. 7.
[54] *Laws of Northern Rhodesia*, Vol. III, chap. 3.
[55] *Memorandum on the Economics of the Cattle Industry in Northern Rhodesia*, p. 18.

pean cattle industry. It was also designed, however, to encourage the production of better grades of beef within the territory.[56]

The Operation of Agricultural Controls

Maize policy.—The introduction of maize control produced a surprising response on the part of African suppliers. Native maize sales jumped from 100,000 bags in the 1934–35 season to 235,000 bags in 1935–36. The season was an especially good one, but the much larger increase in African sales to the maize board (compared with European) appears to confirm the point made in the *Pim Report*. The purchase of African-grown maize by traders previously was limited by the traders' lack of export facilities. With the Maize Control Board standing ready to purchase all maize offered to it, large amounts of native maize, which previously were consumed by Africans, were now marketed commercially. This indicated the willingness of Africans to respond positively when presented with a market opportunity.[57]

The remarkably increased volume of African maize sales, together with the expanded European output, meant that both groups exceeded their respective internal market quotas. Fortunately the world price soared to its 1929 level.[58] The board was not only able to dispose of the surplus produced in the first year of control, but also inherited stocks equivalent to the internal requirements for two and one-half years. Consequently, African producers were not penalized by the small internal market share allotted to them. In the next year the continuance of a favorable export price again saved Africans from having to accept a lower price on a substantial part of their output. Thereafter, European producers regularly fell short of their quota. Indeed,

---

[56] As one member of the Legislative Council commented with regard to the earlier Cattle Levy Ordinance, which had the same objective as the later Cattle Marketing and Control Ordinance: "It will have the effect of raising the quality of cattle in the country, and it will give the consumer a better class of meat than at the present time he is able to buy" (*Legislative Council Debates* [Hansard] First Session, Fifth Council, Nov., Dec., 1935, Northern Rhodesia [Lusaka: Government Printer, 1935], p. 239).

[57] The Director of Agriculture, who was chairman of the subcommittee formulating the maize control measure, was able to point with pride to the benefits accruing to Africans from maize sales. But, the fact that this particular benefit was never mentioned in the arguments made for the introduction of control leads one to suspect that the African response was a complete surprise to the Europeans. They assumed that the African maize marketed prior to control represented the entire surplus available above subsistence needs.

[58] *Annual Report for the Year 1936*, Northern Rhodesia, Department of Agriculture, p. 4.

the internal market expanded so rapidly that heavy importation actually was required. By the time an export surplus reemerged after 1955, the government was guaranteeing the same producer price for African and European maize regardless of whether it was exported or sold internally. As a result, the chairman of the maize board was able to say in 1953: "It is quaint to recall the object for which it [the Maize Control Board] was established, for it has never once had to carry it out. It was created to secure to the European growers of maize a proportion of the internal market at a time when over-production was threatened and the export price was very little more than 3s. a bag." [59]

The African supplier did not receive all revenue resulting from the sale of his maize. Acting as sole purchaser and seller, the board was faced with the problem of having to set a purchase price before it knew how much revenue it would obtain on the basis of its fixed internal selling price and an unknown export price. Fearful of operating at a loss, the board invariably set a lower buying price than it actually realized on the selling side. Supplementary payments were made to European producers but it was impracticable to reach the thousands of African producers. Over the years, a substantial surplus was built up in the native pool. By 1942 this surplus reached £85,000 or an amount equal to 34 percent of the revenue actually paid for native-grown maize since 1936–37. During the first few years the board management argued that the surplus was necessary for price-stabilization purposes. After the size of the fund exceeded what anyone could claim was required for this purpose, the continuing surplus came to be justified on conservation grounds. The additional acreage expansion by Africans that might result from higher prices was to be discouraged because of the harmful effects of African cultivation practices on soil fertility. The matter was finally settled in 1949 in a manner consistent with this point of view, by transferring the existing surplus and any excesses occurring thereafter to a fund used to finance the African Farming Improvement Scheme.[60]

Beginning in the 1942–43 season, the maize board, by means of government subsidies, deliberately began to operate at a loss. From 1943 to 1954, during which time large quantities of maize were imported, the price fixed by the board for consumers was

---

[59] Annual Report, 1952–1953, Northern Rhodesia, Maize Control Board, p. 3.

[60] Annual Report, 1949–1950, Northern Rhodesia, Maize Control Board, p. 3. The operations of this scheme are discussed later (pp. 165–167).

kept below the cost of imports. The producer price, although considerably higher than the selling price, also was held at a level below the cost of importing. The resulting government subsidy to the maize board during these years was more than £7 million.[61] The case for keeping the internal price of maize to consumers below the cost of imported maize rested on the view that the country must have a cheap supply of food for its African labor. Since employers purchased most of the maize as rations for their African employees, this reduces to the argument that the cost of African labor must be kept low. Both European and African maize growers suffered under the arrangement, because they received less during this period than they would have under free-market conditions. Those who benefited from the policy were the employers of African labor.

After 1954 an export surplus developed in the maize industry. The subsidy program continued, but its effects now were totally different. The net proceeds from exports were considerably less per bag than the price paid to producers. Domestic consumers, who were charged more than the net export price, would have fared better under a free-market system. The program subsidized producers—but not all producers benefited. European farmers and those Africans participating in the African Farming Improvement Scheme received more than if they were required to compete in an open market, but the ordinary African farmer did not always gain under the program. To obtain funds for paying cash benefits to African farmers joining the improved farming scheme, the government directed the Grain Marketing Board to collect a levy on all African maize by paying Africans less than the net price received by European producers. This levy averaged about 8s. per bag between 1954 and 1957, but thereafter was reduced to about 2s.[62] In 2 of the 4 years between 1955 and 1960 when maize was exported, namely, 1956 and 1960, the price paid "unimproved" African farmers (typical farmers not covered by the improvement program) was less than the net export price (the export price less all marketing costs incurred between the time the board collected the maize from African producers and delivered

---

[61] Annual Reports, 1943–1954, Northern Rhodesia, Maize Control Board.

[62] The price paid by the marketing board to European and African farmers also differs because of transportation charges. The European farmer must bear the cost of delivering his maize to the board's storage facilities along the line of rail. The African farmer leaves his crop at one of the many depots provided by the board off the railway line. The cost of collecting and transporting this maize is borne by the African producer in the form of a lower price paid to him for this maize.

it overseas). If the subsidy program as well as the special levy on African-grown maize had not existed, the vast majority of African farmers actually would have been better off in these years.

From 1955 to 1957 the maize subsidy program cost the government £2.5 million. The Northern and Southern Rhodesian markets were combined under the Grain Marketing Act of 1957.[63] Thereafter, under federal auspices the domestic consumer price was increased and the producer subsidy on exported maize was removed. This reduced the government's burden somewhat, although the cost in 1960 was still £1 million.[64] Under this federal scheme, Northern Rhodesian farmers ended up subsidizing Southern Rhodesian farmers. The price paid by the marketing board to all producers in the federation was determined by averaging the higher domestic price and the lower international price. Since Southern Rhodesia's export surplus was a larger fraction of internal sales than was Northern Rhodesia's, Northern Rhodesian farmers would have received more under the scheme if it were not tied in with Southern Rhodesia.

Livestock policy.—Market control in the livestock industry worked much better, from a selfish European viewpoint, than in the maize industry. The difficulty with maize is that African and European output is essentially the same in quality. To ensure what was deemed a reasonable income level for the European farmer, it was necessary to increase the price of maize and also to allocate a fixed market share to the European. But even with a high price, European production did not expand rapidly enough to fulfill its assigned market quota. On the other hand, maize prices were sufficiently attractive to induce a very large expansion in African production, and African producers were able to take advantage of the European shortfall.

In the livestock field the greater differentiation between European and African output permitted more selective regulation of the two groups. The need for net imports of cattle that developed in the very first year of the Board's operation, and has persisted to the present time, has enabled a minimum-price scheme, in conjunction with import controls, to operate effectively in raising European incomes above their free-market levels.

---

[63] One feature of this new act that should be noted is that the European-African quota system for the internal market was abandoned.

[64] *Report of the Grain Marketing Board for the Year Ended 30th June, 1960,* Federation of Rhodesia and Nyasaland, Grain Marketing Board (Salisbury: Service Press, n.d.), annexure 9.

Embarrassing open subsidies such as occurred in the maize market were not required. The Cattle Control Board, by allowing large numbers of the lower grades of livestock to enter the internal market from outside, while severely restricting the importation of the better grades,[65] was able to achieve two goals of government policy. First, by raising the producer price of prime cattle 460 percent between 1937 and 1956, it enabled the European livestock industry to flourish and the production of higher quality cattle to increase. Like their counterparts on the maize board, the authorities of the cattle board were extremely concerned about "good production practices"—by which was meant the production of better quality beef. Efficient production for them was related more to this technical concept than to the demands of the market. In addition to the price incentive, a cattle loan scheme and a system of bonuses for good livestock practices were used to achieve this objective. The second goal attained by the cattle board was the maintenance of low prices for poorer quality beef. Compound-grade cattle (the lowest grade) sold for only 200 percent more per 100 pounds in 1956 than 1937.[66] By keeping this "boys' meat" relatively inexpensive, the board was able to hold down the cost of African labor.

As one would expect on economic grounds, the relative market supply offered by African producers declined because of these manipulations. By 1960 the African share of local production had fallen from its 1944 level of 63 percent to only 44 percent.[67] The much larger increase in the price of maize also undoubtedly played a major part in causing this relative decline in cattle sales, especially in the Southern Province. The price paid Africans for maize rose over 200 percent between 1947, and 1959,[68] whereas

---

[65] *Report of the Federal Cattle and Beef Marketing Committee*, Federation of Rhodesia and Nyasaland, Federal Department of Conservation and Extension (Salisbury, 1954), pp. 11, 44.

[66] Most of the widening in the price differential between the poorest and best grade of cattle occurred after 1944. In that year the ratio between the price of prime to inferior grade cattle was 1.87 as compared with 1:62 in 1937. By 1956 the ratio was 2:92 (Annual Reports, 1944–1956, Northern Rhodesia Department of Veterinary Services [Lusaka, Government Printer]).

[67] Annual Report, 1944, Northern Rhodesia, Department of Veterinary Services, p. 9; *Annual Reports of the Departments of Agriculture and Co-operatives and African Marketing for the Year 1960*, Northern Rhodesia, Ministry of African Agriculture (Lusaka: Government Printer, 1961), p. 6.

[68] Annual Report, 1947–1948, Northern Rhodesia, Maize Control Board; *Report of the Grain Marketing Board for the Year Ended 30th June, 1959*, Federation of Rhodesia and Nyasaland, Grain Marketing Board (Salisbury: Service Press, n.d.).

the compound-grade cattle price increased but 70 percent.[69] African producers planted maize on land formerly used as pasture and utilized a larger proportion of their animals for work purposes rather than for cattle sales. In view of the pricing practices of the cattle board it is difficult to sympathize with the continual lament of cattle authorities that African sales have been disappointingly low.

It is important to note the experience of Southern Rhodesia where a similar pricing structure prevailed until 1956.[70] In that year, a free cattle market was established, and the gap between the higher and lower grades of beef promptly and sharply narrowed.[71] The same thing would very likely have occurred in Northern Rhodesia if the market had been less restrictive. In fact, when the Cold Storage Commission of Southern Rhodesia was federalized and eventually extended its operations into Northern Rhodesia in 1960, the price paid for native cattle was increased, and sales by Africans rose.[72]

An Appraisal of Agricultural Policy

The agricultural policy of Northern Rhodesia was based upon the premise that European farmers were entitled to preferential treatment. As noted, even before African farmers exerted any significant competitive pressure on European producers, they were removed from most of the best agricultural land near the line of rail. The European government at that time apparently believed that the African people had no right to share as agricultural producers in the demands generated by the copper industry and, moreover, were incapable of responding to the market demand. When the fallaciousness of this latter view was demonstrated by a rapid growth in the African share of the commercial agricultural market during the early thirties, the government introduced controls that clearly were designed to give preference to European farmers. Fortunately, the controls on maize sales did not operate in as highly a discriminatory manner as

[69] Annual Reports, 1947–1959, Northern Rhodesia, Department of Veterinary Services.

[70] *Report of the Federal Cattle and Beef Marketing Committee.*

[71] *Nineteenth Annual Report and Accounts for the Period 1st January to 31st December, 1956,* Cold Storage Commission of Southern Rhodesia (Bulawayo: Rhodesian Christian Press, 1957), p. 13.

[72] *Annual Report for the Year 1960,* Northern Rhodesia, Ministry of Native Affairs, African Affairs (Lusaka: Government Printer, 1961), p. 67.

they might have, both because of expanding internal markets and because of changes in the control scheme. Nevertheless, around 1960, official agricultural policy still substantially favored the European producer (and now the "improved" African farmer) over the typical African farmer.

The soil-depletion argument.—European agricultural authorities, of course, attempted to justify their policies on grounds other than self-interest. It was alleged that African farmers misused the European productive techniques they adopted. As a result, they were depleting the fertility of the soil so rapidly that a continuance of these practices would ultimately lead to a reduction of African income. The conclusion was reached that the African should be protected from his own folly by limiting his production. This reasoning appears again and again in discussions of native agriculture. For example, in 1942, when the internal market was very favorable because of the war, the government deprecated attempts to increase African acreage because of the soil depletion it would cause.[73]

Like so many conservationist arguments, this view is based on the notion that the valuation system derived from a free market should not be permitted to determine the utilization rate for natural resources. The rabid conservationist wishes to substitute his own rate of discounting future income for those discount rates held by the contemporary members of the community. Such a view runs counter to the concepts of a free economy—certainly counter to the concepts held by Europeans in Rhodesia with regard to their own affairs. No one suggested, for example, that copper should not be mined because it could never be replaced. The crux of the issue was that the European farmers objected to the higher rate of discounting future income used by Africans compared with themselves. The African farmer utilized the soil more intensively and with less regard for its future fertility. This was one of the factors enabling the African to enlarge his share of the grain market. In a free economic society, the competitive pressure resulting from a higher discount of future income by some members of the economy is just as justifiable as that resulting from the willingness of some individuals to work harder than others, or to introduce cost-reducing innovations before other producers.

One view the European population may have held was that

---

[73] *Food Production Committee Progress Report: 1942,* Northern Rhodesia, Department of Agriculture (Lusaka: Government Printer, 1943), p. 4.

they would be obliged to support African producers after they had ruined the soil. They therefore had a right to control African activity in much the same sense that a parent regulates a child. This is like saying that a man should not be permitted to become a drug addict because he eventually imposes costs on the rest of society. Many Europeans undoubtedly looked upon the African as a child, but it is not evident that they were prepared to assume the responsibilities of a parent. Their policy seems to have been that the child should fare largely for himself, provided he did not interfere with European activity.

A case for European-imposed restrictions might be built on this premise, but the evidence does not support the contention that the African was rapidly worsening his own condition. As was noted, there is no lack of declarations deploring the soil-destroying qualities of African agriculture, but the test of the proposition can only be the trend of African output. If it was upward over a long period, it can only be the result of two factors: (1) the extent of the fertility-destroying aspects of native agriculture was vastly exaggerated, and (2) Africans changed their methods of production. Despite statements, even as late as 1941, to the effect that annual African output was not likely to average more than 100,000 bags of maize,[74] output actually averaged 140,000 bags from 1942–43 to 1949–50 and 470,000 bags from 1950–51 to 1959–60. And there has been no decline in per acre yields since 1936, despite continuous cultivation under a system of monoculture.[75] Which of the two factors was more responsible for the remarkable increase in output is impossible to determine. Whatever the causes, the results disprove the predictions of those Europeans who were instrumental in determining African agricultural policy. It was not the African who was shortsighted, but rather the European who neglected to allow for the ability of the African to improve his agricultural practices.

The irregular-supply argument.—With the disproof of the notion that African producers were heading for self-destruction because of ruinous agricultural practices, another argument for a price-support system, based upon European costs of production, became popular: that African farmers cannot be relied upon to

---

[74] *Annual Report for the Year 1941,* Northern Rhodesia, Department of Agriculture, p. 1.

[75] C. E. Johnson, "African Farming Improvement in the Plateau Tonga Maize Areas of Northern Rhodesia," in *Agricultural Bulletin,* no. 11, Northern Rhodesia (Lusaka: Government Printer, 1956), p. 24.

produce a large regular supply of maize for the monetary sector. For example, it was pointed out that African producers delivered 883,000 bags of maize to the maize board in 1958, but only 36,000 bags in 1959, an extremely poor season. European deliveries for these years were 1,174,000 and 544,000 bags, respectively.[76] These figures do not reflect the relative variations in output between the two groups. Maize is a basic foodstuff for African producers, and, even in good years, 75 percent of their output is retained for consumption within the nonmonetary sector of the economy. Because of the low income-elasticity of demand for maize as a consumption commodity among African producers, as much as 98 percent is retained in very poor seasons. Maize is also the basic food for Africans employed on European farms, but, because of a higher output per worker, European farmers usually retain less than 10 percent of their output to feed their workers. Consequently, the same percentage change in output changes the market supply of African producers more than that of European producers.

If output figures, rather than quantities delivered to the maize board are compared, the contrast between the two groups is manifestly different. In each successive year from 1955 to 1960 (the only years for which estimates of total native production are available) the percentage change in African output is less than the percentage change in European production. The fact that the argument based on irregular supply is stated in terms of commercially sold maize illustrates a typical lack of concern about the welfare of the subsistence population. There is more interest in the amounts delivered by Africans to the maize board than in the standard of living of the whole population. Wide fluctuations in supply to any part of a market are certainly undesirable. But there are much better alternatives to meeting the problem than by a costly government subsidization of European farmers that creates an export surplus in all but very poor seasons. Importation of maize is a much cheaper way of meeting internal requirements in poor harvest years. The usual rebuttal to this suggestion is that outside sources of supply are liable to be cut off in times of international emergency. But, the holding of reserve stocks, in conjunction with the ability of Africans to expand production rapidly under price incentives, would meet this contingency.

[76] *Report of the Grain Marketing Board for the Year Ended 30th June, 1960*, tables 9 and 11.

THE RESPONSIVENESS OF AFRICAN FARMERS
TO PRICE INCENTIVES

Many Europeans argue that African farmers are not responsive to price and income opportunities. Or, the claim is made that they do respond to opportunities to raise their income, but not the way European farmers do. For example, when prices rise, they decrease their market offerings, and when prices fall, they increase their market deliveries.[77] Africans are said to possess the target-income notion in agricultural pursuits as well as in urban employment.

The history of African agriculture over the past three decades contradicts these views. The evidence consistently shows that Africans respond positively in terms of supply to better income-earning opportunities. The remarkable growth of African commercial agriculture near the line of rail amply attests to this. In the early twenties the average size of an African family's "garden" was probably about 2 acres. The maize market then began expanding and the Director of Agriculture is quoted as stating, even as early as 1933, that Africans were adopting European methods and were increasing their garden sizes tenfold.[78] Although this estimate of growth seems exaggerated, the Department of Agriculture in 1938 stated that the average African maize farmer cultivated 6 acres.[79] It reported that the typical producer usually owned oxen and, more rarely, a plow and cultivator. By the mid-fifties average family acreages in the maize belt varied from about 10 to 30 acres for "unimproved farmers." [80] As these shifts took place, the tribes in the area actually reduced the proportion of men they sent out to obtain urban employment.[81]

The most arresting aspect of the increase in farm size and

---

[77] Johnson, *op. cit.*, p. 14, notes the prevalence of these views.

[78] *Annual Report for the Year 1933*, Northern Rhodesia, Department of Agriculture, p. 26.

[79] *Annual Report for the Year 1938*, Northern Rhodesia, Department of Agriculture, p. 2.

[80] A. M. Morgan Rees and R. H. Howard, "An Economic Survey of Commercial African Farming among the Sala of the Mumbwa District of Northern Rhodesia," in *Agricultural Bulletin*, no. 10, Northern Rhodesia (Lusaka: Government Printer, 1955), p. 60; Johnson, *op. cit.*

[81] W. Allan *et al.*, *Land Holding and Land Usage among the Plateau Tonga of Mazabuka District*, Rhodes-Livingstone Papers, no. 14 (London: Oxford University Press, 1948), pp. 160–163.

improvement in agricultural practices is that these changes took place without any significant technological assistance by the government, and also without any government-sponsored changes in tribal landholding systems.[82] Economic opportunity was the force that brought about both technical and institutional changes in the African agricultural system near the railway.

A statistical analysis of the very limited agricultural data available also supports the hypothesis that the supply functions for African farmers are positively sloped. Multiple regression equations, where the share of total African production marketed was made a function of the Grain Marketing Board's announced support price and of total African production, were computed for the four main African cereal crops, maize, munga, kaffir corn (finger millet) and rupoko (millet).[83] Letting SM stand for the share marketed by African producers, Q for their total production of the commodity, and P for the price set by the Grain Marketing Board, the equations are as follows:[84]

Maize $SM = -27.81 + .00Q + .21P$; $R = .42$; sample size $= 11$
                        (.40) (1.25)

Munga $SM = -26.99 + .02Q + .12P$; $R = .92$; sample size $= 11$
                        (4.25) (6.34)

Kaffir corn $SM =$ $3.24 + .02Q - .02P$; $R = .39$; sample size $= 11$
                        (1.19) (-.44)

Rupoko $SM = -13.02 + .01Q + .06P$; $R = .77$; sample size $= 10$
                        (.64) (2.79)

A positive regression coefficient for the price variable means that the share marketed increased as price increased, holding total output constant. Similarly, a positive regression coefficient for the output variable means that the share marketed rose as production increased, keeping price constant. All but one of the eight regression coefficients are positive. Before placing confidence in any such results, it is necessary to determine the probability of such coefficients occurring on a random basis. Specifically, in the multiple regression equations given, each of the three regression coefficients with t-values (the numbers within parentheses) of less than 1.00 is not statistically significant. The probability that, on

---

[82] See *ibid.* for a description of the land tenure system.

[83] Southern Rhodesia data was used because it covers a longer time span, but one can be quite confident that the same general relations hold in Northern Rhodesia (*Report of the Secretary for Native Affairs and Chief Native Commissioner for the Year 1960, Southern Rhodesia* [Salisbury: Government Printer, 1961], p. 99).

[84] The bracketed figures are the t-values of the regression coefficients and R is the multiple correlation coefficient.

random sampling, regression coefficients as large as these will occur is as high as 3 out of 10. On the other hand, for the three positive coefficients with *t*-values of 2.79 or more, the chances are only about 1 in 100 (or more, in the case of munga) that coefficients of this size will be obtained from random sampling. The two remaining coefficients are significant at the 15 percent level, that is, regression coefficients of this size would occur randomly about 15 out of 100 times.[85]

This analysis suggests that the positively sloped supply curve hypothesis holds with a high degree of confidence in two of the four product markets, and with a moderate degree of confidence in one of the remaining two.[86] Experience in the kaffir corn market is neither consistent nor inconsistent with the hypothesis. Furthermore, the hypothesis that increases in production increase the proportion marketed also can be accepted with some confidence, as the figures for munga and kaffir corn show.

Yearly acreage data is, unfortunately, not available to correlate against price. The remarkable increase that occurred in groundnut, Turkish tobacco, and cotton production, under the influence of higher prices and better marketing facilities, gives further support to the view that the African is ready and able to take advantage of improved profit opportunities. A reading of official agriculture reports even gives weight to this position. As early as 1944, for example, one finds the Department of Agriculture noting a tendency for Africans to switch to kaffir corn cultivation because of an increase in the price paid for the crop during the year. The report goes on to state that, because kaffir corn does not store as well as other grains, the government reversed this situation by decreasing its support-price for kaffir corn.

An Improved Farming Scheme

One group of the rural African population that definitely benefited from the government's agricultural price-support program are those farmers who participate in the African Farming Improvement Scheme started in 1949. By agreeing to practice soil-conserving methods these farmers receive a cash subsidy from the government. The revenue for the subsidy is derived from

---

[85] The simple correlation coefficient between production and price is .00 for maize, .30 for munga, .30 for kaffir corn, and .33 for rupoko. Consequently except in the kaffir corn equation the multicollinearity problem is not significant.

[86] It should be stressed that the supply curve under discussion is the very short-period schedule in which production is held fixed.

a levy by the government on African maize production. The levy in effect represents an additional tax on the poorest sector of the African population. By 1955, 4 percent of the African farmers in the maize control areas had joined the program and they supplied 10 percent of the African maize sold to the maize board.[87]

Despite the fact that net receipts per bag of maize are about 50 percent higher for improved farmers than unimproved cultivators, the success of the scheme is open to question.[88] The program seems to be based more on the notions of what agricultural experts consider "good practices" than on the real economic opportunities confronting African producers. An improved farmer is permitted to plant only 50 percent of his acreage in maize. The other 50 percent must be planted with legumes, half of which must be plowed in as green manure. This system undoubtedly maintains a higher degree of soil fertility than the practices of unimproved farmers, but it is not necessarily an economically rational policy from a national viewpoint.

A study of the Sala area revealed that the per acre value of maize for improved cultivators was over two and one-half times greater than the per acre value of legumes.[89] Therefore, if an unimproved cultivator, who planted his entire acreage in maize, was able to produce a per acre yield equal to about two-thirds of the yield achieved by improved farmers, he could match the income (excluding the subsidy and neglecting the quantities of other inputs) of the improved farmer. In fact, this study showed the average per acre yield of the area planted with maize actually to be higher for unimproved than improved farmers.[90] The program in this region was clearly uneconomic. In the Tonga area, on the other hand, another study did show substantially higher yields for improved farmers and appeared to justify the scheme from the output side.[91] But when one considers that these improved farmers were much better educated, possessed farms twice as large as the unimproved farms, used substantially more manure, and owned one and three-fourths as many plows, the merits of the improved farming scheme even in this region seem doubtful.[92] It appears that the larger, more efficient unimproved farmers joined the scheme in the first place and, that therefore the generally higher

[87] Johnson, *op. cit.*, p. 13.
[88] *Ibid.*; Rees and Howard, *op. cit.*, p. 60.
[89] *Ibid.*, pp. 18, 40 and 43.
[90] *Ibid.*, p. 25.
[91] Johnson, *op. cit.*, p. 24.
[92] *Ibid.*

yield on improved farms may well merely reflect their higher yields prior to joining the program, rather than their new system of crop cultivation. It paid these farmers individually to join the scheme because of the bonus, but from a national viewpoint the subsidy may not have resulted in any greater output, especially when the output-depressing effect of the levy on unimproved farmers is taken into account. To quote C. E. Johnson's conclusion on the program, the yields of improved versus unimproved farmers are not high enough "to prove decisively the advantages of the improved farming system over the prevalent system of maize monoculture." [93]

Considering only the European farmers, the maize subsidization scheme appears unnecessarily costly. The one-third of the European farmers who produce two-thirds of the European crop, and thus receive two-thirds of the subsidy, are the producers whose yields are sufficiently high to continue production without such a high subsidy. Like so many such subsidy arrangements, the small, less efficient producer is used as the standard in setting the price. The result is that the more efficient farmers reap a large economic rent. The scheme also induced farmers to rely on maize as their main crop. Thus, income stability created by a balanced agricultural system was undermined by the maize program. Moreover, it appears likely that government-sponsored profits in the industry retarded the development of alternative crops that could be profitably exported without artificial price supports. [94]

CONCLUSIONS

In summary, the maize subsidy program represents a costly misallocation of funds. European agriculture was expanded at the expense of growth in other sectors of the economy and the income position of the territory as a whole. Maize purchasers not only benefit from a lower price if controls are removed, but the level of taxation can be reduced. Alternatively, if the tax level is not

---

[93] *Ibid.,* p. 25.

[94] For example, *Agricultural Policy in the Federation of Rhodesia and Nyasaland: Report to the Federal Minister of Agriculture by the Federal Standing Committee on Agricultural Production in Collaboration with Professor Sir Frank Engledow,* C. Fed. 77, Federation of Rhodesia and Nyasaland (Salisbury: Government Printer, 1958), p. 49, notes the detrimental effects of the maize policy on increasing groundnut production. African groundnut production near the line of rail is also retarded by the maize support program (*Report of the Rural Economic Development Working Party,* p. 20).

reduced, the funds released by removing the maize subsidy can
be utilized in more productive ways. It is difficult to imagine a
less useful expenditure of public funds than one for the European-
maize industry. There is general agreement that European costs
are much too high to enable the commodity ever to be profitably
exported on a regular basis, and the European industry is consequently, never likely to be able to stand on its own feet. If the
maize subsidy program is eliminated, the internal price would
fall to a level somewhere between the cost of importing and the
net export price—a difference of about 4s. per bag. European
farmers would suffer from the drop in price. But, in two of the
four surplus years since 1955 the net export price exceeded the
price paid African farmers, so that unimproved African farmers
would not necessarily lose if the maize levy on them also was
removed. The improved African cultivators would find their incomes reduced, but the usefulness of their subsidy is doubtful
anyway. Even if most African farmers should receive a lower
price for their output, an abandonment of the control system is
still desirable.[95] Encouraging African production of a commodity
for which both export possibilities and domestic market-growth
prospects are poor is no more justifiable from a national viewpoint for Africans than for Europeans. If Northern Rhodesian
agriculture is to act as a powerful, long-run force in the process
of raising income levels, agricultural programs must be directed
toward such export commodities as tobacco, livestock, and
groundnuts.

Appendix: A Note on Disguised Unemployment

Disguised unemployment is said to prevail in a rural economy if
part of the labor force can be permanently removed without
causing a decline in agricultural output.[96] In other words, the
concept describes a condition where the marginal productivity
of labor is zero. The Northern Rhodesian economy provides a
good opportunity to test this proposition as a large outflow of
labor took place from the subsistence sector. Cross-sectional and
time-series data on agricultural output are too imperfect to permit any useful statistical test on this point, but there are avail-

---

[95] Some form of price stabilization program is desirable, but it should be closely
related to international market conditions over a series of years.

[96] There must, of course, be no change in the capital stock, the state of technology, and natural resource conditions.

able many general observations concerning the effect on village economic activity of African urban migration. These are unanimous in agreeing that urban migration does reduce significantly the output of the rural economy. For example, Andrey Richards, who made perhaps the most detailed analysis of the effects of the outflow of labor from the villages, writes that "the dead appearance of villages with a large percentage of absent men is one of the most striking features of the country-side." [97] This view also was held for many years by government authorities, and one of their main reasons for proposing rural development schemes was to counter the depressing effects on the rural economy caused by labor migration.[98]

A much better body of evidence, which also does not support a disguised unemployment hypothesis, is the detailed anthropological studies concerning the pattern of work within the rural economy.[99] With respect to crop production in the subsistence sector, the men direct their labor activities primarily toward the capital outlays necessary for cultivation, whereas the women undertake the recurrent activities required for production. For example, clearing new fields, tree-cutting under the chitemene system, building granaries, and fencing the gardens are male activities, whereas weeding and harvesting are mainly female pursuits. The men build and repair the huts, and make most of the durable consumer goods not purchased from the urban economy. The women thresh and grind the grain, collect wild vegetables and edible leaves, brew the beer, and do the cooking. When the men are not needed to perform their capital-creating activities, they fish, hunt, take care of the cattle (in those parts of the country where they can be kept), or simply sit around and talk.

A significant amount of seasonal unemployment does exist in the subsistence sector, especially for men, but there are periods during the year when all available male labor is fully utilized in productive activity: at the beginning of the rainy season in November when planting takes place, and again from May to

---

[97] Audrey I. Richards, *Land, Labour and Diet in Northern Rhodesia* (London: Oxford University Press, 1939), p. 405.

[98] See, for example, *Report of the Rural Economic Development Working Party*, pp. 2–5.

[99] Examples of these studies are Richards, *op. cit.*, pp. 381–405; Edwin W. Smith and A. M. Dale, *The Ila-Speaking Peoples of Northern Rhodesia* (London: Macmillan, 1920), I, 140–142; C. M. Doke, *The Lambas of Northern Rhodesia* (London: George G. Harrap, 1931), pp. 94–99; Max Gluckman, *The Economy of the Central Barotse Plain*, Rhodes-Livingstone Papers, no. 7 (Livingstone: Rhodes-Livingstone Institute, 1941), pp. 53–66.

June when tree-cutting or the clearing of new fields occurs. Studies made by anthropologists frequently point out that the output of families in which most or all of the men are absent during these times is significantly less than the output of families whose male members are at home during these periods.[100] Other indirect evidence that the marginal productivity of labor is well above zero at these times can be found in the time pattern of rural-urban migration. Requests for long leave from the copper mines are so heavy at these times of the year that it would be impossible to grant them all without crippling production. The highest quitting rates in the industry also occur at the beginning of the rainy season and again from May to June.[101] It seems unlikely that the many mine workers who retire to the rural sector before the mandatory age would do so unless their marginal productivity were positive. The same applies to the women in the villages. A significant number of miners leave their wives at home even though married accommodations can now be obtained from the mines. A major cause of this would seem to be that these women do increase the family's income by working in the rural economy. For these reasons, disguised unemployment does not appear to be a condition generally characterizing the subsistence economy in Northern Rhodesia or Central Africa.

[100] Richards, *op. cit.*, p. 298; Elizabeth Colson, *The Social Organization of the Gwembe Tonga* (Manchester: Manchester University Press, 1960), pp. 91–93.

[101] Based on evidence obtained from the Roan Antelope Copper Mines, Luanshya, Northern Rhodesia, in 1961.

7

Transportation, Power, and Secondary Industry

RAILWAYS

One of the first interindustry repercussions touched off by the development of Northern Rhodesian mining was the construction of a railroad into the territory from Southern Rhodesia. Without a railway a significant mining industry could not have been established, and without the mining industry, it is doubtful if the railroad would have been built until many years later. The long distances involved in opening up the country meant that only industries producing commodities with high value:weight ratios were capable of supporting a railroad. Agricultural prospects during the early part of the century were not bright enough to meet this condition, but mineral prospects were sufficiently lucrative to warrant the investment needed to establish simultaneously a mining and a railway industry.

Copper, however, was not the mineral that first sparked Northern Rhodesian railway development. The first stretch of the line was constructed from Livingstone to reach the lead and zinc deposits at Broken Hill. The British South Africa Company, in building this line, was motivated more by the prospects of increased mineral royalties than by transportation receipts. The company's dual financial interest undoubtedly accelerated the development of the railway system beyond what would have taken place if the mines and railroads had represented separate financial interests. The company was able to capture the external economies of the railway industry on the mining industry, and vice versa.

The extension of the railway from Broken Hill to the Congo border in 1909 did not involve these joint interests. The rapidly developing Katanga copper mines wished to connect with the Rhodesian system mainly to obtain coke from the Wankie Colliery deposits in Southern Rhodesia.[1] They also needed a rail link to provide an ocean outlet for their copper until the Benguela line to Lobito Bay, Angola, was completed.[2] But the British South Africa Company did not possess mineral rights in Katanga and was, as usual, hard pressed financially. It refused to build the extension with its own resources. Instead, the company permitted a new firm, the Rhodesian-Katanga Junction Railway and Mineral Company, to be formed for the purpose of extending the line from Broken Hill to the Congo border. The company did, however, retain the option to purchase the extension, and finally exercised this right in 1928, when it was obvious that copper developments within the country would make the railway extremely profitable.

Unfortunately, mineral exploitation after the completion of the rail line from Livingstone to the Congo had little effect in stimulating additional railroad development. The Katanga copper deposits are just across the border from the Rhodesian Copperbelt, and therefore, the line from Broken Hill to the Congo passed very close to the Copperbelt area. When the potential profitability of the Rhodesian ores was finally recognized in the twenties, the only effect on the railway system was the construction of a few short spur lines from the main line into the copper fields. Other than the copper and cobalt deposits near the Katanga border and the lead and zinc deposits at Broken Hill, no mineral wealth has been discovered that is sufficiently attractive to justify large-scale exploitation, with the result that there was no stimulus to the extension of the railway system into other parts of the country. As noted, the best agricultural land happened to be close to the line of rail, a circumstance that provided no stimulus to further railroad expansion when agricultural development of the region began. The construction of a short line from Livingstone to the forest areas northwest of the city, for

---

[1] Emile B. d'Erlanger, *The History of the Construction and Finance of the Rhodesian Transport System* (London: Burrup Mathieson, 1939), p. 29.

[2] There were many delays in the construction of this line, and it was not finished until 1931.

transporting timber to the Zambezi Sawmills, was the only other significant railroad development. Both Southern Rhodesia and the Republic of South Africa were more fortunate. Mineral deposits in these countries are more widely scattered and a more elaborate system of branch lines was constructed. Areas, which could not by themselves attract a railroad, became profitable for agricultural and industrial development because they were located near a rail line.[3] But on the basis of the railway in Northern Rhodesia, only a thin, nearly straight strip of land close to the one line has been able to develop.

There have been many suggestions for extending the Northern Rhodesian rail system. These include running a line from Sinoia (just north of Salisbury) to Kafue (just south of Lusaka), as well as building a link from Ndola to Dar es Salaam in Tanzania. The first project would cut 400 miles off the Copperbelt–Beira, Mozambique, trip, whereas the second would reduce the length of this route by only 100 miles. The conclusion reached by a team appointed to survey the prospects of the Tanzania (Tanganyika) link are relevant to all of the various proposals.

In conclusion we would stress that with the exception of the southwest Tanganyika mineralised area, development must be based almost entirely on agriculture, and those responsible will be wise to consider whether some part of the funds which would be spent on rail construction, equipment and bearing initial losses could not better be devoted in the early phases of development to highgrade all weather roads, to the promotion of agricultural developments of various kinds and possibly, in the early stages, to the lowering of road freights by government assistance. These steps we think would be as helpful in building up food production, which is so essential to Africa, as would be a railway and would cost very much less.[4]

The Benguela railway to Lobito Bay provides an alternative access to the industrial areas of the northern hemisphere via the west coast of Africa, but it has not been utilized very extensively. In order to prevent a loss of traffic to this competitive railroad company, Rhodesia Railways has so controlled its rates on the short part of its line which must be used to reach the Benguela

---

[3] In the Republic of South Africa, for example, with only a few exceptions, no area is more than 50 miles from a railroad, whereas over 5/6 of Northern Rhodesia is more than 50 miles from a railroad (H. R. Fraser, "Economic Survey of the Federation of Rhodesia and Nyasaland" [Salisbury, 1957], I, 58, copy in library of the Anglo-American Corporation of South Africa, Salisbury).

[4] *Report on Central African Rail Link Development Survey*, Great Britain, Colonial Office (London: H.M.S.O., June, 1952), I, 33.

line from the Copperbelt, that the west coast route has not proved particularly attractive.[5]

Besides providing the initial impetus to railway construction, the mining industry has continued to be the major customer of the railways. Table 2-4 shows that in 1957 Rhodesia Railways derived 60 percent of its Northern Rhodesian revenue from the copper industry. The railroad, in turn, made significant purchases of other Northern Rhodesian productive inputs. For example, Rhodesia Railways employed within Northern Rhodesia 5,875 Africans in 1960 and paid these employees wage rates that were second highest in the industrial sector only to the copper industry. The number of Europeans employed by the company was also substantial.[6] An important feature of labor activities in the railway industry is the high skill component (a fact indicated by the comparatively high ratio of Europeans to Africans). An opportunity for acquiring industrial and commercial skills thus existed for the indigenous population. As in the copper industry, the European employees have succeeded in preventing substantial African advancement.

During the late twenties, at the time of extensive construction activity in the Copperbelt and the Congo, the railway enjoyed a comfortable income. But the profit picture suddenly changed with the collapse of the copper market in the thirties, and no dividends were paid from 1931 to 1938.[7] Owing to lack of capital funds in the thirties, and the inability to obtain capital during the war, the railway system by 1946 was in a very poor state of repair. This condition, and the absence of financial resources needed for modernization, were the major factors causing the Southern Rhodesian government to purchase the whole of the share capital of Rhodesia Railways in 1947. Although Southern Rhodesia assumed responsibility for the financial arrangements necessary for acquisition, Northern Rhodesia and Bechuanaland were represented in the management of the railway and agreed to underwrite part of any deficit arising in the future servicing of loans.[8] The railway became a statutory body in 1949, and, after

---

[5] "A Port for the Copperbelt," *Rhodesian Recorder*, May, 1956.

[6] In its annual reports the company unfortunately does not break down its European employees by number employed in Southern versus Northern Rhodesia. In 1960 there were 9,887 European and 21,710 African employees in the entire system.

[7] "Report of the General Manager," 1947, Rhodesia Railways (Bulawayo), p. 2.

[8] "The Industrial Directory and Brand-Names Index of Rhodesia and Nyasaland," Association of Rhodesia and Nyasaland Industries (Salisbury, 1960), p. 5.

federation in 1953, it came under the control of the federal government.

Between 1947 and 1960 average investment expenditure on the railway system exceeded £5 million annually.[9] Much of the capital improvement was directed toward meeting the requirements of the mining industry in Northern and Southern Rhodesia, for the rapid growth in postwar mineral output had placed a tremendous strain on the railway's facilities. Unfortunately, long delays in the delivery of equipment prevented the pressure on the system from being quickly relieved. Immediately after the war, for example, delivery delays on locomotives lasted more than 2 years. The lack of adequate transportation facilities hit the Northern Rhodesian copper mines especially hard with regard to their coal requirements. From 1946 to 1957 almost every annual report of the copper companies stressed the difficulties caused by inadequate coal supplies. On several occasions the mines actually were forced to close down for a few days because of coal shortages. The difficulty did not lie entirely with the railway system, however. Even when railway space was available, the Wankie Colliery in Southern Rhodesia often was not able to supply the coal.

Several steps were taken to alleviate these problems. In order to supply needed electric power, a large cordwood-cutting and -burning operation was instituted on the Copperbelt. Large quantities of coal were also imported from the Republic of South Africa and the United States via the Lobito Bay rail route. For several years the mines even recruited labor for the Wankie Colliery. By doing this, they were given a larger coal quota by the colliery. Finally, in 1953, the Anglo-American Corporation of South Africa assumed the administrative and technical management of the Wankie Colliery.[10] The company guaranteed the Southern Rhodesian government it would raise output from the then prevailing 2.7 million short tons annually to not less than 5 million tons per year, and agreed to invest £6 million in the coal mines. In return, it received a long-term agreement with regard to the rate of profit per ton of coal.

The change in management succeeded in alleviating the coal-production shortage, and soon the railway system again was the

[9] H. B. Muskett, *Steel Highway* (Bulawayo: Rhodesia Railways, 1957); "Annual Report," for the years 1947–1960, Rhodesia Railways (Bulawayo).

[10] "Annual Report," 1954, Anglo-American Corporation of South Africa (Johannesburg), p. 32.

bottleneck. To help ease the situation, Anglo-American purchased nearly £8 million of rolling stock and then rented this equipment to Rhodesia Railways.[11] In addition, Anglo-American lent £1 million to Rhodesia Railways. Most of the funds used to modernize the railway system—and thereby provide adequate capacity—came, however, from the federal and territorial governments, the International Bank for Reconstruction and Development, and the United States. The federal government lent £21.8 million, Southern Rhodesia £35.0 million, and Northern Rhodesia £9.7 million. The International Bank made two loans for railway development, one of $14 million and another of $19 million (a total of about £11.8 million). Two loans also were granted under the United States foreign aid program. These loans were for £5 million and $10 million (a total of about £8.6 million).[12]

ROADS

Good road facilities were not very extensive in Northern Rhodesia, even in 1960. Except for the highway that closely followed the railway line from Livingstone to Ndola, and the roads that connected the Copperbelt towns, surfaces were almost entirely gravel or earth.[13] The number of vehicles using these roads was also small. In 1960 only 37,000 cars, trucks, and buses were registered in the territory.[14]

The government's allocation of funds for road construction—as for most government activities—was directed, until recently, mainly toward the European monetary sector. Since Europeans furnished most of the tax revenue and directed economic activity

[11] Sir Ronald L. Prain, "Building on a Mineral Foundation," in *Rhodesia and East Africa*, ed. F. S. Joelson (London: East Africa and Rhodesia, 1958), p. 246.

[12] Loan data from "Annual Report," 1959, Rhodesia Railways (Bulawayo).

[13] A 1941 study estimated that the cost of motor transportation could be reduced from 15 to 10 pence per mile if "improved road conditions" replaced the then present road conditions (*Memorandum on the Work of the National Development Board*, Northern Rhodesia [Lusaka: Government Printer, 1941], p. 35). Somewhat more specific information on the costs associated with gravel and earth roads versus tarmac roads is contained in a 1951 report on the operations of the major public motor carrier in the country. The company stated that it must overhaul its diesel vehicles every 50,000 miles on earth and gravel roads compared with 100,000 miles on tarmac roads. It also pointed out that only 55 percent of its vehicles were on the road at one time because of the need for repair. With tarmac road conditions, it was claimed that 90 percent of their vehicles would be on the road (*Report of the Motor Transport Commission, 1951*, Northern Rhodesia [Lusaka: Government Printer, 1951], p. 86).

[14] *Annual Report for the Year 1960*, Northern Rhodesia, Ministry of Transport and Works (Lusaka: Government Printer, 1961), p. 113.

in the sector, this expenditure pattern seemed eminently reasonable to the European-dominated legislature. Some roads were needed in rural areas in order to maintain adequate administrative control, but beyond that, objective attempts to provide a road system in the subsistence sector were not given serious consideration. In particular no concerted effort was made to stimulate cash agriculture in some of the subsistence areas by means of a balanced rural development program that included considerable emphasis on better roads.[15] One gains the impression in studying government activities between 1920 and 1960 that, until the late fifties, the fear of African agricultural competition by Europeans prevented the formulation of such a program.

POWER

The development of the electric-power industry in Northern Rhodesia was even more closely linked with the expansion of mining than was the construction of the railway system. In the metal-mining industry of the federation, electricity costs represent 12 percent of the total value of output, illustrating how vitally important adequate power facilities were to the industry.[16] The lead and zinc mine at Broken Hill became the first big user of electricity, when in 1925 the Rhodesia Broken Hill Development Company installed the first hydroelectric plant in the subcontinent.[17] The project was located in the Mulungushi River, about 35 miles east of Broken Hill, and consisted of a 2-Mw generator. This was supplemented in 1927 by two 6-Mw units, and the capacity was eventually increased to 20 Mw in 1945. Another project on the Lunsemfwa River was brought into operation in the same year, so that the company's total capacity rose to 32 Mw in 1945.

The copper mines followed the same practice of building their

[15] The significance of transportation cost in agricultural prices is illustrated by the following data, relating to African farmers in the Eastern Province. In 1959 the price of maize delivered on the line of rail was 35s. per bag, but the cost of transporting the maize to the line of rail was 21s. 6d. per bag. In addition to this charge, 1s. 6d. per bag was subtracted as a levy to be used for improved farming schemes. Consequently, the Eastern Province farmer received only 12s. per bag net. The average sales price of his burley tobacco was 22d. per pound, but transportation and handling costs reduced his net return on this product to 11 1/4d. per pound.

[16] "Economic Development in Northern Rhodesia, Study Conference, number 2," sponsored by the United Northern Rhodesia Association (Lusaka, 1958), p. 53.

[17] G. Bradford, "Electric Power for Future Economic Development of the Rhodesias," *Optima*, III (June, 1953), 9.

own power plants. The four mines that were opened in the thirties—Roan Antelope, Rhokana, Mufulira, and Nchanga— each built steam-power plants. The capacity of these four plants and the power facilities at Broken Hill amounted to 229.8 Mw in 1957, or more than 87 percent of the installed capacity in the territory.[18] In order to reduce costs by meeting the peak-load problem more satisfactorily, the Roan Antelope and Mufulira power systems were interconnected in 1938, and the Rhokana and Nchanga power facilities were joined to these two in 1948. A separate company, the Rhodesian Congo Border Power Corporation, was set up by the copper companies in 1952 to distribute this power among the various mines and municipal townships in the Copperbelt area.

Despite the elaborate power system owned by the mines in the early fifties, the difficulty of obtaining coal supplies from Wankie forced them to seek an alternative source of electric power. In 1954 Rhodesian Selection Trust estimated, for example, that their cost per long ton of copper would be £8.35, instead of £11.57, if all the needed coal could be obtained from Wankie. As a result of this search, a tripartite agreement among the Union Miniere du Haut Katanga, the United States government, and the two Rhodesian copper companies (Rhodesian Selection Trust and Anglo-American) was signed in 1953 with regard to the undertaking of the Marinel Hydro-Electric Scheme in the Congo. The Export-Import Bank of the United States advanced to Union Miniere, who owns and operates the Marinel plant, £8 million to help build the project, and the copper companies themselves lent another £7 million.[19] The terms of the American loan were that the loan was to be repaid in deliveries of copper and cobalt. The Marinel project was commissioned in September, 1956, and the full, long-term contractual supply of 500 million kwh annually was delivered to the Rhodesian copper companies soon thereafter.

This project greatly eased the power shortage for the mines but did not remove it completely. The mining companies were still anxious for expansion of hydroelectric power within the federation in order to obtain electricity at a lower rate than was

[18] *Second Report of the Secretary for Power Covering 1 July 1957 to 30 June 1958*, Federation of Rhodesia and Nyasaland (Salisbury: Government Printer, 1959), p. 13.

[19] "Annual Report, 1955," Rhodesia Congo Border Power Corporation (Kitwe, 1956), p. 2.

possible from their own steam plants. Most Northern Rhodesians favored a hydroelectric project on the Kafue River, but the federal government finally selected a site on the Zambezi River. The construction of a dam at the Kariba gorge on the Zambezi River was selected over a site on the Kafue River mainly because of the larger power potential at Kariba. Although the copper companies preferred the Kafue project on the grounds that it would be completed sooner than Kariba, they did not have strong opinions on the matter and were quite willing to aid in the financing of the Kariba project. This scheme consists of two stages. The first stage was completed in 1962, possessed a power capacity of 600 Mw (initially a 500-Mw capacity was planned for the first stage), and cost approximately £75 million.[20] The second stage will increase capacity to 1,200 Mw and supposedly will be completed by 1971. The original estimate of the two-stage undertaking was £113 million.

The mining companies made a large contribution to the financial requirements of the first stage. Rhodesian Selection Trust and Anglo-American lent £20 million to the federal government for the purpose of building Kariba, and the British South Africa Company contributed another £4 million.[21] In addition to these private firms, two banks—the Standard Bank of South Africa and Barclays Bank, D.C.O.—each made loans of £2 million. Other sources of funds were the International Bank for Reconstruction and Development (£28.5 million), the Colonial Development Corporation (£15 million), and the Commonwealth Development Finance Corporation (£3 million). In addition, the federal government agreed to advance £6 million if needed.

Power first began to flow from Kariba to the Copperbelt in January, 1960, and the project was officially opened in May of that year. The mines immediately curtailed production of power from their own high-cost stations, and in the half year ending June, 1960,[22] derived only about 30 percent of their power consumption from these stations. Since the projected 1970–71 power requirements for Northern and Southern Rhodesia can be met

[20] *Annual Report and Accounts for the Year Ended 30th June, 1960,* Federation of Rhodesia and Nyasaland, Federal Power Board (Salisbury, 1960), p. 25.

[21] The copper companies also agreed to accept a surcharge on Kariba power determined so as to return to the Federal Power Board a total of £10 million between 1961 and 1967 ("Annual Report, 1955," Rhodesia Congo Border Power Corporation, p. 2).

[22] "Interim Accounts for Half Year Ended 30 June 1960," Rhodesia Congo Border Power Corporation (Kitwe).

from Kariba alone, the power-shortage problem appears to be solved for at least several years, providing the second stage of the Kariba project is completed.

One of the most favorable interindustry effects associated with the building of the Kariba project was the expansion impact on the cement industry in Northern Rhodesia. On the basis of contracts to supply cement for the project, the industry increased its annual capacity in 1956 from 60,000 tons annually to 180,000 tons.[23] Construction of the dam, transporting materials to the area, building of houses for employees, and resettling more than 50,000 Africans also provided jobs for large numbers of workers. Between 1956 and 1958 European and African employment averaged 1,240 and 6,200 respectively.[24] Although the labor coefficient for construction activities is high, the labor coefficient is not large for the actual operation of a hydroelectric power station. By 1960, when most construction had been completed, European employment had dropped to 250 and African employment to 1,500.[25]

SECONDARY INDUSTRY

The lack of any substantial manufacturing industry in Northern Rhodesia has already been indicated (see tables 2-3 and 2-4), but the data presented on manufacturing in the territory understates its extent because of the classification system used. Most of the mining companies' activities are lumped together under mining, but many of them are in fact manufacturing activities, the most obvious being smelting and refining. In addition to these two are many other manufacturing activities performed in the mining companies' own workshops. The Central Statistical Office has had to abandon its attempt to split up these processes because of the

---

[23] "Rhodesia," *A Financial Times Survey of Rhodesia and Nyasaland* (London), Oct. 21, 1957. In 1958 the Chilanga Cement Company supplied 115,000 tons for the Kariba project (*Annual Report and Accounts for the Year Ended 30 June, 1958,* Federation of Rhodesia and Nyasaland, Federal Power Board [Salisbury: Rhodesian Printers, 1959], p. 30).

[24] *Annual Report and Accounts for the Year Ended 30th June, 1960,* Federation of Rhodesia and Nyasaland, Federal Power Board.

[25] *Ibid.* The experience with recruiting and holding African workers during the construction of the project was interesting. In 1956 it was necessary to recruit most of the labor from Nyasaland (through the Rhodesia Native Labour Supply Commission) because the supply of voluntary labor was insufficient. By 1958 the voluntary labor supply had improved substantially—though individuals stayed no longer than 3 to 4 months—and only a part of the labor force was recruited. By 1960, however, the statement appears in the annual report of the power board that Africans are reluctant to leave Kariba.

difficulty of securing reliable data. It tried, though, for one in-dustrial-census year, 1956–57. In that year gross output of manu-facturing in Northern Rhodesia was listed as £182 billion, or 75 percent of the combined output of mining, manufacturing, construction, electricity, and water. When the 1956–57 figures were reworked the next year without isolating the manufacturing functions of the mining companies, the manufacturing share dropped to 9 percent.

On the other hand, the failure to classify separately as manu-facturing some of the productive activities of the mines also tends to overstate the recent growth of manufacturing. The mines have deliberately attempted in recent years to turn over these manufacturing functions to outside firms. Specifically, in order to encourage the growth of such enterprises, they purchase needed goods and services from firms located within Northern Rhode-sia as long as the prices charged by these firms are not more than 5 percent higher than those charged by outside companies. The result of this policy of stimulating local manufacturing is that some new lines appearing as manufactures in the industrial census merely represent a classification change. The mill-ball industry is a case in point. Mufulira formerly produced its own mill balls from scrap steel but now buys them from a firm located on the Copperbelt. The new firm even purchased the smelting furnace that Mufulira formerly used for this purpose.

The nature of the manufacturing sector was determined mainly by the technological character of the mining industry. The cop-per industry uses large amounts of highly specialized machinery and supplies. In turn, many of these items require abundant quantities of skilled labor and the existence of large markets to make production profitable. But in Northern Rhodesia skilled-wage rates are very high, and the size of the market for the items is small. Reasonably cheap sources of supply for a number of these commodities do exist in the Republic of South Africa and—to a growing extent—in Southern Rhodesia. The industrial market is much larger in these countries, and this factor more than offsets the transportation advantages of locating in Northern Rhodesia for all but a few industries. Mining machinery, structural steel, electrical apparatus, vehicles, explosives, bearings, rails, fittings, and piping are all imported from these two countries or from overseas. Northern Rhodesia suffers, in other words, both from the narrowness of its industrial market and its nearness to areas where the market is much larger.

The absence of a significant industrial base capable of supplying the needs of the mining industry, and the high degree of foreign ownership of the mining industry, are manifested in the high import content of both exports and investment. A. C. Irvine calculated these ratios for the federation as a whole from 1949 to 1954.[26] He found the import content of exports to be 40 percent over this period and the import content of investment to be 63 percent.[27] Comparable figures for Northern Rhodesia alone would undoubtedly be even higher.

Manufactured commodities produced in the territory usually are characterized by the following features: high transportation costs in relation to the value of the product; the local availability of necessary raw materials; and an ability to produce the product efficiently on a small scale. The cement industry, for example, proved feasible because of the relatively high cost of transporting cement and because a comparatively small plant was efficient. This industry was developed soon after the war under the initiative of the government and with the aid of funds supplied by the Colonial Development Corporation. Subsequently, the cement works, which are located near Lusaka, were sold to a private enterprise. As noted, the cement demand from the Kariba project was responsible for a large expansion of the firm. Another industry whose existence in the country is mainly determined by the transportation factor is the construction industry. The presence of large supplies of Rhodesian teak and native timbers are the significant factors accounting for the sawmill and furniture industries in the country.[28] The meat slaughtering, dairy, and grain-mill industries are also partly dependent on the raw-material factor. Furthermore, the absence of significant economies of scale characterizes all manufacturing, other than copper. The clothing, drink and tobacco, furniture, chemical, and engineering indus-

---

[26] A. G. Irvine, *The Balance of Payments of Rhodesia and Nyasaland, 1945–1954* (London: Oxford University Press, 1959), p. 598.

[27] *Ibid.* The goods and services import content of exports of goods and services, that is, excluding income payments derived from exports, was 17 percent. The same relation for investment was 62 percent.

[28] The main timber firm in the territory is Zambezi Sawmills, which is located near Livingstone. It is also one of the oldest companies in Northern Rhodesia, having started production in 1916. Besides railway sleepers, the firm also manufactures furniture and blocks for parquet flooring (J. D. Martin, "The Mukushi [Baikiaea Plurifuga Harms] Forests of Northern Rhodesia," in *Second Agricultural Bulletin of the Department of Agriculture 1932*, Northern Rhodesia [Livingstone: Government Printer, 1933], p. 74).

tries, for example, owe their existence in the territory largely to this consideration.

One favorable aspect of the copper industry that should be stressed again in discussing local industry is its training of labor. This is illustrated by the mines' gradual shift from performing many construction and manufacturing activities themselves to purchasing the commodities and services produced by such activities from outside firms. At the start, the mines found it necessary to recruit labor from abroad for the purpose of producing these items. Once the mining companies determined that there existed an experienced local group that had acquired the managerial and labor skills necessary to carry on certain manufacturing and construction operations independently, they eliminated those activities from their mining operations. It became cheaper for the companies to purchase many goods and services from outside firms.[29] Some skilled workers and entrepreneurs voluntarily migrated from other countries to the Copperbelt area to establish firms for this purpose, but many of the small industrial firms in the Copperbelt were organized by former European employees of the mines. Had the latter not acquired specialized knowledge and training at the mines, many of these firms would not have been formed. The knowledge of specialized, small market opportunities does not spread easily abroad to those particular individuals who would be willing to exploit them. Moreover, the indivisibilities associated with foreign recruitment efforts apparently made it too costly for the mines themselves to undertake deliberate efforts to obtain these individuals. Once the firms were established, however, they began to branch out into operations beyond servicing the copper industry, thereby stimulating further growth in the economy.

A similar point applies with regard to African labor. The copper mines became the great training school of Northern Rhodesia. Although Africans were blocked from obtaining training in skilled labor, they acquired simple skills and industrial work habits that greatly increased their labor efficiency compared to its level in the early twenties. Entrepreneurs starting small manufacturing firms could hire from this relatively large pool of trained labor at the prevailing rates paid by the mines. In this way they

---

[29] After wage rates at the mines rose to artificially high levels, the labor unions in the industry insisted that the copper companies deal only with local contractors who maintained the same wage scale as that prevailing in the industry.

could avoid the not-inconsiderable costs of familiarizing rural recruits with even the simplest tasks of modern mechanized industry.[30] As a result, small manufacturing firms, which would otherwise not have been profitable, were introduced into the economy. The monopolistic wage structure established in the industrial sector, and the failure to undertake a substantial African advancement program, undoubtedly prevented more domestic industry, but the labor training provided by the copper industry was a most important and favorable development repercussion.

The technology of copper production influenced the development of manufacturing in another important way. As previously discussed (pp. 65 ff.), it was a major factor in accounting for the economy's very unequal distribution of income. The income distribution, together with the comparatively low ratio of total wages to gross output, affected demand and, in turn, manufacturing prospects. The highly paid European sector followed an expenditure pattern similar to that found in rich, developed countries. Yet the total demand by Europeans for many of the items in their budgets was too small to support local industry. The import content of consumption expenditure by Europeans therefore was high. Africans, on the other hand, did not possess the spending power needed to follow the European spending pattern. For example, Europeans devoted 32 percent of their consumption expenditure to food, drink, and tobacco; urban Africans spent 60 percent of their budget on these items (table 7-1). As a consequence, the African propensity to import is significantly lower than the European. It is difficult to estimate the extent of these import propensities, but G. A. Hay and R. W. Jones calculated that the average propensity to import out of domestic market expenditure within the federation was 19 and 43 percent for Africans and non-Africans, respectively, residing in Northern Rhodesia; they estimated the import propensity for the federation as a whole to be 32.5 percent.[31] The result of this high import propensity and the large leakages associated directly with exports and investment expenditure is that the export and investment

---

[30] The labor-supply curve for these trained workers was perfectly elastic for small producers but (until recently) not for the copper mines. Consequently, it did not pay the mines to bid these workers back since it also would necessitate increasing wage rates for the large numbers of the trained workers already employed. Instead, it paid the mines to hire and train additional workers directly from the villages, since this labor-supply curve was highly elastic for the mines.

[31] Data given to the author by G. A. Hay and R. W. Jones in a personal conversation.

TABLE 7-1

EUROPEAN AND AFRICAN CONSUMPTION-EXPENDITURE PATTERNS

Item	Europeans (percentages)	Africans (percentages)	Income elasticity (for urban Africans)[a]
Food, except for servants	25.2	44.4	.68
Housing			
Rents, rates, and water	5.8	—	
Fuel and light	3.0	3.3	.82
Household stores	4.1	6.0	.95
Consumer capital goods	3.6	2.5[b]	1.28
Clothing and footwear	9.4	17.7	1.19
Miscellaneous			
Drink and tobacco	6.9	16.0	.68
Car, motorcycle, cycle	5.3	2.6	2.18
Servants	7.6	—	
Other current	11.3		
Holidays	4.0	7.5	1.76
Other periodical	13.6		
Total	99.8	100.0	

[a] The Central Statistical Office estimated income elasticities for the various items on the basis of the change in consumption resulting from a hypothetical wage increase of £1 per month for all African wage earners. The marginal propensity to save obtained by these calculations amounts to a figure of 13.2 percent. For all Africans and non-Africans in Northern Rhodesia, G. A. Hay and R. W. Jones estimated saving/disposable-income ratios of 7.7 percent and 19.5 percent, respectively (data given to the author in a personal conversation).

[b] Furniture and radios have been taken out of the Central Statistical Office's household stores class to make up the category, consumer capital goods.

SOURCES: European budget from *Report on Northern Rhodesia Family Expenditure Survey, 1951*, Federation of Rhodesia and Nyasaland, Central Statistical Office (Salisbury: Government Printer, 1953), p. 23; African budget from "Second Report on Urban African Budget Survey Held in Northern Rhodesia May to August 1960," Federation of Rhodesia and Nyasaland, Central Statistical Office (Salisbury: Government Printer, 1961), pp. 14–16.

multipliers are very low in Northern Rhodesia. Irvine's estimates for the federation between 1950 and 1954 are an export multiplier of from 1.25 to 1.8 and an investment multiplier of about 0.6.[32] A £1 million increment in exports and in investment, respectively, in other words, increases gross national product only by between £1.25 to £1.8 million and £.6 million respectively.

[32] Irvine, *op. cit.*, pp. 598–608.

8

The Public Sector

One of the most striking features of the copper industry's inter-sector payments pattern is the large flow of tax funds to the government. As is indicated in chapter 2, in 1956–57 taxes paid by the industry equaled its total wage and salary payments (table 2-4). Although profits—and thus taxes—were exceptionally high that year, payments to the government and to households invariably have constituted the two largest sector-outlays made by the industry.

The government's contribution toward stimulating development by means of its expenditure policies depended not only upon the magnitude of available funds, but also how they were spent. In this chapter it is pointed out that the Northern Rhodesian government was in a favorable position with regard to the availability of funds—mainly because of tax revenue from the copper industry. But the government was primarily interested in using its funds to promote growth in the European monetary sector (chaps. 6, 7). Expenditures designed specifically to foster African rural development were surprisingly modest. It is also argued here that the programs of limited expenditures for this purpose were not very effective.

CURRENT REVENUE AND EXPENDITURE

Government revenue originating within Northern Rhodesia increased almost one hundredfold between 1925–26 and 1959–60 (table 8-1). There also was a considerable shift in the source of revenue between these years. Before the copper industry's growth the bulk of the government's revenue receipts came from import

TABLE 8-1

GOVERNMENT REVENUE ORIGINATING IN NORTHERN RHODESIA
FOR SELECTED YEARS
(thousands of pounds)

Revenue category	1925–26	1938	1959–60
Northern Rhodesia government			
Customs and excise	83	265	—
Native tax	111	112	331
Income tax	61	750	5,663
Territorial surcharge	—	—	2,115
Share of revenue from mineral rights	—	—	2,622
Fees and payment for special services and earnings of government departments	55	114	1,189
Reimbursement by federal government	—	—	1,041
Interest	2	30	2,478
All other revenue	59	89	1,283
Total[a]	371	1,360	16,722
Federal revenue from Northern Rhodesia, excluding Northern Rhodesia's share of federal income tax[b]	—	—	19,500
Grand total	371	1,360	36,222

[a] Total and preceding breakdown from *Financial Report for the Year Ended 30th June 1960*, Northern Rhodesia (Lusaka: Government Printer, 1961), pp. 8–13.

[b] Federal revenue for 1959–60 from first column of table 8-2 (£25.2 million), less portion of federal income tax returned to Northern Rhodesia (£5.7 million).

SOURCES: *Financial Report for the Year Ended 30th June 1960*; *Report of the Commission Appointed To Enquire into the Financial and Economic Position of Northern Rhodesia*, Colonial, no. 145, Great Britain, Colonial Office (London: H.M.S.O., 1938), Appendix IX.

duties, the native tax, income from the sale of land, and miscellaneous revenues from school, hospital, post, and telegraph services. Only about 16 percent of the revenue in 1925–26 was accounted for by the income tax, and the contribution by the mining industry was insignificant.[1] By 1938, when the copper mines were well established, the situation was markedly different. In that year 54 percent of the government's revenue was derived from income taxes. Of the £750,000 obtained from this source it was estimated that £585,000, or 43 percent of all government revenue, was furnished by the mining industry.[2]

[1] *Report of the Commission Appointed To Enquire into the Financial and Economic Position of Northern Rhodesia*, Colonial, no. 145, Great Britain, Colonial Office (London: H.M.S.O., 1938), Appendix IX, hereafter referred to as the *Pim Report*.

[2] *Rhodesia-Nyasaland Royal Commission Report*, Cmd. 5949, Great Britain (London: H.M.S.O., 1939), pp. 66, 67, hereafter referred to as the *Bledisloe Commission*.

At this time the tax of companies was at a flat 4s. per pound on realized profits.

A determination of government revenue originating within Northern Rhodesia is complicated after 1953 by the divided revenue responsibilities of the territorial and federal governments. The federal government possessed the sole power to make laws with respect to customs duties and excise taxes (other than on "motor spirits"), taxes on income and profits, and other taxes on the sale of goods (other than motor spirits). The federal government also had the power to impose fees for such services as posts and telegraphs. It was obliged, however, to redistribute part of the proceeds of the basic federal income tax to the territorial governments.[3] The proportions of distribution prevailing in 1960 were: Southern Rhodesia, 14 percent; Northern Rhodesia, 18 percent; and Nyasaland, 6 percent. The remaining 62 percent was used to finance federal activities. In addition to Northern Rhodesia's share of the basic federal income tax, the three main revenue sources of the territorial government were a surcharge on the taxable income of companies equal to 20 percent of the federal income tax,[4] a 20 percent tax on the mineral royalties paid by the mining companies to the British South Africa Company,[5] and interest receipts from loans made primarily to local authorities and public utilities.

On the basis of an analysis made by the federal treasury, A. Hazlewood and P. D. Henderson[6] estimated the volume of federal receipts originating in Northern Rhodesia between 1954–

But a provision to relieve the double income-tax burden on companies registered in foreign countries reduced the tax money collected by the Northern Rhodesian government considerably. Specifically, the fact that the mining companies, the railway companies, and the British South African Company were registered in the United Kingdom meant that their effective rate in Northern Rhodesia was only 2s. 6d. per pound. The *Pim Report* estimated that if the Rhodesian government had received the full 4s. per pound, its income-tax receipts in 1938 would have increased by £250,000 (p. 134).

[3] In 1961 the federal tax on companies was 33.3 percent of taxable income.

[4] The combined federal and territorial tax on corporate income was 40 percent.

[5] In 1950 an agreement was signed among the British South Africa Company, the Secretary of State, and the Northern Rhodesian government whereby the British South Africa Company undertook to pay the Northern Rhodesian government 20 percent of its mineral royalties and to hand over its mineral rights entirely to the Northern Rhodesian government on October 1, 1986. The royalty payments by the copper companies to the British South Africa Company presently are 13.5 percent of the average of the London Metal Exchange quotations for the month, less £8.

[6] Arthur Hazlewood and P. D. Henderson, *Nyasaland: The Economics of Federation* (Oxford: Basil Blackwell, 1960), p. 42.

55 and 1958–59 (table 8-2).[7] On the basis of these figures as well as the revenue raised by the Northern Rhodesian government itself and the taxes paid by the mining companies, the contribution of the mining industry to government revenue originating in Northern Rhodesia since federation was then estimated (table 8-2). During the mid-fifties, when copper profits were extremely high, over 60 percent of all government revenue was paid by the mining industry. Soon after the collapse of the high price of copper in 1956, however, the mining industry share dropped to around 40 percent. But the improved profit position of the industry in 1960 raised this figure sharply in fiscal 1960–61.

The shift in the functional distribution of current government expenditure is shown in table 8-3. As with government revenues, the expenditure breakdown after federation was difficult to determine because of the divided expenditure responsibilities between the territorial and federal government. The major services for which the federal government was responsible were defense; health; primary, secondary and vocational education for non-Africans; higher education for all races; posts, telegraphs, and interterritorial roads; European agriculture; and prisons. In allocating 1959–60 current federal expenditure, the proportions adopted by Hazlewood and Henderson for allocating current federal expenditure in 1958–59 were used.

In the twenties over one-third of the government budget was devoted to native administration and the maintenance of the police and the military. These functions steadily decreased in importance, and in 1959–60 accounted for less than one-fifth of government expenditure. Balancing this relative decline was a rise in the significance of social and economic services. The increase in African educational activities was particularly impressive. Funds set aside for this purpose rose from 1 percent to 6.6 percent of all expenditures between 1925 and 1960, and in the latter year they exceeded the sum spent on European education. Taking health, education, agriculture, natural resources, and communications as a unit, the share of expenditure devoted to these activities

---

[7] The Minister of Finance in his budget message of June 30, 1960 (*Legislative Council Debates* [Hansard no. 100], June-Aug., 1960, Northern Rhodesia [Lusaka: Government Printer, 1960], pt. 2, p. 944), presented a set of figures quite different from those of Hazlewood and Henderson. It appears that the minister excluded that portion of the federal income tax paid to Northern Rhodesia from the federal revenue received from Northern Rhodesia firms and individuals. When this is included the two estimates are the same.

TABLE 8-2

CONTRIBUTION OF THE MINING INDUSTRY TO GOVERNMENT REVENUE ORIGINATING IN NORTHERN RHODESIA SINCE FEDERATION, 1954–1960

Year	Federal revenue originating in Northern Rhodesia[a] (millions of pounds)	Revenue raised by Northern Rhodesia government itself (excluding share of federal income tax)[b] (millions of pounds)	Total government revenue originating in Northern Rhodesia (millions of pounds)	Taxes paid by mining industry[c] (millions of pounds)	Percentage share of mining tax to total revenue
1954–55	25.8	9.4	35.2	21.8	61.9
1955–56	26.9	12.0	38.9	24.5	63.0
1956–57	36.1	12.4	48.5	32.1	66.2
1957–58	36.6	11.7	48.3	26.5	54.9
1958–59	25.4	10.4	35.8	14.4	40.2
1959–60	25.2	11.0	36.2	13.9	38.4

[a] The 1954–55 through 1958–59 figures in this column are from Arthur Hazlewood and P. D. Henderson, *Nyasaland: The Economics of Federation* (Oxford: Basil Blackwell, 1960), p. 42; federal income tax for 1959–60, computed by multiplying territorial surcharge by 5 and adding estimates of income tax paid by individuals, based on *Sixth Report of the Commissioner of Taxes for the Year Ended 30th June, 1960*, Federation of Rhodesia and Nyasaland (Salisbury: Government Printer, 1961), Appendix IV; other federal taxes and revenues for 1959 computed from *Report of the Comptroller and Auditor-General on the Finance Accounts, Appropriation Accounts, and Accounts of Miscellaneous Funds for the Financial Year Ended 30th June, 1960*, Federation of Rhodesia and Nyasaland (Salisbury: Government Printer, 1961), p. 58, and from the average ratios used by Hazlewood and Henderson (*ibid.*, p. 42) in allocating the share of federal receipts originating in Northern Rhodesia.

[b] The 1954–55 through 1958–59 figures calculated from *Report: Appendix VI—Survey of Developments Since 1953*, Great Britain, Advisory Commission on the Review of the Constitution of the Federation of Rhodesia and Nyasaland, Cmnd. 1149 (London: H.M.S.O., 1960), p. 501; 1959–60 figures are from *Financial Report for the Year Ended 30th June 1960*, Northern Rhodesia (Lusaka: Government Printer, 1960), pp. 8–13.

[c] Includes the copper companies, the Broken Hill Development Company, and the British South Africa Company. Income taxes obtained from financial statements of mining companies and allocated to the respective financial years according to the special payment arrangements between the British South Africa Company, the mines, and the government. Mineral royalties from the sources given in preceding note. Customs duties and licenses paid by mining companies computed by taking a 2-year average of the calendar year figures for these items given in *Year Book*, 1956, Northern Rhodesia Chamber of Mines (Kitwe, Rhodesian Printers), table 4.

TABLE 8-3

CURRENT GOVERNMENT EXPENDITURE IN NORTHERN RHODESIA
IN SELECTED YEARS
(thousands of pounds)

Expenditure category	1925–26	1938	1959–60 Current expenditure by territorial government	1959–60 Current expenditure by federal government[a]
Native affairs and provincial administration	102	126	1,925	
Police and military	48	79	2,541	760
Health	35	74	—	2,340
African education	4	33	2,130	
European education	11	39	—	1,485
Agriculture and veterinary	21	36	560[b]	
Land and natural resources	—	—	1,317	
Communications	28	64	1,156	2,047
Pensions and gratuities	16	82	658	
Public works	21	62	2,412	
Public debt	—	134	902	2,910
All other	90	194	2,704	6,291
Total	376	923	16,305	15,833[c]
			32,138[d]	

[a] Current federal expenditure allocated to Northern Rhodesia was based on the 1958–59 proportions determined by Arthur Hazlewood and P. D. Henderson, *Nyasaland: The Economics of Federation* (Oxford: Basil Blackwell, 1960), pp. 44–45, in conjunction with the federal treasury.

[b] African agriculture only; European agriculture included in "All other."

[c] Total current federal expenditure allocated to Northern Rhodesia.

[d] The total of current territorial expenditure and allocated current federal expenditure.

SOURCES: 1925–26 and 1938 figures from *Report of the Commission Appointed To Enquire into the Financial and Economic Position of Northern Rhodesia*, Colonial, no. 145, Great Britain, Colonial Office (London: H.M.S.O., 1938), Appendix XA; 1959–60 figures from *Financial Report for the Financial Year Ended 30th June 1960*, Northern Rhodesia (Lusaka: Government Printer, 1960), p. 7; *Report of the Comptroller and Auditor-General on the Finance Accounts, Appropriation Accounts, and Accounts of Miscellaneous Funds for the Financial Year Ended 30th June, 1960*, Federation of Rhodesia and Nyasaland (Salisbury: Government Printer, 1961), p. 78.

increased from 25 percent in 1925–26 to 30 percent in 1938, and 34 percent in 1959–60.[8] In addition to the growth of these services, the major change in the composition of the budget was the emergence of interest charges on the public debt between 1925–26

[8] If European agriculture had been included in 1959–60, the figure would have been still higher.

and 1938. Thereafter, the share of interest charges in the total budget decline in importance.

Using the estimates of federal receipts originating in Northern Rhodesia and federal expenditures allocated to the territory, the extent to which Northern Rhodesia subsidized the rest of the federation can be computed. Federal receipts originating in Northern Rhodesia in 1959–60 were estimated to be £25.2 million, whereas federal expenditure in the territory was estimated (table 8-3) to be £15.9 million. To this latter figure must be added the share of federal income tax paid to the Northern Rhodesian government.[9] This brings the total of federal current payments to Northern Rhodesia in 1959–60 to £21.5 million. Northern Rhodesia consequently contributed £3.7 million more to the federal government as receipts than it received from it as payments. This net drain to the rest of the federation has been typical since the federation was formed. In 1956–57 the figure was £13.6 million, and for the entire period from 1954–55 to 1959–60 the loss amounted to £56.1 million.[10] This sum is all the more meaningful when compared with total capital expenditures by the Northern Rhodesian government in the same period of only £49.9 million.[11]

CAPITAL EXPENDITURE AND DEVELOPMENT PLANS

During the twenties and thirties, nonrecurrent expenditures by the Northern Rhodesian government were very small. In 1925–26, for example, only £18,000, an amount equal to less than 5 percent of the recurrent expenditure in that year, was devoted to capital items. Excluding £270,000 set aside as a reserve fund, the 1938 nonrecurrent expenditure level was £142,000, or 15 percent of current expenditure in that year. Native affairs and provincial administration absorbed £31,000 of this total spending, whereas public works accounted for another £82,000. Expenditures for agriculture (£2,800), health (£1,400), European educa-

[9] Federal receipts include the entire income tax originating in the country, whereas federal spending in the territory is derived from the federal budget, that is, the sum at the federal government's disposal after the payment to the territories of their share of the federal income tax.

[10] Hazlewood and Henderson, *op. cit.*, p. 46; tables 8-1, 8-3, above.

[11] *Report: Appendix VI—Survey of Developments Since 1953*, Great Britain, Advisory Commission on the Review of the Constitution of the Federation of Rhodesia and Nyasaland, Cmd. 1149 (London: H.M.S.O., 1960), p. 502, hereafter referred to as the *Monckton Report*.

tion (£900), and African education (£2,500) came to but £7,600. Capital outlays during the twenties and thirties were also directed mainly toward the thin strip of land along the railway where the country's money economy existed. Between 1927 and 1937, 70 percent of the country's £2 million expenditure of loan proceeds was spent along the line of rail and in the Copperbelt.[12]

Ten-Year Development Plan

At the end of World War II the government embarked on a serious program to accelerate social and economic development. A 10-year development plan was inaugurated in 1947. It differed from the detailed plan followed in many underdeveloped countries where production targets for individual commodities, together with estimates of the labor and capital requirements needed to fulfill these goals, were established. Instead, it was formulated merely by asking the heads of the various departments dealing with social and economic services to draw up detailed plans and estimates for their departments over the next 10 years. Then, to these expenditure estimates for health, African and European education, agriculture, forestry, veterinary services, and game and tsetse-fly control, were added sums for African housing, communications, water supplies, and the creation of rural development centers for the African population.

A breakdown of the £13 million plan by various activities is shown in table 8-4. The sum, it should be noted, did not represent just capital expenditures for the various departments concerned. It was composed of £7.8 million of capital expenditures and £5.2 million of recurrent expenses. In order to finance the program the government hoped to secure £2.5 million from colonial development and welfare funds, £5 million from loans, and the balance of £5.5 million from future revenue surpluses of the government.

Despite the great divergence in the degree of detail presented by various departments in their estimates of future requirements, and the almost haphazard manner in which the plan evolved, there were definite objectives embodied in the plan. Specifically, there were three goals:

---

[12] *Pim Report*, p. 93. The copper companies, in particular, benefited from the activities of the Colonial Development Fund. Of the £433,000 that this organization granted or lent the government, £240,000 was re-lent to Rhokana in 1934 in order to build a refinery. The interest rate was 5 percent and the loan was repayable at the option of the company (*Bledisloe Commission*, pp. 80–81).

TABLE 8-4

PLANNED EXPENDITURE UNDER FIRST (1947) VERSION OF TEN-YEAR
DEVELOPMENT PLAN, 1947–1957

Expenditure category	Amount (millions of pounds)	Percent
Health	1.60	12.3
African education	1.54	11.8
European education	.25	1.9
Agriculture, forestry, and veterinary	2.11	16.2
Communications	1.82	14.0
Rural development	1.50	11.5
Water development	.97	7.5
Agricultural development, marketing, and secondary industries	.50	3.8
African housing	1.00	7.7
General building and public works	1.30	10.0
Loan to local authorities	.25	1.9
Unallocated balance	.17	1.3
Total	13.01	99.9

SOURCE: *Ten-Year Development Plan for Northern Rhodesia as Approved by Legislative Council on 11th February 1947*, Northern Rhodesia (Lusaka: Government Printer, 1951).

i. To give, on a modest scale, the bare essentials of social and economic services which all sections of the community require.

ii. To encourage development of the natural and potential assets of the Territory but at the same time to prevent "exploitation" (used in its worst sense) of these assets.

iii. To assist the African population to develop itself under its Native Authority with all possible speed. This is urgent because a higher standard of living must be earned and cannot be awarded. To achieve it the Africans require better health and increased knowledge, energy, industrial or agricultural skill. Also, a more efficient and less wasteful use of natural assets can only follow a better understanding of the principles involved if it is to be willingly adopted.[13]

These goals, taken in conjunction with the proposed functional distribution of the expenditure, make it evident that the program was heavily weighted toward improving living standards for the African population. African education, African housing, and rural development together account for 31 percent of the planned expenditure. The African population also was to receive signifi-

---

[13] *Ten-Year Development Plan for Northern Rhodesia as Approved by Legislative Council on 11th February, 1947*, Northern Rhodesia (Lusaka: Government Printer, 1951), p. 8.

cant benefits from the outlays on health, communications, and agriculture.[14]

The development program had hardly started in 1947, when a shift in emphasis occurred. Under pressure from the legislature, three short-term goals were superimposed upon the longer run objectives. These were: (1) increased food production; (2) more European and African housing; and (3) improved roads.[15] With these new objectives, the general goal of stimulating the rural, nonmonetary sector soon was relegated to a relatively minor position in the development program. As the 1953 version of the program indicates (table 8-5), such items as European education,

TABLE 8-5

1953 VERSION OF TEN-YEAR (1947–1957) DEVELOPMENT PLAN
FOR NORTHERN RHODESIA

Expenditure category	Amount (millions of pounds)	Percent
Health	3.6	6.6
African education	1.8	3.3
European education	5.1	9.4
Agriculture, forestry, and veterinary	1.9	3.5
Communications	9.2	17.0
Rural development	1.0	1.8
Water development	1.5	2.8
African housing	6.6	12.1
General building and public works	9.5	17.5
Law and order	1.8	3.3
Loans to local authorities	5.5	10.1
Public utilities	5.9	10.8
Other	1.0	1.8
Total	54.2	100.0

SOURCE: *Approved Estimates of the Development Fund, 1954–55,* Northern Rhodesia (Lusaka: Government Printer, 1954), p. 3.

general building and public works (which included European housing), loans to local authorities, and public utilities increased markedly in relative importance. Sums devoted to purposes only remotely connected with social and economic development, such

[14] For example, 83 percent of expenditure proposed by the Department of Agriculture was devoted to African agriculture (C. J. Lewin, *Agriculture and Forestry Development Plans for Ten Years,* Northern Rhodesia [Lusaka: Government Printer, 1945], p. 15).

[15] *Review of Ten-Year Development Plan of Northern Rhodesia,* Northern Rhodesia (Lusaka: Government Printer, 1948), p. 3.

as prisons and police stations, also became significant in the program. The share devoted to African housing, African education, and rural development fell from 31 percent in the original plan to 17 percent in the 1953 version.

The fate of the rural development program illustrates the change in emphasis. Originally, a series of development centers were to be established at which subordinate European and African agricultural officers were to be trained for extension work. Each center was designed with a hospital, a normal school, an agricultural and veterinary research station, a model rural community, lecture rooms, and adequate housing for the entire staff.[16] Actually, the legislature authorized only one such center, and it was never completed. By 1953 the sum for rural development had been reduced from its initial £1.5 million level to £1 million—less than that allocated to the police.

Rapid expansion of the economy after the war created pressing needs for capital in the monetary sector. To take full advantage of these new capital opportunities, greatly enlarged outlays on roads, housing, medical facilities, power, water, and the like, were urgently needed, and gave every indication of yielding a higher short-run return than spending on uncertain rural projects. The government soon shifted the main part of its development efforts toward the monetary sector. The urban African shared in the benefits from this change in policy, but the rural, nonmonetary African sector did not receive proportionately much more in the way of development aid than it had in the thirties.

The change in direction of development activity also made unnecessary the existence of a special development authority: a rural development center required a development commissioner to coordinate the activities of established departments. But the extension of capital facilities in the monetary sector, where no coordinated production goals were set forth, could be handled adequately through established departmental channels. In fact, the development plan became merely the aggregate of the capital expenditures traditionally carried out by the existing departments. Friction between the development commission and the heads of departments gradually reduced the commissioner's authority and finally the position was abolished in 1956.[17] After

---

[16] G. F. Clay, *Memorandum on Post-War Development Planning in Northern Rhodesia*, Northern Rhodesia (Lusaka: Government Printer, 1945), pp. 10–17.

[17] *Legislative Council Debates* (Hansard no. 88), 28th June–24th Aug., 1956, Northern Rhodesia (Lusaka: Government Printer, 1956), p. 3.

that date, the Capital Expenditure Planning Committee, consisting of members of the Executive Council, directed the capital-spending activities of the government.

In addition to a change in the composition of development spending, another major feature of the development program, over the years, was the remarkable increase in its size. A plan that began in 1947 as a £13 million effort reached £54 million by 1954. The main reason for this increase was the unexpected expansion in tax revenues—largely from the copper industry. The initial plan called for 42 percent of the program to be financed from general revenue sources. Actually 59 percent of the funds were obtained from general revenue sources up to 1958. Thereafter, however, there was greater reliance on loan proceeds, so that by the end of 1960, 55 percent of the development receipts (table 8-6) had been secured from the general revenue of the territory.

TABLE 8-6

SOURCES OF REVENUE FOR DEVELOPMENT SPENDING, 1947 TO 1959–60

Source	Amount (millions of pounds)	Percent
Appropriations from territorial funds	41.5	55.3
Colonial welfare and development schemes	3.8	5.1
Loans	23.4	31.1
Miscellaneous receipts	6.4	8.5
Total	75.1	100.0

SOURCE: Financial Reports, 1947–1960, Northern Rhodesia (Lusaka: Government Printer).

Federal Development Plans

After 1954, development activity by the federal government augmented the capital expenditure program of the Northern Rhodesian government. Federal development plans were directed mainly toward two activities, namely, the development of power (especially the Kariba hydroelectric project) and the modernization of the railway system (table 8-7). Together these projects accounted for 73 percent of the proposed expenditure in the revised 1957–1961 plan. Unlike the Northern Rhodesia government's development program, the federal government planned to rely very heavily on loan funds. In the 1957–1961 version of the plan it was estimated that 76 percent of the funds would come from

TABLE 8-7

FEDERAL DEVELOPMENT PLANS, 1957–1961 AND 1959–1963
(millions of pounds)

Planned expenditure	1957–1961	1959–1963
Rhodesia Railways	28.8	10.7
Roads and bridges	4.8	7.1
Post and telegraphs	6.9	6.0
Power	60.5	31.0
Agriculture	.9	.4
Other economic services	1.9	1.8
Education	4.8	5.1
Health	4.3	4.0
Other social services	.3	.5
Housing	1.3	1.5
Other	7.2	8.7
Total	121.7	76.8

SOURCES: *Review of the Development Plan 1957–1961*, Federation of Rhodesia and Nyasaland (Salisbury: Government Printer, 1958), p. 9; *Review of the Development Plan 1959–1963*, Federation of Rhodesia and Nyasaland (Salisbury: Government Printer, 1959).

loans, and in the regular revision of the plan two years later, 85 percent of the financial resources were listed as loans (table 8-8).

The capital expenditures by the federal government in Northern Rhodesia between 1954–55 and 1960–61 are shown in table 8-9. Although the federal treasury broke down its total capital

TABLE 8-8

ESTIMATED SOURCES OF REVENUE AVAILABLE FOR FEDERAL
DEVELOPMENT PLANS, 1957–1961 AND 1959–1963

Revenue source	1957–1961		1959–1963	
	Amount (millions of pounds)	Percent	Amount (millions of pounds)	Percent
Reserve funds	13.8	11.3	3.0	3.9
Loans	92.6	76.1	65.4	85.2
Rhodesia Railway's own development resources	9.6	7.9	2.6	3.4
Miscellaneous receipts	5.7	4.7	5.8	7.6
Total	121.7	100.0	76.8	100.1

SOURCES: *Review of the Development Plan 1957–1961*, Federation of Rhodesia and Nyasaland (Salisbury: Government Printer, 1958), p. 8; *Review of the Development Plan 1959–1963*, Federation of Rhodesia and Nyasaland (Salisbury: Government Printer, 1960).

TABLE 8-9

Public Capital Expenditures in Northern Rhodesia, 1947–1961[a]

Expenditure category	Northern Rhodesian government's capital fund expenditures[b] (millions of pounds)	Northern Rhodesia's share of federal loan vote expenditure[c] (percent)	Northern Rhodesia's share of federal power board expenditure[d] (millions of pounds)	Total (millions of pounds)	Percent
Health	1.2	2.6		3.8	2.64
European education	1.7	2.1		3.8	2.64
African education	4.2			4.2	2.92
African housing	11.7			11.7	8.14
European housing	8.3			8.3	5.77
Agriculture, forestry, and veterinary	4.8			4.8	3.34
Power and water	7.2	16.9	14.5	38.6	26.86
Rural development	3.5			3.5	2.43
Land and natural resources	.6			.6	.41
Communications	7.8	18.1		25.9	18.02
Public utilities	1.5			1.5	1.04
Law and order	4.8			4.8	3.34
Industry	1.1			1.1	.76
Loans for nonspecified purposes	15.6			15.6	10.85
Other public works	3.3			3.3	2.29
All other	6.5	5.7		12.2	8.49
Total	83.8	45.4	14.5	143.7	99.94

[a] Figures for 1960–61 based on expenditure estimates.

[b] Figures for 1947–1952 from *Approved Estimates of the Department Fund, 1953–54*, Northern Rhodesia (Lusaka: Government Printer, 1953); 1953–1960 computed from Financial Statements, 1952–1960, Northern Rhodesia (Lusaka: Government Printer); 1960–61 from *Estimates of Revenue and Expenditure*, Northern Rhodesia (Lusaka: Government Printer, 1960).

[c] Determined as explained in text (p. 200) from Arthur Hazlewood and P. D. Henderson, *Nyasaland: The Economics of Federation* (Oxford: Basil Blackwell, 1960), p. 56; *Report: Appendix VI—Survey of Developments Since 1953*, Great Britain, Advisory Commission on the Review of the Constitution of the Federation of Rhodesia and Nyasaland, Cmnd. 1149 (London: H.M.S.O., 1960), pp. 491–492; *Report of the Comptroller and Auditor-General on the Finance Accounts, Appropriation Accounts, and Accounts of Miscellaneous Funds for the Financial Year Ended 30th June, 1960*, Federation of Rhodesia and Nyasaland (Salisbury: Government Printer, 1961); *Estimates of Expenditure during the Year Ending 30th June, 1961*, Federation of Rhodesia and Nyasaland (Salisbury: Government Printer, 1960). The "All other" category includes outlays on agriculture, housing, prisons, as well as miscellaneous items.

[d] To June, 1960.

expenditures by territories at the request of Hazelwood and Henderson, it did not present the territorial distribution of the various expenditure components, except for Rhodesia Railways and the Federal Power Board.[18] Federal loan vote expenditures were distributed in the same ratios as current federal expenditures for these services between 1954–55 and 1959–60 (table 8-9). The federal loan vote for power, however, also did not include all of the capital funds spent for the Kariba project. The sums made available by the copper companies, the British South Africa Company, the Standard Bank of South Africa, and Barclays Bank, D.C.O., were lent directly to the federal government and then re-lent to the Federal Power Board. In addition, the power board borrowed £43.5 million directly from the International Bank for Reconstruction and Development and from the Colonial Development Corporation. Half the £29 million that was withdrawn from these loans up to 1960 is listed in table 8-9 under capital expenditures by the Federal Power Board.[19] The table itemizes all expenditures from the Development Fund (now termed "Capital Fund") between 1947 and 1961 by the Northern Rhodesian government. The final column is an estimate, therefore, of the capital spending by all government authorities since development planning began soon after the war. It should be emphasized that the total figure and, particularly, the functional distribution of this sum give only a rough picture of development spending, because it was necessary to use somewhat arbitrary methods in allocating the various expenditures.

The remarkable difference in the final pattern of development spending from that envisaged in 1947 is clearly brought out in table 8-9. What started out as a plan aimed primarily at providing economic and social services for the rural African population turned into a program designed to strengthen the urban monetary sector. Power and water services and communications (almost entirely along the line of rail) absorbed 45 percent of all funds spent. The three next largest categories, namely, loans to local authorities, African housing, and European housing, account for another 25 percent and also represent urban spending. The sums spent for rural development and part of the funds assigned to

---

[18] The expenditure on Rhodesia Railways is divided between Southern Rhodesia (60 percent) and Northern Rhodesia (40 percent). Advances to the power board in connection with Kariba are divided equally between Northern and Southern Rhodesia.

[19] *Annual Report and Accounts for the Year Ended 30th June, 1960,* Federation of Rhodesia and Nyasaland, Federal Power Board (Salisbury, 1960).

agriculture were the only major economic outlays designed to stimulate agricultural development in the subsistence sector.

RURAL DEVELOPMENT

From the point of view of maximizing national product, heavy spending in the expanding monetary sector undoubtedly was a good policy. But it is not evident that the near neglect of economic expenditure in the rural, subsistence sector was justifiable on these same economic grounds. Moreover, on grounds of equity—a consideration that most governments are prepared to use to modify the goal of maximizing national product—the pattern of expenditures is one-sided. For years, government officials deplored the extent of the imbalance between economic development in the monetary versus the subsistence sector. But, under political pressures of the moment, the Legislative Council invariably responded to the wishes of the European electorate and channeled most of the funds available into the money economy. Without significant political representation, the rural African population, understandably, was seriously neglected.

Government Programs

The fact that those endeavors actually undertaken to raise living standards in the subsistence sector did not prove very successful also played an important part in keeping down spending for rural development. The usual approach employed in attempting to increase African agricultural output was to concentrate upon a relatively small number of African farmers in the hope that other farmers would then copy the modern practices adopted by this small group. The demonstration method seemed to offer an inexpensive yet effective manner of introducing modern agricultural techniques. The Intensive Rural Development Program for the Northern and Luapula provinces described below illustrates this approach. In 1956 Rhodesian Selection Trust lent the government £2 million to encourage rural development in the areas from which the copper mines drew much of their labor. The Northern Rhodesian government responded by initiating an intensive £2 million development program in the Northern and Luapula provinces for the period 1957–1960. At the beginning, about one-quarter of the funds was allocated for the establishment of a depot farm to train Africans in the techniques of modern farming.[20] The trainees were to be provided with land nearby in order to form the core of an agricultural community that, it was hoped, would influence farming practices in the entire area. The regular rural development program also operated on this principle. Development Area Training centers were established to train men and women in such activities as constructing better houses, improving health conditions, and making clothing. When these people returned to their villages, it was hoped that their knowledge would spread through the entire community. Similarly, the various peasant-farming improvement schemes were designed to spread better agricultural practices by the demonstration method.

The various programs did not work out as planned, unfortunately. The persons participating in them were disappointingly few, and their influence on others was not very great. The Rural Development Commission found, for example, that the 1,000 men and women who attended courses in 1959 faced ridicule when they returned home and often quickly abandoned what they had learned.[21] As a result, the notion of the rural training center as an institution was abandoned, and the program was modified to concentrate upon extension work in the villages themselves. Those directing the African Farming Improvement Scheme also concluded that greater emphasis was needed within the village areas. The same fate apparently befell the Northern and Luapala provinces program. Facilities were established for training only about 30 individuals annually, and there was no evidence of an agricultural revolution starting in the area.[22] Other parts of this plan also fared badly. The Luapula Transport Cooperative which operated buses went bankrupt; the Bangweulu Water Transport Company, with assets of £61,000, earned only £3,500 in 1960 and sustained a net loss of £10,000 that year; the Luebwe and Nchelenga sawmills, with assets of £42,000, suffered a loss of £11,000; and the Lake Tanganyika Commercial Fisheries incurred a trading loss of £5,000 on assets of £34,000 in 1960.[23]

---

[20] M. Halcrow, "Intensive Rural Development Plans for the Northern and Luapula Provinces, 1957–1961," Northern Rhodesia (Lusaka, 1958).

[21] *Annual Report of the Commissioner for Rural Development, 1959,* Northern Rhodesia, Ministry of Native Affairs (Lusaka: Government Printer, 1960), p. 1.

[22] *Report on Intensive Rural Development in the Northern and Luapula Provinces of Northern Rhodesia, 1957–1961,* Northern Rhodesia (Lusaka: Government Printer, 1961).

[23] *Financial Report for the Financial Year Ended 30th June 1960,* Northern Rhodesia (Lusaka: Government Printer, 1960).

Objections to Government Planning

Several observations may be made in connection with the lack of success of the various rural programs. The most obvious is the lack of any substantial sums devoted to such programs. The Intensive Rural Development Program, for example, could hardly be expected to revolutionize the rural life of millions of people with a nonclerical staff of only 22 Europeans and 80 Africans. But there was more to the problem than mere lack of funds. The approach used was to present the African with the opportunity of raising his agricultural income by adopting modern European practices. The required practices, at worst, seemed to be based more on physical conditions in the European areas than on economic conditions in the rural sector, and, at best, were too complex for any but a few already progressive Africans to understand. The introduction of successively less stringent conditions of qualification for the African Farming Improvement Scheme was a recognition of this point. Too much emphasis also was placed upon the necessity for the immediate adoption of European methods of agriculture as the condition for raising income. Attempts to raise agricultural income would have been more successful if there had been greater efforts made to provide better marketing and transport facilities. This would have created an opportunity for African farmers to earn more by expanding output under their existing methods. Despite the frequent arguments to the contrary, the African farmer is profit oriented. If he can see the chance of raising his income with existing methods he will do so, and he is then more likely to adopt European methods gradually in an effort to raise his income still more. This is the lesson of successful commercial farming by Africans along the line of rail. Elaborate farm-extension work should go hand in hand with these market-creating opportunities, but the African must not be expected to jump immediately into better practices as the condition for raising his living standard. He must be induced to adopt these new methods by the creation of profit opportunities within his own standards of cultivation.

A final observation concerns the failure to utilize existing social structures in African rural society in attempts to raise agricultural productivity. The usual practice was to select Africans, remove them from the village environment, and place them in a European-oriented training establishment. For a population that long distrusted the motives of the European, it is no wonder that the few who left were treated as political "sell-outs" and had little influence upon their return.

Some of these objections to agricultural planning apply to the Kafue Flats Pilot Polder Scheme begun in 1956 under the auspices of Rhodesian Selection Trust. Under this program dikes were erected to prevent the land from being flooded during the rainy season, and an irrigation system was established to permit intensive cultivation of the soil with such commodities as wheat, barley, livestock, vegetables, and maize. By 1962 only a small pilot scheme (700 acres) had been constructed, but the eventual goal was the irrigation of an area of 450,000 acres comprising 20,000 African farms of 20 acres each, and 3,000 European farms of 150 acres each.[24] The capital cost of the entire undertaking was estimated at £90 million in 1955 prices.[25]

There is more engineering than economics in the scheme. Before a significant output can be obtained from the area, several years of work lie ahead in perfecting the irrigation system and determining what crops can be successfully grown on the land. After this has been accomplished, there still remains the fundamental problem of inducing African producers to follow the complicated system of intensive agriculture required. There is a great difference between creating a potentially profitable agricultural opportunity for highly trained European farmers and inducing untrained African farmers to exploit this opportunity. Plunging African farmers into a situation that requires the immediate adoption of specialized European practices for its success is likely to prove extremely expensive at best and more likely to result in complete failure. The polder scheme already has two strikes against it. A profitable system of agriculture under the best European practices must first be established, and then this system must be adapted to the capabilities of the present-day African farmer. One cannot help but question the economic wisdom of the scheme. Instead of the 20,000 African farms that might perhaps be established for the £90 million, there could be established in the present African agricultural areas with the same sum 180,000 "improved" farms, each with an income of the same order as planned

---

[24] *Kafue Flats, the Granary of the Federation?* Rhodesian Selection Trust (Salisbury, 1958).

[25] Unfortunately, in February, 1963, one of the surrounding walls of the polder collapsed and the flood waters of the Kafue River covered the entire area with 7 feet of water (*Horizon*, V [March, 1963], published by Rhodesian Selection Trust).

in the polder scheme.[26] In short, the program may be economical in 50 years' time, when capital-intensive agriculture is more appropriate, but it does not represent a wise use of present development resources.

A comprehensive report on rural economic development in 1961 recognized some of the objections to previous development efforts noted above.[27] It was encouraging to see, for example, that the report stressed the prime importance of creating better marketing facilities rather than concentrating upon improving agricultural practices among African farmers as a method of stimulating rural growth. Both approaches are certainly needed, but the earlier planning overemphasized the technical side. The large outlay recommended in the 1961 report for improving rural transportation facilities illustrates the emphasis on marketing opportunities.[28] Suggested communications expenditure totaled £7.05 million, or 21 percent of a proposed £33 million 4-year comprehensive rural development plan. Other major expenditures in the plan were agriculture (£8 million), African rural education (£5 million), and power supplies (£2 million).[29]

Another excellent feature of the new plan was the proposed expansion in the production of commodities such as tobacco, groundnuts, cotton, and cattle, which could be sold on the international market. It is by means of relying on international demand rather than local demand that rapid rural development can best be achieved. With the existing low level of incomes any bootstrap method of development, relying on local demand, is bound to result in slow progress. Furthermore, the income elasticity of demand for many of the domestically produced and consumed foodstuffs is quite low. The income elasticity for the major single food item consumed, mealie meal (corn meal), is, for example, only .35 among urban families.[30] A rising level of income among the African population, therefore, will not increase the market for maize very much.

[26] Calculated from *Report of the Rural Economic Development Working Party,* Northern Rhodesia (Lusaka: Government Printer, 1961), p. 35.

[27] *Ibid.,* pp. 17–41.

[28] Roads in themselves are not enough. Provision should also be made—by the government, if necessary—for trucks and vans to carry commodities at reasonably low rates.

[29] *Report of the Rural Economic Development Working Party,* p. 164.

[30] Calculated from "Second Report on Urban African Budget Survey Held in Northern Rhodesia May to August 1960," Federation of Rhodesia and Nyasaland, Central Statistical Office (Salisbury, 1961), p. 7.

Most farmers are reluctant, however, to shift to such cash crops as burley tobacco and cotton. They are well aware from past experience how extreme the cyclical price fluctuations in these commodities can be. Wide price fluctuations, together with low-income levels and the inability to borrow sufficient funds during periods of low commodity prices, imply that the farmers' risk of earning a very low real income in some periods is unusually high. Farmers also realize that there may be wide fluctuations in the output of these cash commodities. Their local planting and processing experience is limited: an unexpected plant disease or insect problem may completely destroy a farmer's crop before the difficulty is solved by agricultural research. The individual farmer knows that his own lack of experience in growing these commodities may result in a costly error on his part. The greater possibility of earning a disastrously low income by cultivating the new products, in contrast with a standard commodity like maize, acts to discourage their production, even though the long-run average income associated with them might be considerably higher than with maize. The producer—quite sensibly—reasons that he may not be around to enjoy "the long-run" under these probability conditions.

As the rural development report states, a statutory marketing board providing a guaranteed market at reasonably stable prices seems necessary to meet part of the problem of cyclically unstable prices. But, such arrangements must not turn either into permanent tax or subsidy schemes. The problem of wide variations in price and output can also be helped by research programs designed to yield the information needed to protect against plant diseases and destructive insects, and to provide technical services to individual farmers. To repeat, greater efforts of work within the village social structure are needed to provide this information. Another desirable measure is some type of subsidy arrangement for new producers which protects them from economic failure based on inexperience. This, too, must not be used to keep inefficient farmers in business indefinitely or to subsidize the efficient producers on a permanent basis.

A 4-year development plan, based in part upon the 1961 rural development report discussed above, was drafted.[31] But, as might be expected, the funds for the plan were reduced from £33 million to £30 million, and—what is much more important—a signifi-

---

[31] *Draft Development Plan for the Period 1st July, 1961 to 30th June, 1965,* Northern Rhodesia (Lusaka: Government Printer, 1962).

cant share was devoted to urban development activities. The funds allocated to African rural development amounted to only £10.5 million. African education was still assigned £5 million, but this covered both rural and urban educational facilities.

EDUCATION

Another especially important part of any Northern Rhodesian development planning is the amount and distribution of expenditures on African education. From the first development plan in 1947, great emphasis has been placed upon the objective of providing 4 years of education (through Standard II) for all African children.[32] It was obvious at that time that the general shortage of funds required a decision on whether to concentrate upon this approach or upon the more intensive training of fewer individuals. Why the mass education goal was selected is not exactly clear. Egalitarian grounds or political considerations may have been the basis of the decision. On the other hand, perhaps Europeans wished to train the African somewhat, but not enough so that he might seriously compete with European workers.[33] Still another factor that may have guided educators in making this decision was the economic gains the country could expect from this type of education. In other words, they may have considered simple, mass education to be a highly productive form of investment in people. This is not the place to analyze the political consequences of various distributions of educational expenditures, but in the rest of this section an attempt is made to outline a method of evaluating quantitatively the economic benefits to the country of education expenditures.

When viewed as an investment in people, educational expenditures can be analyzed from the same economic viewpoint as can investment in a factory or in a machine.[34] When deciding whether

---

[32] A. M. Frisby, *African Education Development Plans, 1945–1955*, Northern Rhodesia (Lusaka: Government Printer, 1945), p. 6.

[33] This view was stated explicitly as early as 1920 in a meeting of the Advisory Council. One member "believed in the advancement of the native to a certain extent, but not to such an extent that he would compete with the white artizan." The administrator stated that there was "a mean somewhere beween educating the native to compete with the white artizan and refusing him any training and so compelling them [him] to compete with the farmer" (*Report of the Proceedings of the Second Advisory Council*, First Meeting June 21st to 29th, 1920, Northern Rhodesia [Livingstone: Government Printer, 1920], pp. 7–8).

[34] It should be pointed out at the outset that one is not de-emphasizing the importance of free choice by individuals, when spending for education is treated

to build a new factory, a businessman must first estimate for the lifetime of the factory the stream of costs and receipts associated with the project. In early periods, construction and equipment costs are generally greater than any revenue obtained from selling the output of the plant, that is, net receipts are negative. Once most of these outlays are undertaken, sales receipts usually exceed operating costs over the factory's remaining lifetime, that is, net receipts are positive during this time. Having estimated the net receipts stream over the project's lifetime, the investor should then capitalize this stream at an appropriate discount rate and thereby determine the present value of the stream of net receipts. If the present value is positive, the investment is profitable; if negative, the project should not be undertaken.

The question of providing additional educational facilities can be treated in a similar way.[35] The main economic costs to society are construction and equipment costs associated with more class-rooms, salaries of teachers, and any output students would have produced during the additional time they attend school. On the other hand, the total receipts stream consists of the extra income earned over their lifetime by the individuals who receive additional training in the new facilities. One factor that complicates any estimate of net receipts or benefits from education is possible technological spillovers. For example, a better educated person may freely pass on to others part of his increased knowledge, so that they too may become better educated and thereby earn more income. The additional income earned by these people should also be included in the benefit stream.

Another matter frequently pointed out is that formal education is a consumption commodity as well as an investment good. Like food, for example, an individual may desire more education not just because it enables him to increase his earnings but also because he derives utility from the additional knowledge.

as investment in people. Quite the contrary, this approach helps those in positions of public authority to determine the type and amount of educational expenditures the people want.

[35] The economics of public investment policy in underdeveloped nations is a complex topic that can be considered here only in a very limited manner. Two books that examine in much more detail some of the issues raised in the discussion that follows are Jack Hirshleifer, James C. DeHaven, and Jerome W. Milliman, *Water Supply: Economics, Technology, and Policy* (Chicago: University of Chicago Press, 1960), and Roland N. McKean, *Efficiency in Government through Systems Analysis* (New York: John Wiley & Sons, 1958); see also R. E. Baldwin, "Investment Policy in Underdeveloped Countries," in *Economic Development in Africa*, ed. E. F. Jackson (Oxford: Basil Blackwell, 1965).

Therefore, the maximum sum that he would pay for additional education—this being the economic measure of his benefits— equals the additional income he can earn plus an extra sum amounting to his valuation of education as a consumption good. A comprehensive evaluation of education would have to attempt to estimate this additional benefit.

Data concerning income earned by level of education are available in the 1960 African demographic survey of urban areas in Northern Rhodesia (table 8-10). This data clearly leaves much to

TABLE 8-10

AVERAGE AFRICAN WAGE RATES
BY LEVEL OF EDUCATION, 1960

Education	Monthly wages (shillings)
No education	163
Below Standard I	162
Standard I	168
Standard II	171
Standard III	174
Standard IV	188
Standard V	204
Standard VI	230
Above Standard VI	316

SOURCE: *Report on Northern Rhodesia African Demographic Surveys, May to August, 1960*, Federation of Rhodesia and Nyasaland, Central Statistical Office (Salisbury: Government Printer, 1961), p. 20.

be desired for our purposes. It does not indicate what a new graduate from each of the grades earns, but instead gives averages covering individuals of various ages. Furthermore, for an investment calculation one should estimate what will be earned in the future and not just what is currently earned. If one assumes, however, that the relative differences in earnings, according to educational attainment, do not change in the future, the correct ordering relation will still be achieved. The same difficulties apply on the cost side. It is possible to estimate present costs, but one wishes to know future costs, too. For the rough calculations here, present costs will also be projected into the future.

An estimate of the present value of additional educational facilities can be made in the following way. Assume that the investment project is the establishment of classroom capacity for one more pupil. The cost stream involved in the project is, therefore, the initial per student construction and equipment cost and the per student cost of operating the classroom over its life. Another cost to society is the loss of income resulting from the student's attendance at school rather than his presence as a worker in the subsistence economy. The benefit stream, on the other hand, is the additional income earned by the additional students educated (i.e., one each year) during the life of the classroom.[36] It is assumed in the first set of calculations, as in fact is the case, that there already exists an excess pool of available students one grade below the standard being considered. To educate more individuals to the level of (say) Standard IV, it is not necessary to expand the capacity of all the standards preceding this one. This is the noncumulative case. Next, it is assumed that to increase, for example, Standard IV facilities, it is necessary also to provide additional Standards I–III facilities.[37] This is the cumulative case. In both calculations the typical individual is assumed to begin work for money wages outside of the subsistence sector when he is 18 years old and to continue employment until he is 60 years old.

The cost and benefit streams resulting from these assumptions are summarized in table 8-11. Take, for example, the streams arising from the expansion of Standard IV capacity by one more pupil in the noncumulative case. The initial cost is £40 and the operating costs each year over the 35-year life of the classroom are £8.8 (table 8-11, n. *a*). In addition, it is assumed that each of the 35 students who attend the class over its life costs the subsistence economy £9 per year in terms of output he would have produced had he remained at home. Since it is assumed each student returns to the rural life after his year in school and works there until he is 18, he loses only one year of production because of his extra education. The benefit stream begins 8 years after the classroom capacity is built, when the first pupil reaches 18. Each pupil enters Standard IV when he is 11 years old, receives one more year of education, returns to the family farm thereafter, and finally

---

[36] No attempt is made to include in the benefit stream an estimate of the spillover effects or an estimate of the value of education as a consumption good.

[37] It is supposed, however, that there is already a sufficient pool of students so that one does not have to wait until new pupils are trained in the first 3 standards before students are available for Standard IV.

TABLE 8-11

PRESENT VALUES (AT VARIOUS DISCOUNT RATES) OF THE NET BENEFIT STREAMS DERIVED FROM PROVIDING CLASSROOM FACILITIES FOR AN ADDITIONAL STUDENT[a]

(in pounds)

Standard	Values	Alternative Discount Rates						
		2 percent	5 percent	10 percent	12 percent	16 percent	20 percent	24 percent
I	Noncumulative	871.62	313.02	41.23	5.44	−27.62	−39.63	−44.19
	Cumulative	871.62	313.02	41.23	5.44	−27.62	−39.63	−44.19
II	Noncumulative	515.53	171.72	5.09	−16.68	−36.61	−43.63	−46.10
	Cumulative	1,387.15	484.74	46.32	−11.24	−64.23	−83.26	−90.52
III	Noncumulative	179.18	−54.30	−131.57	−133.38	−126.43	−116.42	−107.23
	Cumulative	1,566.33	430.44	−85.25	−144.62	−190.66	−199.68	−197.52
IV	Noncumulative	2,822.97	1,030.83	200.15	87.39	−19.52	−59.20	−74.19
	Cumulative	4,389.30	1,461.27	114.90	−57.23	−210.18	−258.88	−271.71
V	Noncumulative	2,375.33	1,280.86	273.07	133.71	−1.09	−53.15	−74.11
	Cumulative	6,764.63	2,742.13	387.97	76.48	−211.27	−312.03	−345.82
VI	Noncumulative	5,982.80	2,544.97	692.39	424.87	154.07	37.89	−16.51
	Cumulative	12,747.43	5,287.10	1,080.36	501.35	−57.20	−274.14	−362.33

a Initial construction and equipment costs £40; operating costs £40; operating costs: Standards I and II, £2.8; III and IV, £8.8, and V and VI, £12.8. An individual who attends school when he is at least 10 years of age is assumed to cost the economy £9 in lost subsistence output. Using the wage data in table 8-10, the additional annual income that an individual receives as he moves from less than Standard I to Standard I, from Standard I to Standard II, and so on, is assumed to be: less than I to I, £3; I to II, £1.8; II to III, £1.8; III to IV, £8.4; IV to V, £9.6; V to VI, £15.6. Each student starts Standard I at age 8 and begins to work for money wages when he is 18 and continues until he is 60. The life of the schoolroom facilities is assumed to be 35 years. The present values are based upon net benefit streams of 45 periods.

SOURCES: Wage data from table 8-10; construction and equipment costs based on information supplied by the Director of Native Education in Southern Rhodesia; operating costs from *Triennial Survey, 1958–1960*, Northern Rhodesia, Ministry of African Education (Lusaka: Government Printer, 1961), p. 16.

goes into the wage economy at 18 years of age. From then on, he earns £8.4 more per year over his working life than if he had only completed Standard III. Since one more pupil is educated each of the 35 years of the classroom, the benefit stream, which begins 8 years after the classroom is constructed, rises by £8.4 per year for 35 years, remains at this level for 7 years, and begins to decline thereafter by £8.4 per year for the next 35 years as retirements gradually occur. For simplicity of calculation, instead of discounting at various rates over this entire period of time, net benefit streams were calculated for only 45 years in all cases. Cutting off the net benefit stream at this point also helps to correct for two factors not taken into account in the computations. One is the lack of any allowance for the death of some individuals before the age of 60.[38] The other is the shape of the usual age-income curve for individuals. When an individual first enters the labor market, he earns less than the lifetime average for his educational group. During his middle working years his wage is above the average, while in his latter years it is again below the average. The nature of the discounting process causes the present value of this type of benefit stream to be less than a constant stream with the same (undiscounted) average.

It should be noted that the present values presented in table 8-11 are relevant for only a relatively small increase in educational investment. After a point, the building of large numbers of classrooms for any grade causes costs to rise and the income earned by graduates of the grade to decline. A running set of calculations is needed as investment rises in order to take account of such changes. But the calculation at any time always indicates the direction in which investment should occur to maximize national product.

The matter of deciding—solely on economic grounds—whether additional educational facilities should be provided depends upon what is regarded as the proper discount rate. If benefit and cost streams can be regarded as certainty-equivalents (the expected values associated with the probability distributions of costs and benefits), the pure rate of interest for long-term investments (perhaps 4 percent) should be used.[39] It is evident however, that the actual figures used in the table cannot be regarded as certainty-equivalents. In order to account for the risk involved in these estimates, one should discount at the rate private in-

---

[38] Sixty years of age may also be too high as the assumed retirement age.
[39] Hirshleifer *et al., op. cit.,* pp. 140–150.

vestors insist upon when providing capital to private companies comparable in risk (perhaps 10 percent). As no attempt is made here to calculate carefully the degree of risk actually associated with cost and benefit estimates, present value data are given for a range of discount rates.

One interesting result apparent from the table is that, as one discounts at higher rates, the lower standards tend to become unprofitable first. In other words, if 12 percent is in fact the proper discount rate, additional facilities for Standards II and III (by themselves) are not economically worthwhile, whereas additional investment in facilities for Standards IV, V, and VI are. In this case, funds should be shifted from lower to higher standards.[40] The economic aspects of education must not be overstressed—there are important political and social considerations that should also be taken into account. These may well override any conclusions reached on economic grounds. But, if one does argue on economic grounds for greater expenditures on a particular type of education or education in general, he should be prepared to support his case by the kind of calculations outlined.

---

[40] In evaluating the cumulative alternatives (which are mutually exclusive), the correct procedure, given the proper discount rate, is to stop at the educational level with the highest positive present value at discount rate of 12 percent or less; this means that facilities through Standard VI should be built. At discount rates of 16 percent or more, however, all cumulative present values are negative.

It may be helpful to note here that the reason the present value of the net benefits stream in the noncumulative, Standard III case becomes larger as the discount rate rises from 12 percent to 24 percent is that in this instance the decrease in gross benefits is less than the decrease in the cost stream.

9

General Conclusions

THE EXPORT-TECHNOLOGY HYPOTHESIS

The analysis of Northern Rhodesia's development reveals that the pattern of its growth has been consistent with the development model outlined in chapter 3. Not only has the copper industry been responsible for most of the increase in national product over the last 35 years, but the technological nature of this export industry's production function has mainly determined the structural components of the rise in output. As has been detailed, the engineering constraints on the manner of producing copper, and the early relative factor endowments were not favorable for initiating a broadly based, self-sustaining development process. Instead, they were such that Northern Rhodesia became a markedly dualistic economy whose prosperity was largely dependent upon world-market conditions for copper.

The number of workers employed per unit value of copper output was relatively small, and the skill requirements for a significant proportion of these workers were fairly high. Initially it was cheaper to import skilled workers from abroad rather than to train unskilled African labor. The direct employment and immediate skill-imparting effects on African labor were consequently comparatively slight, as were the cash-spending repercussions touched off by these workers. The consumption spending of the skilled European workers added somewhat to the indirect demand for African workers, but because of their high income levels and their foreign-oriented taste patterns their import propensity tended to be high.

The capital requirements of the industry were not very favorable for demand-induced development. Unlike the capital requirements for export commodities produced under a plantation system, a large fraction of the fixed-capital requirement for copper consisted of complex machinery whose production in turn required highly skilled labor and complicated capital goods. There was no likelihood that these items could be supplied domestically in the early stages of Rhodesia's growth. There were, however, some favorable repercussions set off by the nonlabor, current inputs needed for copper production. By far the most important inputs of this type were transportation services and electric power. The demand for transportation services produced the most important secondary repercussion from the copper industry. The railroad, built in response to this demand, directly employed large numbers of workers and facilitated growth in such sectors as agriculture. The electric-power industry established under the impetus provided by copper expansion also was an important factor in permitting growth in other industrial sectors, but the industry did not furnish much employment itself.

As detailed in chapter 3, the key aspects of export expansion are its effects in stimulating the use of improved techniques in other parts of the economy and in improving the skills of the labor force (pp. 64–70). Unlike economies in which resources are fully employed and efficiently allocated, changes in demand conditions, that is, pecuniary spillovers, in underdeveloped areas do affect the quantitative and qualitative features of the basic means of production. Specifically, when traditional producers receive larger incomes because of an increase in demand derived directly or indirectly from the export industry, they do more than try to expand output under existing techniques. They tend to introduce improved productive techniques previously unfeasible because of such factors as the relation between their income level and the risks involved in using these techniques, and the conditions of capital rationing which operate against them. The greater the increase in the demand for products already being produced, or that can be produced rather easily with existing factor supplies, the more extensive the adoption of better technology in these product lines. Demand repercussions, in other words, cause not just a shift in resource allocation but lead to an increase in the productive powers of existing resources. Unfortunately, the nature of the production function for copper was such that the direct and indirect demand effects derived from the industry were not very large.

The technological spillovers from the copper industry, on the other hand, were favorable for inducing further growth. Besides important locational benefits owing to the building of a railroad extending the entire length of the country, the copper industry also provided important skill-acquiring opportunities. The proportion of skilled workers in the total work force employed by the copper industry was significant, and the nature of the skill ladder in the industry was such that unskilled workers could gradually advance by means of on-the-job training. Moreover, most of the skills acquired in the copper industry were general ones that were easily used in other industries.

The combined impact of the pecuniary and technological externalities derived from the technological features of copper production caused Rhodesian development to be confined to a relatively small number of industries and to a relatively small proportion of the available labor force. Although certain forces were established within the monetary sector which acted to bring about its continued expansion, its size and growth were insufficient to produce other than a dualistic development pattern within the country.

THE RELEVANCE OF OTHER GROWTH THEORIES

Although the main contours of Rhodesia's growth have been fashioned by technological factors, this growth has also been significantly affected by the use of monopolistic power by special groups. The most important way this monopoly power has been used is to influence the distribution of the benefits from development. The European population, who from the outset possessed almost all political and economic power in the territory, followed a policy over the years which served to retain a major share of the economic gains from growth for themselves. In agriculture, they first excluded African producers from most of the land that could be used to meet the food demands stimulated by the expansion of the mining industry. Later they established marketing controls over such major products as maize and cattle for the purpose of protecting these markets against African penetration. In industry, the story was the same. Tightly organized European unions were permitted to use their powerful bargaining position to prevent any significant advancement in labor skills by African workers. The policy seemed to be that the benefits to the African of urban development were to extend only as far as becoming an unskilled worker. Where he could live in the towns and, indeed, *if* he could live in them, were determined by the Europeans.

What is important in affecting the distribution of income is not just what the Europeans did but what they did not do. Until recent years there were very few positive programs for improving the African's status. There were many good intentions but few actual programs. Such rural programs as improving roads and transport services, furnishing efficient storage facilities, training farmers in the use of better techniques, and providing special credit facilities were extremely modest in size and scope. Such basic welfare activities as education and medical care in African rural areas also received minimal attention from the state.

European monopolistic efforts did much more than affect the distribution of income. They retarded the overall rate of development itself. The larger skilled-labor force that would exist, if monopolistic government and union policies had not been followed, could be employed not only in the production of more copper but also in more numerous secondary industries than presently exist. Agricultural output also would be larger and better balanced if Africans had been permitted to compete freely in the market place. The economy would still be dualistic and heavily dependent upon the copper industry, but compared with its present extreme narrowness, the faster, more-balanced growth that would have resulted could have made an important contribution to the country's present development goals.

One development hypothesis that is not consistent with Rhodesian growth experience is the theory that stresses such factors as limited wants and lack of response to price incentive as causes of dualistic development (see pp. 6–8). Contrary to what this theory predicts, the people of Central Africa respond positively and quickly to market opportunities for raising their living standards. The manner in which Africans living near the line of rail reacted to the cash opportunities for marketing maize by increasing production and adopting better methods of farming provides a vivid example of the nonapplicability of this hypothesis. Their positive behavior toward market opportunities for other agricultural products confirms this experience with maize. With respect to urban employment, available evidence does not support the hypothesis that the individual Africans' supply curve of urban labor is backward-bending. The wants-horizon of the migrant

African has widened tremendously over the last 30 years, and he is now eager to spend a large fraction of his working years within the urban areas.

My analysis of Rhodesian growth does not support a development theory that ascribes the lack of broadly based growth in the country to a deterioration of the terms of trade. The years from 1940 to 1960 were the period of great export expansion and of dualistic growth in Northern Rhodesia, and yet the country's terms of trade were more favorable at the end of this period than at the beginning. But, even setting this factual evidence aside, the terms-of-trade argument is not particularly relevant for a mineral-exporting economy like Northern Rhodesia. The fundamental problem was that an increase in copper exports induced very little other domestic spending and production. In other words, the multiplier effect of an export increase on real income elsewhere in the economy was low. If the ratio of copper prices to import prices had risen more rapidly than it did, the increase in induced real income would obviously have been larger. But it is doubtful if this would have resulted in the establishment of a much larger number of domestically based industries. The problem was not getting a little more of what the Rhodesians already had. Rather, it was that an expansion of their export industry was incapable of triggering the development of a diversified domestic industrial structure.

GROWTH PROSPECTS IN ZAMBIA

Does the analysis of the effects of copper technology on development mean that the growth prospects of Northern Rhodesia (or Zambia as it is now called) are poor? Not at all. The new nation of Zambia faces development prospects that surpass those in almost all the rest of Africa. What it does mean is that expanding the development base will not be an easy task. It requires strong and imaginative political leadership backed by careful, practicable economic planning.

To begin with, better economic statistics must be obtained. In particular, a much more detailed census of production is necessary in order to obtain an accurate estimate of the flow of intersector purchases within the economy. It appears that considerably more can and should be done in the way of supplying domestically the input requirements of the copper industry. The possibilities are limited enough because of general economic constraints; they should not be further limited because of lack of knowledge. Similarly, in assessing the feasibility of other new industries, it is important to know the interindustry repercussions that will be created. Formulating policy in the field of African agriculture is badly hampered by lack of economic information. For example, present income estimates in the subsistence sector are only rough guesses. Even knowledge concerning the number of African farmers in the money economy, the commodity composition of their output, and their production techniques is very inadequate.

The agricultural sector is the main problem in Zambia. For, if one sets as his prime objective the raising of income levels for the great mass of people living in the subsistence sector, then it is clear that this must be done mainly by raising agricultural incomes. In the immediate future, employment possibilities in industry will be insufficient to tap more than a small part of the labor force, even under the most optimistic assumptions about industrial expansion possibilities. The great question, therefore, is how to raise agricultural productivity.

Experience shows that one way not to approach this goal is to concentrate almost exclusively upon getting African farmers to make significant technological improvements in their productive practices. Starting out with training schemes is not only costly but does not seem to work. A better way is to raise the cash-earnings prospects of African farmers under present techniques by improving the facilities for marketing their products in the money economy. Rhodesian experience shows that African farmers will take advantage of better cash opportunities not only by expanding output under existing practices but by adopting improved techniques in order to improve their position still more. It is at this stage that they can be most usefully helped by those who can teach them the new techniques.

With respect to specific policy, greater emphasis should be placed upon improving marketing facilities than in previous rural development efforts. This means devoting more development funds for extending and improving the road system in African rural areas and providing better transport services (probably at subsidized rates) into these areas. When a new commodity is introduced into African agriculture and pushed for export, action must also be taken by the government to prevent its price from fluctuating widely during the early years of its cultivation. The fear—based on past experience—of switching to the production of an economically attractive item, only to have its price drop drastically because of some short-run cyclical pressure, is a major reason why some products that look promising from a long-run viewpoint do not catch on with African producers.

Any agricultural program should be directed toward producing items that can be exported. The internal demand for agricultural products is nowhere near enough to raise rural incomes to any appreciable extent. Tobacco—Turkish, burley, and Virginia—groundnuts, cotton, and cattle appear to offer the best prospects for export expansion. Every effort must be made to take advantage of these opportunities as well as to seek new ones.

The only product that is an important exception to the generalization that African agricultural income can be raised appreciably only by relying on international market demand is maize. If the costly subsidization of European maize producers is stopped, and if the monopoly use of Crown Lands by European farmers is brought to an end, African farmers are very likely to take over almost all of the maize market. In the face of African competition, Europeans will find it much more profitable to specialize in those agricultural products that require a high degree of technical and managerial know-how.

The more agricultural incomes rise, the more extensive can become the industrial base of Zambia. To repeat, the present internal market for most consumer goods is so small as to limit severely the possibilities for establishing local industry to supply it. Further industrialization is immediately possible to take advantage of certain direct and indirect industrial demands generated by the copper industry, but it is limited in terms of the number of higher-earning, employment opportunities needed in the economy. Significant long-run expansion of industry directed at internal demand must await a significant improvement in rural incomes.

Like agriculture, if major industrial expansion is to occur in the near future, it must be directed at export markets. Clearly, copper does not offer any unusual prospects in this regard. The basis on which Zambia may be able to increase exports significantly is not the presence of some special natural resource but of a well-trained labor force. Copper production, as pointed out many times, does have favorable labor-training effects. So far, the labor-training repercussions on the African labor force have been largely blocked by the monopolistic pressures from European trade unions. If this monopoly is broken and—what is economically crucial but politically very difficult—the wages of African skilled workers are not set at the artificially high European levels, Zambia could become a major exporter of manufactured products in Africa. Most countries to the north, east, and west are not automatically training skilled labor within the export process itself. Countries to the south do possess a skilled labor force, but its wage level is set at the monopolistic European level. If wages for skilled and semiskilled labor in Zambia could be set at levels that are based on economic fairness as well as social fairness, the country might be able to take advantage of its unique position and become an important industrial exporter.

For most emerging nations, questions of finance dominate the scope and composition of any development program. Zambia is, of course, not free from financial constraints, but the copper industry does provide tax revenues the size of which is envied by all governments in Africa. Because of these revenues, the ability of the government to borrow internationally is much greater than of most of the less-developed countries. By means of redirecting the use of existing tax revenues, tapping additional sources of tax revenues, and borrowing both internally and internationally, the government should be able to provide effective leadership in taking advantage of the favorable development opportunities that exist for the country.

Bibliography

Books

Baldwin, Robert E. "Investment Policy in Underdeveloped Countries," in *Economic Development in Africa,* ed. E. F. Jackson. Oxford: Basil Blackwell, 1965.

Balten, T. R. *Problems of African Development.* London: Oxford University Press, 1947.

Baran, Paul A. *The Political Economy of Growth.* New York: Monthly Review Press, 1957.

Barber, William J. *The Economy of British Central Africa.* Stanford: Stanford University Press, 1961.

Bézy, F. *Problèmes Structurels de l'Économie Congolaise.* Louvain: Institut de Recherches Économiques et Sociales, 1957.

Boeke, J. H. *Economics and Economic Policy of Dual Societies.* New York: Institute of Pacific Relations, 1953.

Bradley, Kenneth. *Copper Venture.* London: Mufulira Copper Mines, 1952.

Butts, A., ed. *Copper: The Science and Technology of the Metal, Its Alloys and Compounds.* New York: Reinhold, 1954.

Cannisen, Jan. *The Luapula Peoples of Northern Rhodesia.* Manchester: Manchester University Press, 1959.

Clegg, Edward. *Race and Politics.* London: Oxford University Press, 1960.

Colson, Elizabeth. *The Social Organization of the Gwembe Tonga.* Manchester: Manchester University Press, 1960.

Coulter, Charles W. "The Sociological Problem," in *Modern Industry and the African,* ed. J. Merle Davis. London: Macmillan, 1933.

Davidson, J. W. *The Northern Rhodesian Legislative Council.* London: Faber and Faber, 1948.

Deane, Phyllis. *Colonial Social Accounting.* Cambridge: Cambridge University Press, 1953.

———. *The Measurement of Colonial National Incomes.* National Institute of Economic and Social Research, Occasional Paper, no. 12. Cambridge: Cambridge University Press, 1948.

Doke, C. M. *The Lambas of Northern Rhodesia.* London: George G. Harrap, 1931.

Elliott, William Y., *et al. International Control in the Non-Ferrous Metals.* New York: Macmillan, 1937.

D'Erlanger, Emile B. *The History of the Construction and Finance of the Rhodesian Transport System.* London: Burrup Mathieson, 1939.

Forde, D. *Ethnographic Survey of Africa.* London: International African Institute, 1950.

Frankel, S. Herbert. *Capital Investment in Africa.* London: Oxford University Press, 1938.

Gann, L. H. *The Birth of a Plural Society.* Manchester: Manchester University Press, 1958.

———. *A History of Northern Rhodesia.* London: Chatto and Windus, 1964.

Gelfand, M. *The Sick African.* 3d ed. Cape Town: Juta, 1957.

———. *Tropical Victory.* Cape Town: Juta, 1953.

Gouldsbury, C., and H. Sheane. *The Great Plateau of Northern Rhodesia.* London: Edward Arnold, 1911.

Graves, I. C. *Modern Production among Backward People.* London: George Allen and Unwin, 1935.

Gray, Richard. *The Two Nations.* London: Oxford University Press, 1960.

Haberler, Gottfried. "Terms of Trade and Economic Development," in *Economic Development for Latin America,* ed. Howard Ellis. New York: St. Martin's Press, 1961.

Hagen, Everett E. *On the Theory of Social Change.* Homewood: Dorsey Press, 1962.

Hazlewood, Arthur, and P. D. Henderson. *Nyasaland: The Economics of Federation.* Oxford: Basil Blackwell, 1960.

Higgins, Benjamin. *Economic Development: Problems, Principles, and Policies.* New York: W. W. Norton, 1959.

Hirshleifer, Jack, James C. DeHaven, and Jerome W. Milliman. *Water Supply: Economics, Technology, and Policy.* Chicago: University of Chicago Press, 1960.

International Labour Office. *African Labour Survey.* Geneva, 1958.

Irvine, A. G. *The Balance of Payments of Rhodesia and Nyasaland, 1945–1954.* London: Oxford University Press, 1959.

Joelson, F. S., ed. *Rhodesia and East Africa.* London: East Africa and Rhodesia, 1958.

Keatley, P. *The Politics of Partnership*. Baltimore: Penguin Books, 1963.

Kindleberger, Charles P. *The Terms of Trade*. New York: John Wiley & Sons, 1956.

Kuczynski, R. R. *Demographic Survey of the British Colonial Empire*. Vol. II. London: Oxford University Press, 1949.

Lewin, Julius. *The Colour Bar in the Copper Belt*. Johannesburg: South African Institute of Race Relations, 1941.

Leys, Colin, and Crawford Pratt, eds. *A New Deal in Central Africa*. London: Heinemann, 1960.

McKean, Roland N. *Efficiency in Government through Systems Analysis*. New York: John Wiley & Sons, 1958.

Malcolm, Dougal O. *The British South Africa Company, 1889–1939*. London: Herbert Fitch, 1939.

Mason, Philip. *Year of Decision: Rhodesia and Nyasaland in 1960*. London: Oxford University Press, 1960.

Meier, Gerald M. *International Trade and Development*. New York: Harper and Row, 1963.

Meier, Gerald M., and Robert E. Baldwin. *Economic Development: Theory, History, Policy*. New York: John Wiley & Sons, 1957.

Mill, John Stuart. *Principles of Political Economy*. London: Longmans Green, 1940.

Mitchell, J. Clyde. "Demographic Appendix," in *Social Relations in Central African Industry*, eds. D. Mathews and R. Apthorpe. Twelfth Conference Proceedings of the Rhodes-Livingstone Institute for Social Research. Lusaka, 1958.

Nurkse, R. *Problems of Capital Formation in Underdeveloped Countries*. Oxford: Basil Blackwell, 1953.

Organization for European Economic Co-operation. *The Non-Ferrous Metal Industry*. Paris, 1956.

Prain, Sir Ronald L. "Building on a Mineral Foundation," in *Rhodesia and East Africa*, ed. F. S. Joelson. London: East Africa and Rhodesia, 1958.

———. "The Copper Industry: Some Factors Affecting Its Future," in his *Selected Papers*, Vol. II, 1958–1960. Address to the Mining Club, New York, Feb. 4, 1959. London: B. T. Batsford, 1961. Pp. 57–67.

———. *The Copperbelt of Northern Rhodesia*. London: Royal Society of Arts, 1955.

Prebisch, Raul. *The Economic Development of Latin America and Its Principal Problems*. New York: United Nations, Department of Economic Affairs, 1950.

Ricardo, David. *Principles of Political Economy and Taxation*. Everyman's Library. London: J. M. Dent and Sons, 1911.

Richards, Audrey I., ed. *Economic Development and Tribal Change*. Cambridge: W. Heffer and Sons, 1957.

———. *Land, Labour and Diet in Northern Rhodesia.* London: Oxford University Press, 1939.

Robinson, E. A. G. "The Economic Problem," in *Modern Industry and the African,* ed. J. Merle Davis. London: Macmillan, 1933.

Schumpeter, J. A. *Capitalism, Socialism and Democracy.* New York: Harper, 1947.

———. *The Theory of Economic Development.* New York: Oxford University Press, 1961.

Skelton, Alex. "Copper," in *International Control in the Non-Ferrous Metals,* ed. W. Y. Elliott *et al.* New York: Macmillan, 1937.

Smith, Adam. *An Inquiry into the Nature and Causes of the Wealth of Nations.* New York: Modern Library, 1937.

Smith, Edwin W., and A. M. Dale. *The Ila-Speaking Peoples of Northern Rhodesia.* London: Macmillan, 1920. 2 vols.

Smith, Prudence, ed. *Africa in Transition.* London: Max Reinhardt, 1958.

Thompson, C. H., and H. W. Woodruff. *Economic Development in Rhodesia and Nyasaland.* London: E. Dobson, 1954.

Turner, V. W. *Schism and Continuity in an African Society: A Study of Ndembu Village Life.* Manchester: Manchester University Press, 1957.

Watson, Sir Malcolm. *African Highway.* London: John Murray, 1953.

Watson, W. *Tribal Cohesion in a Money Economy.* Manchester: Manchester University Press, 1958.

Worthington, E. B. *Science in Africa.* London: Oxford University Press, 1938.

Youngson, A. J. *Possibilities of Economic Progress.* Cambridge: Cambridge University Press, 1959.

PAMPHLETS AND PERIODICALS

Allan, W., *et al. Land Holding and Land Usage among the Plateau Tonga of Mazabuka District.* Rhodes-Livingstone Papers, no. 14. London: Oxford University Press, 1948.

Allan, William. *Studies in African Land Usage in Northern Rhodesia.* Rhodes-Livingstone Papers, no. 15. London: Oxford University Press, 1949.

Anderson, D. L. "Kariba Hydro-Electric Power for Central African Development," *Optima,* VI (June, 1956), 37–43.

Austin, F. W. "Fifty Years of the Rhodesia Railways," in *African World Annual,* 1948.

Baldwin, R. E. "Patterns of Development in Newly Settled Regions," *Manchester School of Economic and Social Studies,* XXIV (May, 1956), 161–179.

———. "Secular Movements in the Terms of Trade," *American Eco-*

nomic Review, Papers and Proceedings, XLV (May, 1955), 259–269.

Barnes, J. A. *Marriage in a Changing Society*. Rhodes-Livingstone Papers, no. 20. London: Oxford University Press, 1951.

Bennett, O. B., "The Improvement in Plant Practice and Labour Utilisation at Rhokana Corporation," *Journal of the South African Institute of Mining and Metallurgy* (May and Sept., 1958).

———. "Large-Scale Mining Methods on the Copperbelt," *Optima*, III (June, 1953), 19–24.

Berg, E. J. "Backward-Sloping Labor Supply Functions in Dual Economies: The Africa Case," *Quarterly Journal of Economics*, LXXV (Aug., 1961), 468–492.

Bettison, David G. *Numerical Data on African Dwellers in Lusaka, Northern Rhodesia*. Rhodes-Livingstone Communication, no. 16. Lusaka: Rhodes-Livingstone Institute, 1959.

Bradford, G. "Electric Power for Future Economic Development of the Rhodesias," *Optima*, III (June, 1953), 8–13.

Cole, D. T. "Fanagalo and the Bantu Languages in South Africa," *African Studies*, XII (March, 1953), 1–9.

Cole, L. S. "Hard Metal: The New Rock Drilling Medium," *Optima*, II (June, 1952), 20–23.

Colebrook, M. R. "Economic Factors in Farm Planning," *Rhodesia Agricultural Journal*, LVII (March-April, 1961).

Colsen, E. *Life among the Cattle-Owning Plateau Tonga*. Occasional Papers of the Rhodes-Livingstone Museum, no. 6 Livingstone, 1949.

———. "Plateau Tonga Diet," *Rhodes-Livingstone Journal*, XXIV (Dec., 1958), 51–62.

Cooper, G. "Village Crafts in Barotseland," *Rhodes-Livingstone Journal*, XI (1951), 47–60.

Duff, C. E. "Preservative Tests and Durability Trials with Native Timbers of the Copper Belt of Northern Rhodesia," *British Wood Preserving Association Journal*, V.

Eckaus, R. S. "Factor Proportions in Underdeveloped Areas," *American Economic Review*, XLV (Sept., 1955), 539–565.

Elkan, W. *An African Labour Force*. East African Studies, no. 7. Kampala: East African Institute of Social Research, 1956.

———. "The Persistence of Migrant Labour," *Inter-African Labour Institute Bulletin*, VI (Sept. 1, 1959), 36–43.

Flanders, M. June. "Prebisch on Protection: An Evaluation," *Economic Journal*, LXXIV (June, 1964), 305–327.

Fosbrooke, H. A. "Social Security as a Felt Want in East and Central Africa," *Inter-African Labour Institute Bulletin*, VI (May 1, 1959), 8–57.

Gann, L. H. "The Northern Rhodesian Copper Industry and the World of Copper: 1923–1952," *Rhodes-Livingstone Journal*, XVIII 1955), 1–18.

Gleeson, P. J. "The Story of the Broken Hill Mine in Northern Rhodesia," *Optima,* II (Sept., 1952), 5–10.

Gluckman, Max. *The Economy of the Central Barotse Plain.* Rhodes-Livingstone Papers, no. 7. Livingstone: Rhodes-Livingstone Institute, 1941.

Gulliver, P. H. *Labour Migration in a Rural Economy.* East African Studies, no. 6. Kampala: East African Institute of Social Research, 1955.

Gussman, B. S. "Industrial Efficiency and Urban Africa," *Africa,* XXIII (1953), 135–144.

Hoselitz, Bert F. "Social Implications of Economic Growth," *Economic Weekly,* Feb. 14, 21, 1959. Reprinted in T. Morgan, G. W. Betz, and W. K. Choudhry, eds., *Readings in Economic Development,* no. 9. Belmont, Calif.: Wadsworth, 1963.

Johnson, R. W. M. *The Economics of Subsistence.* Technical Paper in Agricultural Economics, no. 1. Salisbury: University College of Rhodesia and Nyasaland, 1963.

Leontief, Wassily W. "Domestic Production and Foreign Trade: The American Capital Position Re-examined," *Proceedings of the American Philosophical Society,* XCVII (Sept., 1953), 332–349.

———. "The Structure of Development," *Scientific American,* CCIX (Sept., 1963), 148–166.

McCulloch, Merran. *A Social Survey of the African Population of Livingstone.* Rhodes-Livingstone Papers, no. 26. Manchester: Manchester University Press, 1956.

Miracle, M. P. "Plateau Tonga Entrepreneurs in Historical Inter-Regional Trade," *Rhodes-Livingstone Journal,* XXVI (Dec., 1959), 34–50.

Mitchell, J. Clyde. *African Urbanization in Ndola and Luanshya.* Rhodes-Livingstone Communication, no. 6. Lusaka: Rhodes-Livingstone Institute, 1954.

———. "Aspects of African Marriage on the Copperbelt of Northern Rhodesia," *Rhodes-Livingstone Journal,* XXII (Sept., 1957), 1–30.

———. "The Distribution of African Labour by Area of Origin in the Copper Mines of Northern Rhodesia," *Rhodes-Livingstone Journal,* XIV (1954), 30–36.

———. "An Estimate of Fertility among Africans on the Copperbelt of Northern Rhodesia," *Rhodes-Livingstone Journal,* XIII (1953), 18–29.

———. "Migrant Labour in Africa South of the Sahara: The Causes of Labour Migration," *Inter-African Labour Institute Bulletin,* VI (Jan. 1, 1959).

———. "A Note on the Urbanization of Africans on the Copperbelt," *Rhodes-Livingstone Journal,* XII (1951), 20–27.

Moore, R. J. B. "Native Wages and Standard of Living in Northern Rhodesia," *African Studies,* I (June, 1942), 142–148.

Morgan, T. "The Long-Run Terms of Trade Between Agriculture and Manufacturing," *Economic Development and Cultural Change,* VIII (Oct., 1959), pp. 1–23.

Myint, H. N. "An Interpretation of Economic Backwardness," *Oxford Economic Papers,* VI (June, 1954), 132–163.

Nelems, H. E. "Open Pit Mining at Nchanga," *Optima,* V (March, 1955), 6–14.

Nichols, C. P. "The Bancroft Mine: A Tale of Tribulation and Triumph," *Optima,* VI (Sept., 1956), 65–70.

Oppenheimer, Sir Ernest. "The Advancement of Africans in Industry," *Optima,* III (Sept., 1953), 1–3.

Peters, D. U. *Land Usage in Barotseland.* Rhodes-Livingstone Communication, no. 19. Lusaka: Rhodes-Livingstone Institute, 1960.

————. *Land Usage in Serenje District; A Survey of Land Usage and the Agricultural System of the Lalu of the Serenje Plateau.* Rhodes-Livingstone Papers, no. 19. London: Oxford University Press, 1950.

Prain, Sir Ronald L. "The Development of the Copper Industry," in *Royal School of Mines, University of London,* Special University Lectures, no. 3. London: Portsoken Press, Nov., 1957. Pp. 27–45.

————. "The Northern Rhodesia Copperbelt," *New Commonwealth,* XXVI (Dec. 7, 1953), 601–607.

————. "The Problem of African Advancement on the Copperbelt of Northern Rhodesia," *African Affairs,* LIII (April, 1954), 91–103.

————. "The Stabilization of Labour in the Rhodesian Copper Belt," *African Affairs,* LV (Oct., 1956), 305–312.

"Reading Habits in a Part of the Mushiri Reserve," *Rhodes-Livingstone Journal,* XI (1951), 61–73.

Rhodesian–Anglo-American. *Mining Developments in Northern Rhodesia.* London, 1929. Copy in Colonial Office Library, London.

Richardson, E. M. *Ausli Village Structure in the Fort Rosebery District of Northern Rhodesia.* Rhodes-Livingstone Communication, no. 13. Lusaka: Rhodes-Livingstone Institute, 1959.

Royal Colonial Institute. *Proceedings.* Vol. XXXVIII. London, 1907.

Singer, H. W. "The Distribution of Gains between Investing and Borrowing Countries," *American Economic Review, Papers and Proceedings,* XL (May, 1950), 473–485.

Slevers, W., *et al.* "Safety Practices in Mining at Rhokana, Northern Rhodesia," *Journal of the Chemical, Metallurgical and Mining Society of South Africa,* LIII (Oct., 1953).

"Social Problems of the Northern Rhodesia Copperbelt," *International Labour Review,* XLIII (May, 1941), 542–551.

Spearpoint, C. F. "The African Native and the Rhodesian Copper Mines," *African Affairs,* XXXVI (July, 1937), 1–56.

Talbot, H. L. "Nchanga Mine's New Copper Leach Plant," *Optima,* II (June, 1952), 10–14.

Tarring, L. H. "Prospects for More Stability in Metal Prices," *Optima,* IX (Sept., 1959), 135–148.

Thompson, C. H. "Some Factors in the Economic Development of the Federation," *Proceedings of the Rhodesian Economic Society,* I (April, 1959).

Thomson, Betty Preston. *Two Studies in African Nutrition.* Rhodes-Livingstone Papers, no. 24. Manchester: Manchester University Press, 1954.

Van Bloommestein, J. H. G. "Conquest of Malaria in the Copperbelt," *Optima,* I (Dec., 1951), 19–21.

Watson, W. "Migrant Labour in Africa South of the Sahara: Migrant Labour and Detribalization," *Inter-African Labour Institute Bulletin,* VI (March 1, 1959), 8–33.

White, C. M. N. *An Outline of Luvale Social and Political Origin.* Rhodes-Livingstone Papers, no. 30. Manchester: Manchester University Press, 1960.

———. *A Preliminary Survey of Luvale Rural Economy.* Rhodes-Livingstone Papers, no. 29. Manchester: Manchester University Press, 1959.

Wilson, Godfrey. *An Essay on the Economics of Detribalization in Northern Rhodesia.* Rhodes-Livingstone Papers, no. 5. Livingstone: Rhodes-Livingstone Institute, 1941.

GOVERNMENT REPORTS AND PUBLICATIONS

Federation of Rhodesia and Nyasaland

Federation of Rhodesia and Nyasaland. *Agricultural Policy in the Federation of Rhodesia and Nyasaland: Report to the Federal Minister of Agriculture by the Federal Standing Committee on Agricultural Production in Collaboration with Professor Sir Frank Engledow,* C. Fed. 77. Salisbury: Government Printer, 1958.

———. *Annual Report on the Public Health of the Federation of Rhodesia and Nyasaland, 1959.* Salisbury: Government Printer, 1960.

———. Annual Reports on Education. Salisbury: Government Printer.

———. "Development Plan 1954–57." Presented to the Federation Assembly June 29, 1954. Mimeographed.

———. *Development Plan 1957–61.* Salisbury: Government Printer, 1957.

———. *Estimates of Expenditure during the Year Ending 30th June, 1960.* Salisbury: Government Printer, 1959.

———. *Estimates of Expenditure during the Year Ending 30th June, 1961.* Salisbury: Government Printer, 1960.

———. *Fifth Report of the Commissioner of Taxes for the Year Ended 30th June 1959.* Salisbury: Government Printer, 1960.

———. *Financial Statement 1960–61.* Salisbury: Government Printer, 1960.

———. *First Report of the Secretary for Power Covering 6 April 1955 to 30 June 1957.* Salisbury: Government Printer, 1958.

———. *Parliamentary Debates* (Hansard no. 10) , Salisbury, July-Aug., 1960.

———. *Report of Commission of Inquiry into Rating Structure of the Rhodesia Railways,* C. Fed. 117. Salisbury: Government Printer, 1959.

———. *Report of the Commission of Inquiry into the Health and Medical Services of the Federation, 1959.* Salisbury: Government Printer, 1960.

———. *Report of the Comptroller and Auditor-General on the Finance Accounts, Appropriation Accounts, and Accounts of Miscellaneous Funds for the Financial Year Ended 30th June, 1960.* Salisbury: Government Printer, 1961.

———. *Report of the Comptroller and Auditor-General on the Finance Accounts, Appropriation Accounts and Accounts of Miscellaneous Funds for the Financial Year Ended 30th June, 1961.* Salisbury: Government Printer, 1962.

———. *Report of the Comptroller of Customs and Excise for the Period 1 April 1954–30 June 1959.* Salisbury: Government Printer, 1960.

———. *Review of the Development Plan 1957–1961.* Salisbury: Government Printer, 1958.

———. *Review of the Development Plan 1959–1963.* Salisbury: Government Printer, 1959.

———. *Second Report of the Secretary for Power Covering 1 July 1957 to 30 June 1958.* Salisbury: Government Printer, 1959.

———. *Sixth Report of the Commissioner of Taxes for the Year Ended 30th June 1960.* Salisbury: Government Printer, 1961.

———. Central Statistical Office. Annual Statements of External Trade. 1954–1960. Salisbury: Government Printer.

———. ———. *Census of Industrial Production, 1956–1957.* Salisbury: Government Printer, 1958.

———. ———. *Census of Population 1956.* Salisbury: Government Printer, 1960.

———. ———. *The Census of Production of the Federation of Rhodesia and Nyasaland, 1958–1959.* Salisbury: Government Printer, 1961.

———. ———. "First Report on Urban African Budget Surveys Held in Northern Rhodesia, May to August, 1960." Salisbury, 1960. Mimeographed.

———. ———. *Monthly Digest of Statistics,* VII (Dec., 1960).

———. ———. *National Accounts of the Federation of Rhodesia and Nyasaland, 1954–1959.* Salisbury: Government Printer, 1960.

————. ————. *National Accounts of the Federation of Rhodesia and Nyasaland, 1954–1960.* Salisbury: Government Printer, 1961.

————. ————. *National Accounts of the Federation of Rhodesia and Nyasaland, 1954–1961.* Salisbury: Government Printer, 1962.

————. ————. *National Income and Social Accounts of Northern Rhodesia, 1945–1953.* Salisbury: Government Printer, 1954.

————. ————. "Preliminary Results of Federal Censuses of Population and of Employees: (1) Industrial and Racial Distribution of Employees." Salisbury, 1962. Mimeographed.

————. ————. *Report on the Agricultural and Pastoral Production of Southern Rhodesia, Northern Rhodesia, and Nyasaland, 1958–59.* Salisbury: Government Printer, 1960.

————. ————. *Report on the Agricultural Production of Southern Rhodesia, Northern Rhodesia, and Nyasaland, 1960.* Salisbury: Government Printer, 1961.

————. ————. *Report on the Agricultural Production of Southern Rhodesia, Northern Rhodesia, and Nyasaland, 1961.* Salisbury: Government Printer, 1962.

————. ————. *Report on the Census of Industrial Production, 1956–1957.* Salisbury: Government Printer, 1958.

————. ————. *Report on the Census of Industrial Production, 1957–1958.* Salisbury: Government Printer, 1959.

————. ————. "Report on Northern Rhodesia African Demographic Surveys, May to August, 1960." Salisbury, January, 1961. Mimeographed.

————. ————. *Report on Northern Rhodesian Family Expenditure Survey 1951.* Salisbury: Government Printer, 1953.

————. ————. "Second Report on Urban African Budget Survey Held in Northern Rhodesia May to August 1960." Salisbury. 1961. Mimeographed.

————. Federal Department of Conservation and Extension. *Report of the Federal Cattle and Beef Marketing Committee.* Salisbury, 1954.

————. Federal Power Board. *Annual Report and Accounts for the Year Ended 30th June, 1958.* Salisbury: Rhodesian Printers, 1959.

————. ————. *Annual Report and Accounts for the Year Ended 30th June, 1960.* Salisbury, 1960.

————. Grain Marketing Board. *Report of the Grain Marketing Board and Memorandum on Grain Marketing in Northern and Southern Rhodesia during the Period Ended 30th June, 1958.* Salisbury, n.d.

————. ————. *Report of the Grain Marketing Board for the Year Ended 30th June, 1959.* Salisbury: Service Press, n.d.

————. ————. *Report of the Grain Marketing Board for the Year Ended 30th June, 1960.* Salisbury: Service Press, n.d.

————. Ministry of Agriculture. *Proceedings of the Second Annual*

Conference of the Professional Officers of the Department of Research and Specialist Services. Salisbury: Government Printer, 1956.
————. Ministry of Economic Affairs. *Economic Report 1961.* Salisbury: Government Printer, 1961.
————. ————. *Federal Government Development Plan, 1962–1965.* Salisbury: Government Printer, 1962.

Great Britain

Browne, Major G. St. J. Orde. *Labour Conditions in East Africa.* Colonial Office. Colonial, no. 193. London: H.M.S.O., 1946.
————. *Labour Conditions in Northern Rhodesia.* Colonial Office. Colonial, no. 150. London: H.M.S.O., 1938.
Great Britain. *Correspondence with Regard to Native Policy in Northern Rhodesia.* Cmd. 3731. London: H.M.S.O., 1930.
————. *Memorandum on Native Policy in East Africa.* Cmd. 3573. London: H.M.S.O., 1930.
————. *Report of the Advisory Commission on the Review of the Constitution of Rhodesia and Nyasaland.* Cmd. 1148. London: H.M.S.O., 1960.
————. *Report of the Commission Appointed To Enquire into the Disturbances in the Copperbelt, Northern Rhodesia.* Cmd. 5009. London: H.M.S.O., 1935.
————. *Rhodesia-Nyasaland Royal Commission Report.* Cmd. 5949. London: H.M.S.O., 1939.
————. Advisory Commission on the Review of the Constitution of the Federation of Rhodesia and Nyasaland. *Report: Appendix VI— Survey of Developments Since 1953.* Cmd. 1149. London: H.M.S.O. October, 1960.
————. Colonial Office. *Advisory Committee on Education in the Colonies.* Colonial, no. 186. London: H.M.S.O., 1944.
————. ————. *North Charterland Concession Inquiry: Report to the Governor of Northern Rhodesia by the Commissioner, Mr. Justice Maugham.* Colonial, no. 73. London: H.M.S.O., 1932.
————. ————. *Northern Rhodesia, Report for 1924–25.* Colonial, no. 1292. London: H.M.S.O., 1925.
————. ————. *Northern Rhodesia, Report for 1926.* Colonial, no. 1380. London: H.M.S.O., 1928.
————. ————. *Report of the Commission Appointed To Enquire into the Financial and Economic Position of Northern Rhodesia.* Colonial, no. 145. London: H.M.S.O., 1938.
————. ————. *Report on Central African Rail Link Development Survey.* 2 vols. London: H.M.S.O., June, 1952.
————. ————. *Report on Northern Rhodesia for the Year 1959.* Lusaka: Government Printer, 1960.
Hailey, Lord William Malcolm. *Native Administration in the British*

African Territories. Part II. Central Africa: Zanzibar, Nyasaland, Northern Rhodesia. Colonial Office. London: H.M.S.O., 1950.

Howitt, Sir Harold. *Rhodesian Railways Ltd. Report on State Ownership.* Dominions Office. Dominions, no. 3. London: H.M.S.O., 1946.

Northcott, C. H. *African Labour Efficiency Survey.* Colonial Office. Colonial Research Publication, no. 3. London: H.M.S.O., 1949.

Northern Rhodesia

(The Office of Government Printers moved from Livingstone to Lusaka in 1935.)

Brannigan, P. F. *Report of Commission Appointed To Inquire into the Unrest in the Mining Industry of Northern Rhodesia in Recent Months.* Lusaka: Government Printer, 1946.

Brelsford, W. V. *Northern Rhodesia Copperbelt Markets: A Social and Economic Study.* Lusaka: Government Printer, 1947.

Busschau, W. J. *Report on Development of Secondary Industries in Northern Rhodesia.* Lusaka: Government Printer, 1945.

Carr, Allan. "The Production of Flue-Cured Virginia Tobacco in Northern Rhodesia," in *Agricultural Bulletin,* no. 2. Lusaka: Government Printer, 1950.

Clay, G. F. *Memorandum on Post-War Development Planning in Northern Rhodesia.* Lusaka: Government Printer, 1945.

Clifford, W. *Physical Handicap amongst Africans in Broken Hill,* Social Welfare Research Monograph, no. 2. Lusaka: Government Printer, 1960.

Collins, J. C. "Review of Research on Flue-Cured Virginia Tobacco in Northern Rhodesia," in *Agricultural Bulletin,* no. 12. Lusaka: Government Printer, 1956.

Coster, R. N. "Peasant Farming the Petauke and Katete Areas of the Eastern Province of Northern Rhodesia," in *Agricultural Bulletin,* no. 15. Lusaka: Government Printer, 1958.

Dalgleish, A. *Report of the Commission Appointed To Inquire into the Advancement of Africans in Industry.* Lusaka: Government Printer, 1948.

DeBoer, H. S. *Following Tour through North-Eastern and Portions of North-Western Rhodesia.* Lusaka: Government Printer, 1934.

Forster, Sir John. *Report of Board of Inquiry Appointed To Inquire into the Advancement of Africans in the Copper Mining Industry in Northern Rhodesia.* Lusaka: Government Printer, 1954.

Fraser, R. H. *A Report on the Marketing of Northern Rhodesian Tobacco in Great Britain.* Lusaka: Government Printer, 1936.

Frisby, A. W. *African Education Development Plans, 1945–1955.* Lusaka: Government Printer, 1945.

Hadfield, J. "Aspects of the African Agrarian Economy in Northern

Rhodesia," in *Agricultural Bulletin,* no. 17. Lusaka: Government Printer, n.d.

Halcrow, M. "Intensive Rural Development Plans for the Northern and Luapula Provinces, 1957–1961." Lusaka, 1958.

———. *Recent Advance in the Northern and Luapula Provinces of Northern Rhodesia, Being a Report on Intensive Rural Development.* Lusaka: Government Printer, 1958.

Hobday, J. H. N. *Livestock Industry Development Plans, 1945–55.* Lusaka: Government Printer, 1945.

Jack, D. T. *Report of the Board of Inquiry To Consider the Proposed 40-Hour Week in the Copper Mining Industry of Northern Rhodesia.* Lusaka: Government Printer, 1950.

Johnson, C. E. "African Farming Improvement in the Plateau Tonga Maize Areas of Northern Rhodesia," in *Agricultural Bulletin,* no. 11. Lusaka: Government Printer, 1956.

Keith, J. L., and Lt. Col. Hon. A. Stephenson. *Report of the Sub-Committee of the Native Industrial Labour Advisory Board.* Lusaka: Government Printer, 1936.

Lambrechts, J. de V. *Report on Investigation into Dust and Ventilation Conditions in the Copper Mines and the Broken Hill Mine in Northern Rhodesia with Particular Reference to Silicosis.* Lusaka: Government Printer, 1945.

Lewin, C. J. *Agriculture and Forestry Development Plans for Ten Years.* Lusaka: Government Printer, 1945.

MacDonald, R. A. S. *Further Memorandum on the Economics of the Cattle Industry in Northern Rhodesia with Special Reference to the Native Cattle Industry.* Department of Veterinary Services. Lusaka: Government Printer, 1937.

Martin, J. D. "The Mukushi (Baikiaea Plurifuga Harms) Forests of Northern Rhodesia," in *Second Annual Bulletin of the Department of Agriculture.* Livingstone: Government Printer, 1933.

Milligan, S. *Report on the Present Position of the Agricultural Industry and the Necessity, or Otherwise, of Encouraging Further European Settlement in Agricultural Areas.* Livingstone: Government Printer, 1931.

Moffat, U. J. "Native Agriculture in the Abercorn District," in *Second Annual Bulletin of the Department of Agriculture.* Livingstone: Government Printer, 1933.

Moore, T. C. *Report on the Possibilities of Developing a Cotton Growing Industry on the North-Eastern Plateau and Neighboring Valleys of Northern Rhodesia.* Agriculture Department. Livingstone: Government Printer, 1926.

Northern Rhodesia. *Agricultural Advisory Board, 2nd Report.* Lusaka: Government Printer, 1936.

———. *The Agricultural Survey Commission Report, 1930–1932.* Livingstone: Government Printer, 1933.

————. *Annual Report of the Director of Native Education for the Year 1929*. London: Crown Agents for the Colonies, 1931.

————. "Annual Report of the Income Tax Department for the Year Ended 31st March 1931." Copy in National Archives of Rhodesia and Nyasaland, Salisbury.

————. *Annual Report upon Native Affairs, 1933*. Livingstone: Government Printer, 1934.

————. Annual Statements of the Trade of Northern Rhodesia. 1949–1953. Lusaka, Government Printer.

————. *Approved Estimates of the Development Fund, 1953–54*. Lusaka: Government Printer, 1953.

————. *Approved Estimates of the Development Fund, 1954–55*. Lusaka: Government Printer, 1954.

————. *Approved Estimates of Revenues and Expenditures for the Year 1958–59*. Lusaka: Government Printer, 1958.

————. *Blue Book for the Year Ended 31 December 1924*. No. 1. Livingstone: Government Printer, 1925.

————. *Blue Book for the Year Ended 31 December 1928*. No. 5. Livingstone: Government Printer, 1929.

————. "Census of Northern Rhodesia Taken 3 May 1921." Copy in National Archives of Rhodesia and Nyasaland, Salisbury. Item No. A 3/19/2/5. Handwritten.

————. *Commission on Development in Northern Rhodesia: Correspondence between Secretary of State for the Colonies and the Government of Northern Rhodesia, 1952*. Lusaka: Government Printer, 1953.

————. *Development of Social Services for Africans: Development Centres*. Lusaka: Government Printer, 1945.

————. *Draft Development Plan for the Period 1st July, 1961, to 30th June, 1965*. Lusaka: Government Printer, 1962.

————. *Economic Survey of Livingstone*. Lusaka: Government Printer, 1957.

————. *Estimates of Revenue and Expenditure*. Lusaka: Government Printer, 1960.

————. *European Education Commission, 1929 Report*. Livingstone: Government Printer, 1929.

————. *Evidence Taken by the Commission Appointed To Enquire into the Disturbances in the Copperbelt, Northern Rhodesia July-September 1935*, Vols. I, II. Lusaka: Government Printer, 1936.

————. *Final Report of the Commission of Inquiry into the Cost of Living*. Lusaka: Government Printer, 1950.

————. Financial Reports. 1947–1960. Lusaka: Government Printer.

————. Financial Statements. Lusaka: Government Printer.

————. *First Report on a Regional Survey of the Copperbelt, 1959*. Lusaka: Government Printer, 1960.

————. *Laws of Northern Rhodesia,* Vol. III. Lusaka: Government Printer, 1948.

————. *Legislative Council Debates* (no. 11), Second Session, Third Council, 7th March–1st April 1930. Livingstone: Government Printer, 1930.

————. *Legislative Council Debates* (Hansard), First Session, Fifth Council, Nov., Dec., 1935. Lusaka: Government Printer, 1935.

————. *Legislative Council Debates* (Hansard), Dec. 12, 1940. Lusaka: Government Printer, 1940.

————. *Legislative Council Debates* (Hansard nos. 60–62), June 29, 1951. Lusaka: Government Printer, 1951.

————. *Legislative Council Debates* (Hansard no. 87), 6th March–23rd March, 1956. Lusaka: Government Printer, 1956.

————. *Legislative Council Debates* (Hansard no. 88), 28th June–24th Aug., 1956). Lusaka: Government Printer, 1956.

————. *Legislative Council Debates* (Hansard no. 95), July–October, 1958. Lusaka: Government Printer, 1958.

————. *Legislative Council Debates* (Hansard no. 100), June–Aug., 1960. Lusaka: Government Printer, 1960.

————. *Medical Report on Health and Sanitary Conditions for the Years 1925 and 1926.* London: Crown Agents for the Colonies, 1928.

————. *Medical Report on Health and Sanitary Conditions for the Year 1928.* London: Crown Agents for the Colonies, 1929.

————. *Medical Report on Health and Sanitary Conditions for the Year 1929.* London: Crown Agents for the Colonies, 1930.

————. *Memorandum on the Work of the National Development Board.* Lusaka: Government Printer, 1941.

————. *Report of Agricultural Advisory Board, Third Report.* Lusaka: Government Printer, 1937.

————. *Report of Chairman of the National Industrial Labour Advisory Board.* Lusaka: Government Printer, 1936.

————. *Report of Chairman of the Native Industrial Labour Advisory Board, Ndola, November 7 and 8, December 16 and 17, 1935.* Lusaka: Government Printer, 1936.

————. *Report of Committee Appointed To Enquire into the Development of the European Farming Industry.* Lusaka: Government Printer, 1946.

————. *Report of Committee Appointed To Investigate European Education in Northern Rhodesia.* Lusaka: Government Printer, 1948.

————. *Report of Committee on Trade Testing and Apprenticeship for Africans.* Lusaka: Government Printer, 1957.

————. *Report of Land Commission.* Lusaka: Government Printer, 1946.

————. *Report of Ndola Anti-Malarial Scheme 1931.* Livingstone: Government Printer, 1931.

————. *Report of Taxation Review Committee.* Lusaka: Government Printer, 1946.

————. *Report of the Board of Inquiry Appointed To Inquire into the Advancement of Africans in the Copper Mining Industry in Northern Rhodesia.* Lusaka: Government Printer, 1954.

————. *Report of the Commission Appointed To Inquire into the Administration and Finances of Native Locations in Urban Areas.* Lusaka: Government Printer, 1944.

————. *Report of the Commission Appointed To Inquire the Disturbances in the Copperbelt, Northern Rhodesia, July 1940.* Lusaka: Government Printer, 1941.

————. *Report of the Commission Appointed To Inquire into the Mining Industry in Northern Rhodesia.* Lusaka: Government Printer, 1962.

————. *Report of the Commission Appointed To Review the Salary Structure, Remuneration and Terms of the Civil Service of Northern Rhodesia.* Lusaka: Government Printer, 1952.

————. *Report of the Commission To Inquire into the Organization and Operation of the Lusaka Power Station.* Lusaka: Government Printer, 1950.

————. "Report of the Committee Appointed To Inquire into the High Cost of Building in the Territory, 1951." Copy in the Colonial Office library, London. Mimeographed.

————. *Report of the Committee on Further Secondary Education for European Children.* Lusaka: Government Printer, 1946.

————. *Report of the Development Authority for the Year 1955.* Lusaka: Government Printer, 1956.

————. *Report of the Director of Census Regarding the Census Taken on 5 May 1931.* London: Crown Agents for Colonies, 1931.

————. *Report of the Finance Commission.* Livingstone: Government Printer, 1932.

————. *Report of the Government Unemployment Committee, 1932.* Livingstone: Government Printer, 1933.

————. *Report of the Land Commission on the Area Acquired by Government from the North Charterland Exploration Co.* Lusaka: Government Printer, 1944.

————. *Report of the Maize Sub-Committee of the Northern Rhodesia Agricultural Advisory Board.* Lusaka: Government Printer, 1935.

————. *Report of the Motor Transport Commission, 1951.* Lusaka: Government Printer, 1951.

————. "Report of the Native Labour Board into Conditions of Employment." Copy in National Archives of Rhodesia and Nyasaland, Salisbury. Mimeographed.

————. *Report of the Proceedings of the Second Advisory Council.*

First meeting June 21st to 29th, 1920. Livingstone: Government Printer, 1920.

———. *Report of the Rural Economic Development Working Party.* Lusaka: Government Printer, 1961.

———. *Report of the Taxation Committee, April 1934.* Livingstone: Government Printer, 1934.

———. *Report on Intensive Rural Development in the Northern and Luapula Provinces of Northern Rhodesia, 1957–1961.* Lusaka: Government Printer, 1961.

———. *Report on the Census of Population, 1951.* Lusaka: Government Printer, 1954.

———. *Report on the Census of Population, 1946.* Lusaka: Government Printer, 1949.

———. *Report to Government of Northern Rhodesia on Preliminary Survey of Stores, Public Works and Water Development and Irrigation Departments.* Lusaka: Government Printer, 1956.

———. *Review of Ten-Year Development Plan of Northern Rhodesia.* Lusaka: Government Printer, 1948.

———. *Revision of the Northern Rhodesia Ten-Year Development Plan, November 1953.* Lusaka: Government Printer, 1953.

———. *Second (1951) Review of the Ten-Year Development Plan of Northern Rhodesia.* Lusaka: Government Printer, 1951.

———. *Ten-Year Development Plan for Northern Rhodesia as Approved by Legislative Council on 11th February, 1947.* Lusaka: Government Printer, 1951.

———. Africa Education. *Annual Report for the Year 1955.* Lusaka: Government Printer, 1956.

———. Building, Mechanical, Road, Communication and Electrical Services. *Annual Report for the Year 1958.* Lusaka: Government Printer, 1959.

———. Central African Council. *Report on African Housing.* Lusaka: Government Printer, 1949.

———. Central African Statistical Office. "First Report on the Census of Industrial Production, 1947." Copy in National Archives of Rhodesia and Nyasaland, Salisbury. Mimeographed.

———. Chief Secretary's Office. *Government Circular No. 1 of 1957.* Lusaka: Government Printer, 1957.

———. Department of Agriculture. "Agricultural Report, 1926." Copy in National Archives of Rhodesia and Nyasaland, Salisbury. Mimeographed.

———. ———. Annual Reports. Livingstone and Lusaka: Government Printer, 1926–1960.

———. ———. *Food Production Committee, Progress Report, 1942.* Lusaka: Government Printer, 1943.

———. ———. *Report of a Soil and Land-Use Survey, Copperbelt, Northern Rhodesia.* Lusaka: Government Printer, 1956.

————. Department of Animal Health. Annual Reports. 1935–1936. Lusaka: Government Printer.

————. ————. *Memorandum on the Economics of the Cattle Industry in Northern Rhodesia.* Livingstone: Government Printer, 1935.

————. Department of Labour. Annual Reports. 1947–1958. Lusaka: Government Printer.

————. Department of Lands, Mines and Surveys. Annual Reports. 1937–1938. Lusaka: Government Printer.

————. Department of Veterinary Services. Annual Reports. 1926–1959. Lusaka: Government Printer.

————. Joint Fisheries Research Organization. *Annual Report No. 8, 1958.* Lusaka: Government Printer, 1959.

————. Labour and Mines Department. Annual Reports. 1946–1952. Lusaka: Government Printer.

————. Maize Control Board. Annual Reports. 1936–1953. Lusaka: Government Printer.

————. Mines Department. Annual Reports. 1926–1958. Lusaka: Government Printer.

————. Ministry of African Agriculture. *Annual Reports of the Departments of Agriculture and Co-operatives and African Marketing for the Year 1960.* Lusaka: Government Printer, 1961.

————. Ministry of African Education. *Triennial Survey, 1958–1960.* Lusaka: Government Printer, 1961.

————. Ministry of Labour and Mines. Annual Reports of the Department of Labour. 1959–1963. Lusaka: Government Printer.

————. Ministry of Land and Natural Resources. Department of Veterinary and Tsetse Control Services. *Annual Report for the Year 1959.* Lusaka: Government Printer, 1960.

————. Ministry of Native Affairs. *Annual Report of the Commissioner for Rural Development, 1959.* Lusaka: Government Printer, 1960.

————. ————. African Affairs. *Annual Report for the Year 1960.* Lusaka: Government Printer, 1961.

————. Ministry of Transport and Works. *Annual Report for the Year 1960.* Lusaka: Government Printer, 1961.

————. Native Affairs Department. "Annual Report on Native Education for the Year Ending 31 December 1926." Livingstone. Mimeographed.

————. ————. *North-Western Rhodesia Statistical Report, 1907–1909.* Livingstone, Government Printer.

————. ————. Report upon Native Affairs. 1926–1929. Livingstone. Mimeographed.

————. Native Reserves Commission. Tanganyika District. "Report of the Native Reserves Commission, 1927." Copy in National Archives of Rhodesia and Nyasaland. Salisbury. Typewritten.

————. Office of the Development Commissioner. Northern Province. *Twelfth Quarterly Report.* Kasama, July 27, 1960.

————. Secretary for Native Affairs. "Annual Report for the Year Ended 31st March 1922." Copy in National Archives of Rhodesia and Nyasaland. Salisbury. Typewritten.

Patersen, J. *Report of Committee Appointed by the Government of Northern Rhodesia To Investigate the Cost of Maize Production in Northern Rhodesia.* Supplement, *Northern Rhodesia Government Gazette.* Feb. 4, 1949.

Read, J. Gordon. *Report on Famine Relief: Gwembe, 1931–32.* Livingstone: Government Printer, 1932.

Rees, A. M. Morgan. "An Economic Survey of Plateau Tonga Improved Farms," in *Agricultural Bulletin,* no. 14. Lusaka: Government Printer, 1958.

Rees, A. M. Morgan, and R. H. Howard. "An Economic Survey of Commercial African Farming among the Sala of the Mumbwa District of Northern Rhodesia," in *Agricultural Bulletin,* no. 10. Lusaka: Government Printer, 1955.

Robertson, P. A. P. *Report of a Commission of Inquiry Appointed To Inquire into Causes of Wastage of Personnel from the Police Force.* Lusaka: Government Printer, 1957.

Robinson, H. F. C. *Report of the Financial Relationship Committee.* Lusaka: Government Printer, 1949.

Saffery, A. Lynn. *A Report on Some Aspects of African Living Conditions on the Copperbelt of Northern Rhodesia.* Lusaka: Government Printer, 1943.

Smith, Dean A. *Report of a Nutrition and Health Survey in the Kawambwa District.* Lusaka: Government Printer, 1950.

Stent, H. B. "Observations on the Fertilizer Effect of Wood Burning in the 'Chitemene' System," in *Second Annual Bulletin of Department of Agriculture.* Livingstone: Government Printer, 1933.

Stevensen, D. "Some Important Native Timbers," in *First Annual Bulletin of the Department of Agriculture 1931.* Livingstone: Government Printer, 1931.

Thomson, J. Moffat. *Memorandum on the Native Tribes and Tribal Areas of Northern Rhodesia.* Native Affairs Department. Livingstone: Government Printer, 1934.

————. *Report on the Native Fishing Industry.* Native Affairs Department. Livingstone: Government Printer, 1930.

Trapnell, C. G. *The Soils, Vegetation and Agriculture of North-Eastern Rhodesia.* Lusaka: Government Printer, 1953.

Trapnell, C. G., and J. N. Clothier. *The Soils, Vegetation and Agricultural Systems of North-Western Rhodesia,* 2d ed. Lusaka: Government Printer, 1957.

Trapnell, C. G., J. D. Martin, and W. Allen. *Vegetation: Soil Map of Northern Rhodesia.* Lusaka: Government Printer, 1950.

Tredgold, R. C. *Report of Investigation into Grievance Which Gave Rise to Strike Amongst the African Employees of the Rhodesia Railways.* Lusaka: Government Printer, 1945.

Troup, L. G. *Report of a Commission of Inquiry into the Future of the European Farming Industry of Northern Rhodesia.* Lusaka: Government Printer, 1954.

Vaughan-Jones, T. G. C. *Preliminary Report on the Fishing Industry and Its Markets.* Lusaka: Government Printer.

Worthington, F. V. "Proposed Native Reserves." 1913. Copy in National Archives of Rhodesia and Nyasaland. Salisbury. Typewritten.

Southern Rhodesia

Cold Storage Commission of Southern Rhodesia. *Nineteenth Annual Report and Accounts for the Period 1st January to 31st December, 1956.* Bulawayo: Rhodesian Christian Press, 1957.

Southern Rhodesia. *Interim Report of Commission To Report on Railway Dispute.* Salisbury: Government Printer, 1927.

———. *Report by Brigadier-General F. D. Hammond on the Railway System of Southern Rhodesia,* Vol. I. Salisbury: Government Printer, 1925.

———. *Report of Commission Appointed by His Excellency the Governor To Investigate the Grievances Which Gave Rise to the Strike among the African Employees of the Rhodesia Railways and Certain Other Matters Affecting Africans Employed in Industry.* Salisbury: Government Printer, 1946.

———. *Report of Commission of Enquiry into the Mining Industry of Southern Rhodesia.* Salisbury: Government Printer, 1945.

———. *Report of Railway Court of Enquiry, 1929.* Bulawayo: Government Printer, 1929.

———. *Report of the Secretary for Native Affairs and Chief Native Commissioner for the Year 1959.* Salisbury: Government Printer, 1960.

———. *Report of the Secretary for Native Affairs and Chief Native Commissioner for the Year 1960.* Salisbury: Government Printer, 1961.

———. Central African Statistical Office. "1954–55 Sample Census of African Agriculture." Copy in National Archives of Rhodesia and Nyasaland. Salisbury. Unpublished records.

———. ———. "Report of the 1950 Demographic Sample Survey of the African Population of Northern Rhodesia." Salisbury, 1952. Mimeographed.

————. ————. *Report on the Sample Census of African Agriculture of Southern Rhodesia.* Salisbury: Government Printer, July, 1951.

United States

Bolton, Frances P. *Report of the Special Study Mission to Africa, South and East of the Sahara.* Congress. House. Committee on Foreign Affairs. Washington: Government Printing Office, 1956.

Meyer, Helena M. "Copper," in *Mineral Facts and Problems.* Department of the Interior. Bureau of Mines, Bulletin no. 556. Washington: Government Printing Office, 1956. Pp. 219–245.

Sonenblum, Sidney. "A Report on Capital Purchases by the Copper Mining and Milling Industry." Department of the Interior. Bureau of Mines, Inter-Industry Analysis Branch. Item no. 21. Feb., 1953. Mimeographed.

United States. Department of Commerce. Bureau of the Census. *Statistical Abstract of the United States, 1962.* Washington: Government Printing Office, 1962.

————. ————. Bureau of Mines. *Mineral Resources of the United States.* Washington: Government Printing Office, 1926–1932.

————. Department of the Interior. Bureau of Mines. *Minerals Yearbook.* Washington: Government Printing Office. 1933–1960.

————. Federal Trade Commission. *Report on the Copper Industry.* Washington: Government Printing Office, 1947.

Other Government Publications

British Guiana. "Report of the Lands and Mines Department for 1959." Georgetown, British Guiana, 1960.

Gopalaswami, R. A. *Census of India, 1951.* Vol. I. Part II-B. Calcutta: Government of India Press, 1954.

Venezuela. Ministerio de Minas e Hidrocarburos, *Anuario Petrolero y Minero de Venezuela, 1952.* Caracas, 1957.

MANUSCRIPTS AND REPORTS

"Agreement between Northern Rhodesia Mine Workers Union and Mufulira Copper Mines, Ltd., Nchanga Consolidated Copper Mines Ltd. . . ." Ndola: Rhodesian Printers, 1956.

Anglo-American Corporation of South Africa. "Annual Report, 1954." Johannesburg.

————. "Medical Consultants Report, 1959." Johannesburg.

Arabian American Oil Company. *1956 Report of Operations to the Saudi Arab Government.* Saudi Arabia, April 15, 1957.

Association of Rhodesia and Nyasaland Industries. "The Industrial Director and Brand-Names Index of Rhodesia and Nyasaland." Salisbury. 1960.

Bancroft Mines, Annual Reports. 1954–1960. Salisbury.

Beira and Mashonaland and Rhodesia Railways. Reports of the General Manager. 1922–1932. Bulawayo.

British South Africa Company. *Estimates of Revenue and Expenditure for the Year Ended 31 March 1923*. Livingstone: Government Printer, 1922.

———. *Directors' Report and Accounts for the Year Ended 31 March 1920*. London, 1921.

———. *Directors' Report and Accounts for the Years Ended 31 March 1921 and 31 March 1922*. London, 1923.

Broken Hill Development Co. "General Managers Report, 1929." Copy in the Anglo-American Corporation of South Africa library, Salisbury. Mimeographed.

Bromwich, E. C. "Problems of Arresting Cost Increases in Our Mines." Speech delivered at Rhodesian Selection Trust Symposium, Lusaka, Sept. 25, 26, 1959. Copy at Rhodesian Selection Trust, Salisbury. Mimeographed.

Chibuluma Mines. Annual Reports, 1951–1960. Salisbury.

East African Railways and Harbors. *Report on an Engineering Survey of a Rail Link between the East African and Rhodesian Railway System*. 2 vols. Nairobi, June, 1952.

Empire Parliamentary Association. United Kingdom Branch. *Report on the Parliamentary Visit to Northern Rhodesia, 1930*. London, 1930.

Fosbrooke, H. "Effect of Economic Change on African Society," in "Economic Development in Northern Rhodesia." Study Conference, no. 2, sponsored by the United Northern Rhodesia Association. Oct., 1958. Copy in library of Rhodesian Selection Trust, Salisbury. Mimeographed.

Fraser, H. R. "Economic Survey of the Federation of Rhodesia and Nyasaland." Vol. I. Salisbury. 1957. Copy in library of the Anglo-American Corporation of South Africa. Salisbury. Mimeographed.

Geddes, A. C. *Memorandum Prepared by Rhokana Corporation Limited on the Copper Mining Industry of Northern Rhodesia*. Colonial Office Library. East Africa Pamphlet, no. 249. London, 1932.

Higham, F., ed. "Fourth Empire Mining and Metallurgical Congress, Proceedings." Part I. London: Offices of the Congress, 1950.

Kelley, T. B. "Paternalism versus Greater Responsibility and Independence in Relation to African Life on the Copper Mines, Paper no. 1." Speech delivered at Rhodesian Selection Trust Symposium, Sept. 25, 26, 1959, Lusaka. Copy at Rhodesian Selection Trust. Salisbury. Mimeographed.

Lynn, C. W. "Agricultural Development," in "Economic Development in Northern Rhodesia," Study Conference, no. 2, sponsored by the United Northern Rhodesia Association. Salisbury, Oct. 1958.

Copy at Rhodesian Selection Trust library, Salisbury. Mimeographed.

Mattushek, P. B. "The Future of Mechanization in Our Mines, Paper no. 2." Speech delivered at Rhodesian Selection Trust Symposium, Sept. 25, 26, 1959, Lusaka. Copy at Rhodesian Selection Trust, Salisbury. Mimeographed.

Mufulira Copper Mines. Annual Reports. 1934–1961. Salisbury.

————. "Progress Report." Sept. 30, 1930; June, 1931. Mufulira.

Muskett, H. B. *Steel Highway*. Bulawayo. Rhodesia Railways, 1957.

National Industrial Conference Board. *Copper: Basic Industrial Data.* New York, 1958.

Nchanga Consolidated Copper Mines. Annual Reports. 1947–1960. Salisbury.

————. Directors' Reports and Statements of Accounts. 1938.

Norrie, J. P. and W. T. Pettijohn. "An Outline of Underground Operations at Mufulira Copper Mines Ltd.," in *Transactions of the Institution of Mining and Metallurgy, Fifty-ninth Session, 1949–50,* Vol. LIX. London: Office of the Institution, Salisbury House, 1953.

Northern Rhodesia Chamber of Mines. "Statement of Case To Be Submitted on Behalf of Copper Mining Companies to the Commission of Inquiry 1957." Kitwe.

————. Year books. 1955–1960. Kitwe, Rhodesian Printers.

Northern Rhodesia Mine Workers' Union. "African Advancement Proposals." Chingola Printers, 1960.

Prain, Sir Ronald L. "The Copper Industry: Some Factors Affecting Its Future." Speech delivered at the Mining Club, New York, Feb., 1959.

————. "Statement to Stockholders," In *Annual Report, 1951.* Rhodesian Selection Trust. Lusaka.

Rhodesia Congo Border Power Corporation. "Annual Report, 1955." Kitwe, 1956. Mimeographed.

————. *Directors' Report and Accounts, Year Ended December 31, 1957.* Kitwe.

————. "Interim Accounts for Half Year Ended 30 June 1960." Copy at Rhodesian Selection Trust. Salisbury. Mimeographed.

————. *Operating Report 1959.* Kitwe, 1959.

Rhodesia Congo Border Timber Company. "Sixth Annual Report, 31st March 1960." Kitwe, 1960. Copy at Rhodesian Selection Trust. Salisbury. Mimeographed.

Rhodesia Railways. Annual Reports. 1950–1960. Bulawayo.

————. Reports of General Manager. 1947, 1949. Bulawayo.

Rhodesian Selection Trust. Annual Reports. 1954–1961. Salisbury.

————. "On Price Fixing Agreement of Copper." May 2, 1955. Salisbury. Mimeographed.

————. *Kafue Flats, the Granary of the Federation?* Salisbury, 1958.

Rhokana Corporation. "Compound Manager's Report on Native Diet, Year Ended 30 June 1939." Nkana. Mimeographed.

————. Annual Reports. 1949–1960. Salisbury.

————. "The Utilisation of African Labour, Cost Trends, Policy and Programme To Meet the Situation." Nkana, 1956. Mimeographed.

Roan Antelope Copper Mines. "African Advancement." 1960. Luanshya. Mimeographed.

————. Annual Reports. 1928–1961. London and Salisbury.

————. Progress Report. March 31, 1930. London.

————. "Human Problems at Roan Antelope." 1961. Luanshya. Mimeographed.

Schumann, A. W. "The Future of Mechanization in Our Mines, Paper No. 3." Speech delivered at a Rhodesian Selection Trust Symposium. Sept. 25, 26, 1959. Lusaka Copy at Rhodesian Selection Trust, Salisbury. Mimeographed.

Scott, J. G. "Memorandum Submitted to the Commission of Inquiry at the Request of the African Mineworkers' Union, May 23, 1962." Kitwe. Mimeographed.

Simpson, Samuel. *Report on the Cotton Growing Industry.* African Pamphlet, no. 792. Colonial Office Library, London. (1905).

Soper, J. P. "A Comparative Analysis of the Causes and Effects of Labour Migration in Selected African Territories." Unpublished thesis. Rhodes House, Oxford University.

Tata Industries. "Statistical Outline of India, 1959." Bombay: Bombay House, 1959.

United Northern Rhodesia Association. "Economic Development in Northern Rhodesia, Study Conference no. 2." Lusaka, 1958. Mimeographed.

Young, D. "The Future of Mechanization in Our Mines, Paper No. 1." Speech delivered at a Rhodesian Selection Trust Symposium, Sept. 25, 26, 1959. Lusaka. Copy at Rhodesian Selection Trust, Salisbury. Mimeographed.

Index

DATE DUE

31 1981   MAY 29 1975

JUN 1 1968   S.

AUG 20 1968   S.E.   AUG 29 1978

DEC 8 1969   S.A